AFFORDABLE CONTEMPORARY ART

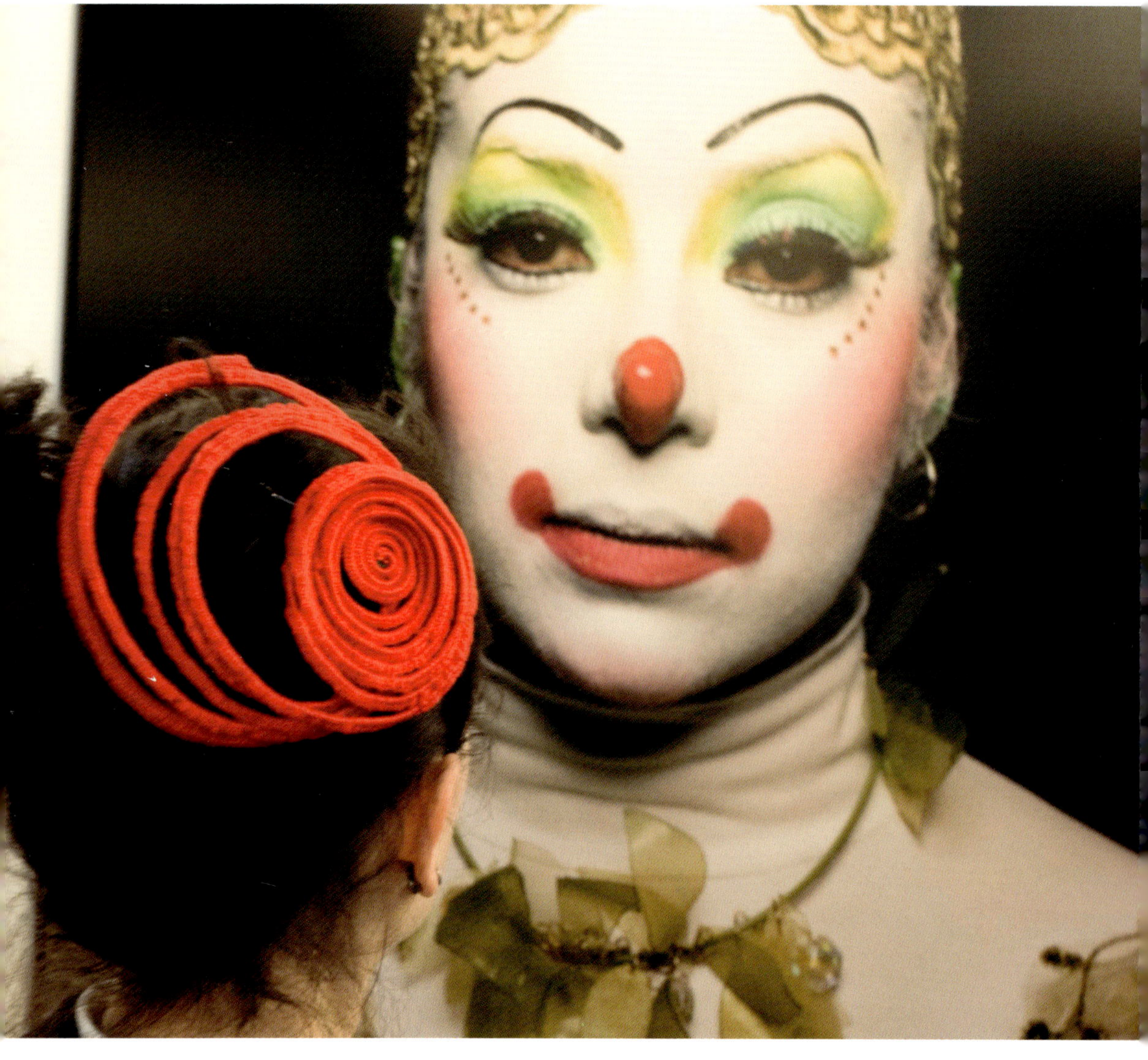

A guide to buying and collecting

AFFORDABLE CONTEMPORARY ART

Beatrice Hodgkin

VIVAYS PUBLISHING

Contemporary art

"term loosely used to denote art of the present day and of the relatively recent past, of an innovatory or avant-garde nature..." Tate Collection

VIVAYS PUBLISHING

Published by Vivays Publishing
www.vivays-publishing.com

A catalogue record for this book is available from the British Library

ISBN 978-1-908126-06-1

Publishing Director: Lee Ripley
Design: Price Watkins
Illustrations: Louisa Jones
Photographs: Amy Gwatkin

Printed in China

Contents

Introduction

HAVE YOU EVER wandered into a contemporary art gallery and liked the art but felt unsure or nervous when it came to buying something? Perhaps you were intimidated by the style, the prices, the art speak, or the gallery assistant (whether they talked to you or categorically ignored you). Were you afraid to ask questions for fear of showing that you weren't an art expert, and, if you did, were you worried that you'd automatically be expected to buy something? Your heart raced – if you bought something, would it be the right thing? If not, how to leave the gallery without being pressured into buying? You felt stuck in an agonizing limbo between buying and not – both seemed filled with the potential for making the wrong decision. If a scene like this sounds even vaguely familiar, then this is the book for you.

Buying and collecting art with confidence comes from understanding the landscape of the art world, of which you, as a collector (however extravagant or modest your budget), are a vital component. This book sets out to be a map by which collectors might more easily engage with the art world and navigate their way through the contours and undulations of the terrain, so they can find and buy art that they love for the right price, and build a collection that's more than the sum of its parts.

However, you won't find specific suggestions about which artists you should buy or which galleries you should visit (although both artists and galleries are mentioned). It's up to collectors to find their own niche of trusted galleries and favourite artists, so outlined here are ways in which collectors and potential collectors can arm themselves with the know-how and confidence to find these and decide for themselves which works of art will be both worthwhile investments and a pleasure to own.

This involves developing a better understanding of the art world (how it operates and how to translate its jargon and often idiosyncratic practices), honing the ability to analyze your own tastes, how to keep an ear to the ground in order to engage fully with the art world, knowing what to look out for and where, and understanding both the practicalities of actually buying works and whether you are paying the right price.

'Affordable' is often viewed by the art world as a derogatory term (if you were an artist you might also be a bit irked by being relegated to the 'cheap' section), but it is not used here in the 'cheap' sense, rather as a way of referring to prices that are accessible, attractive and entry level. It is also undeniably a subjective term, but those with a budget of less than, say, £5,000/€6,000/$8,000 (and often substantially less than this) will want to get the most out of whatever they have to invest in art as much as someone buying a piece for a million – perhaps more so. And while buying art for investment is both generally frowned upon by the art world and a dangerous and tricky game to play, you still want to be sure that what you've spent on a piece of art is worthwhile.

There are many things you can spend money on where you might see a better rate of return on your investment (property?), or which provide you with a certain amount of practical usage for your money (shoes?), but contemporary art is not only a pleasure to live with, it is an exciting process to buy because of the world it draws you into. Buying any art is a luxury, but the distinguishing feature of contemporary art is that it is the art of the here and now. Definitive categorization may have its problems – the UK's Tate Collection defines contemporary art as a "term loosely used to denote art of the present day and of the relatively recent past, of an innovatory or avant-garde nature..."; many auction houses commonly group post-war and contemporary art together as if the lines between the two are so blurred as to prevent distinction (i.e. suggesting that contemporary art can be by artists who aren't living), while the Getty Museum, Los Angeles says the term refers "to art made and produced by artists living today" – but this shape-shifting nature adds to its thrilling lustre. The cutting-edge contemporary art world (as opposed to the artists working today in a more traditionalist vein) is a world where avant-garde is king, where concept can trump skill, and no single authority can define whether something is 'good' art or not. The absence of rules, unifying style or set time-frame, contribute to making buying contemporary art and being part of its world an exhilarating and stimulating experience on a multitude of levels.

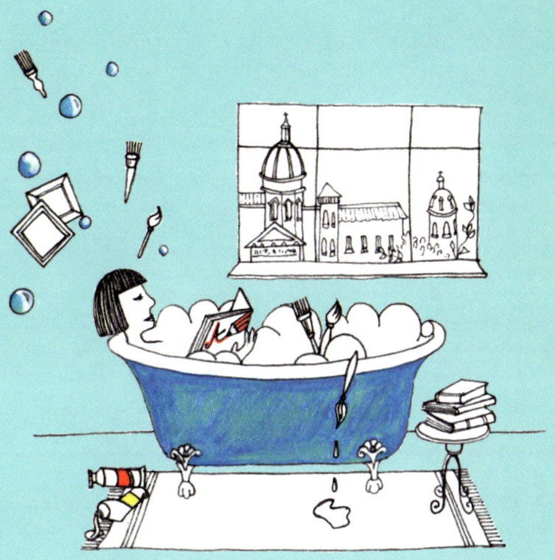

01

Immerse yourself in the art world

Knowledge is power: immerse yourself in the art world

BY IMMERSING YOURSELF in the art world and familiarising yourself with its idiosyncrasies you'll understand it better, and this means you'll then be able to buy more confidently – works which have a greater chance of appreciating both and in terms of your enjoyment of them and, hopefully, financially too. And the best thing? It is hugely enjoyable.

Keep your wits about you and listen out for a buzz around certain artists, trends for particular styles and movements, and auction news and gallery gossip, and you'll get a better feel for the landscape of the art world. Feel your way around so you learn the lingo, understand the rituals and practices and know what to look out for.

Visit public art museums and galleries, especially institutes of contemporary art

Public museums and galleries exhibit work by internationally renowned, respected and recognised contemporary artists, so take full advantage and make going to major national and international exhibitions of contemporary art (both permanent and temporary exhibitions) a priority (if you haven't already), and focus your visits to get the most out of them. It's worth noting that membership can often save a considerable amount of money and avoid queuing.

The ICA in Boston.

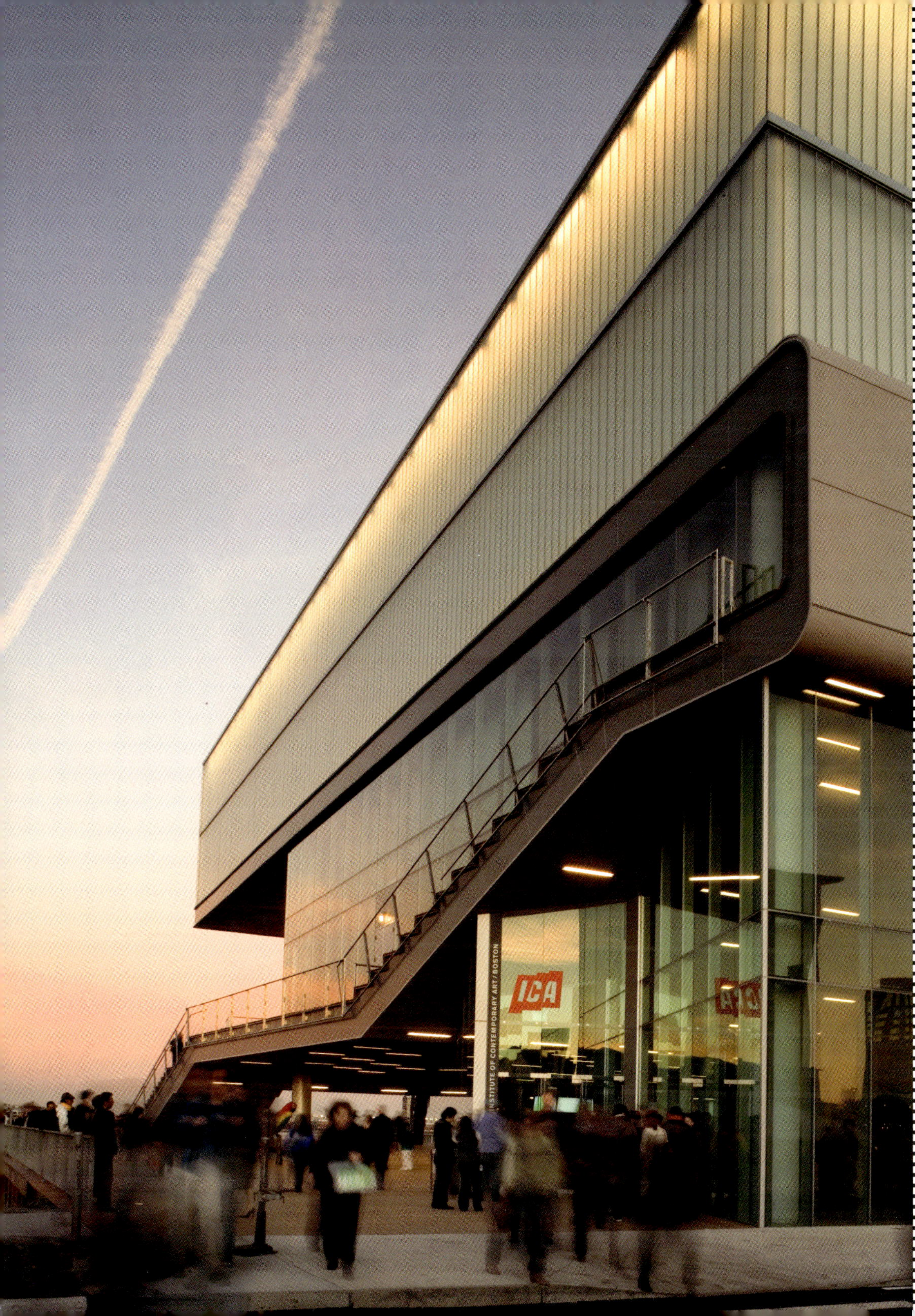
INSTITUTE OF CONTEMPORARY ART / BOSTON
ICA

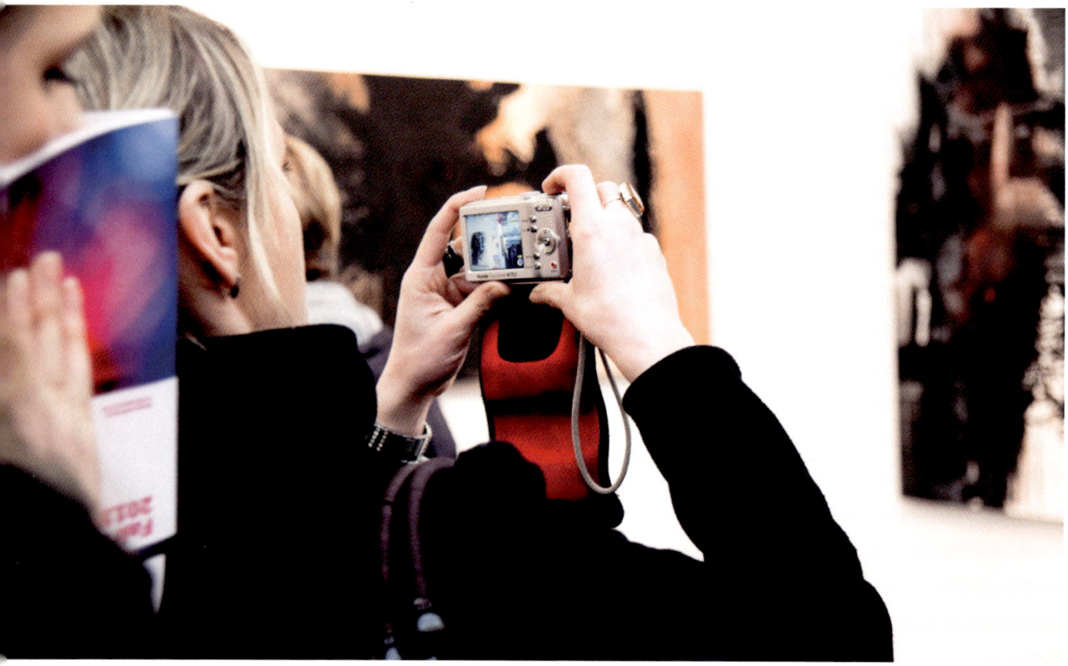

Familiarise yourself with the names and styles of the artists on display

The contemporary art in national galleries and museums is work that the art world holds in the highest regard (and will pay top dollar for). The art world speaks a language made up of these artists' names, their style and the media they work in. To gain access to, and communicate and engage with, this world you'll have to speak this language too, and the basics involve being familiar with revered and celebrated contemporary artists.

Note the artists whose work you have a strong reaction to

The easiest way to get to know the contemporary art landscape is to come at it from your own angle. Single out the artists who you are especially drawn to – or indeed the opposite. You'll instantly create active parameters for your tastes – this is the start of navigating your own path through the contemporary art landscape.

Consider and articulate the conversation you're having with each piece

Once you have singled out a work, think about what makes it stand out, and why it is you like it – how the artwork is communicating with you and how you are responding. Imagine having to articulate that into a conversation with an art dealer or artist when having to describe your tastes. Start by trying to jot down key words, both about the works themselves and your reactions – beginning with

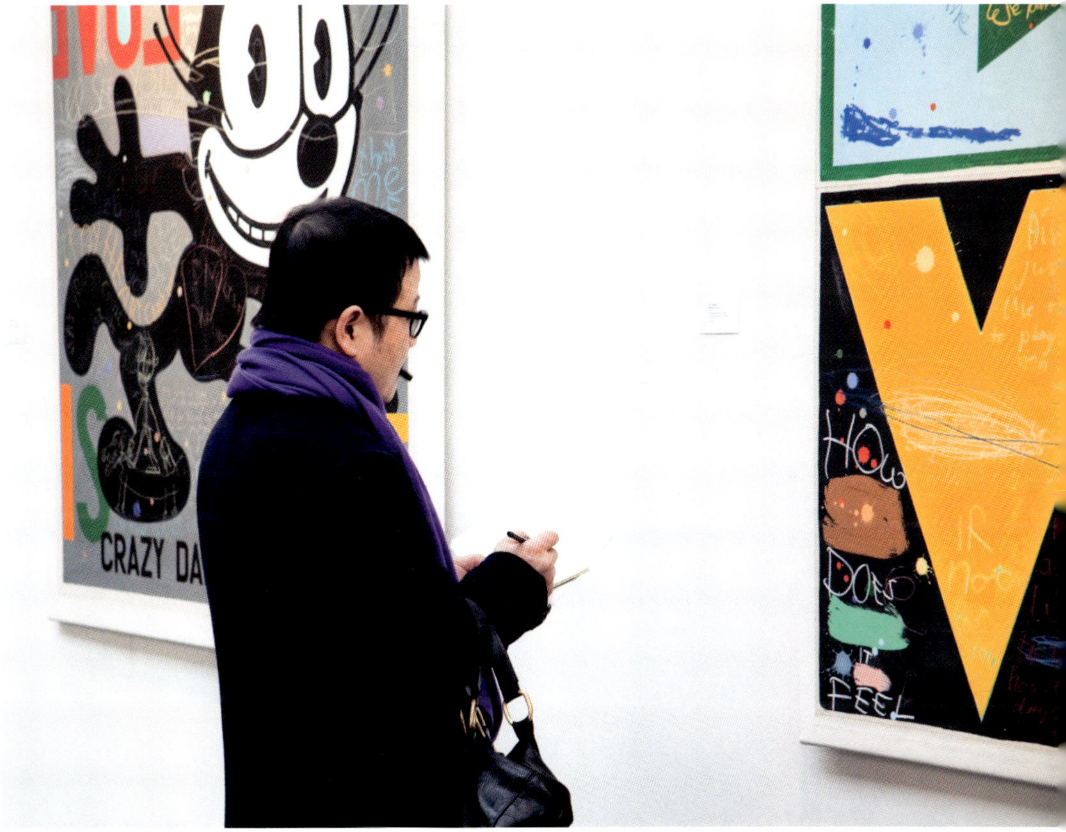

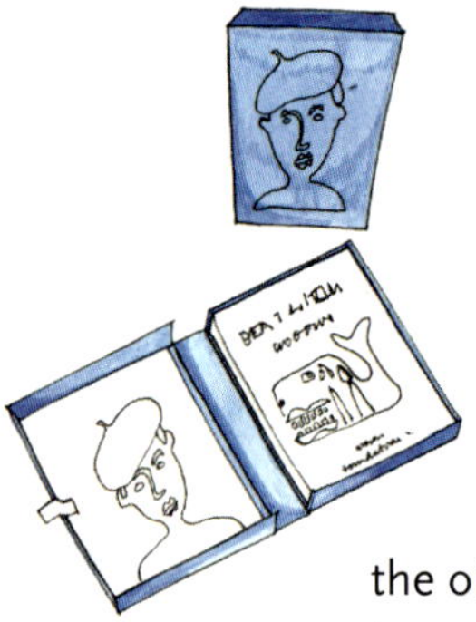

the obvious. This could be anything from the bold colours, shocking imagery, simple shapes or sharp lines of the work, to your own angry, sympathetic, amused, confused or outraged reactions. Then try to think about the relationship between the two (the work's style and your reaction) and shape that into a more structured and eloquent reaction, something you think sums up what you've liked about individual works, groups of pieces, or the body of work by a particular artist. See how reading about and around the work or artist changes your opinions, and if it does, how (see below).

As you feel more comfortable articulating your reactions towards established artists, it'll help build your confidence when assessing artists you discover outside of such an obviously 'hallowed' setting, or, indeed, emerging artists with a lower profile, and it also means you'll be able to spot and snap up works by established artists should you come across their limited-edition prints or more accessibly priced works.

Take advantage of the curatorial explanations and exhibition guides

Public galleries are there to explain and help guide you through a world notoriously prickly about explaining or justifying itself, and a discipline that's often defiantly oblique. Whereas commercial galleries often won't have explanations of particular artworks, public galleries and museums can actively help you understand contemporary art in context – in terms of style, period, movement, agenda and the playful dialogues between artists – so don't underestimate the value of these to provide a comprehensive framework for your understanding.

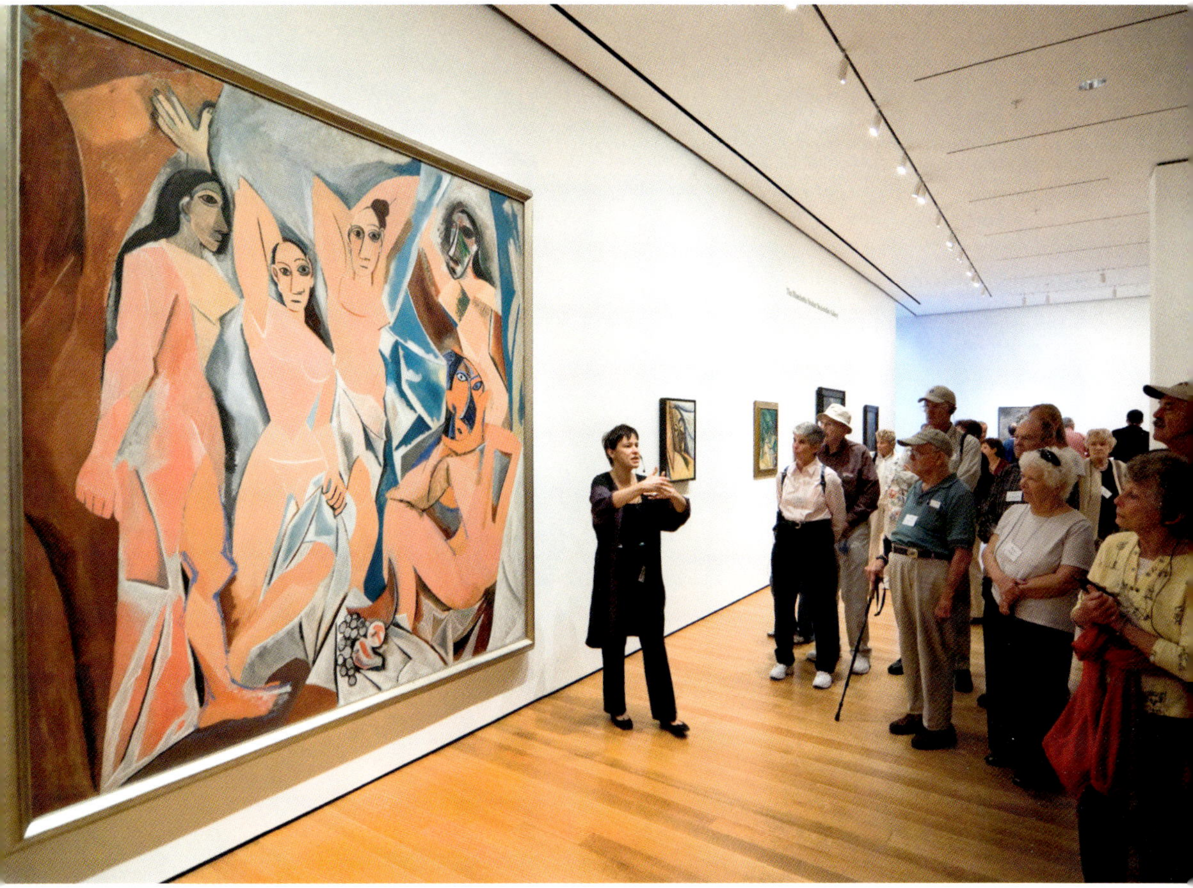

Visitors on a guided tour.

Public art galleries and museums can actively help you understand contemporary art in context so don't underestimate the value of these to provide a comprehensive framework for your understanding.

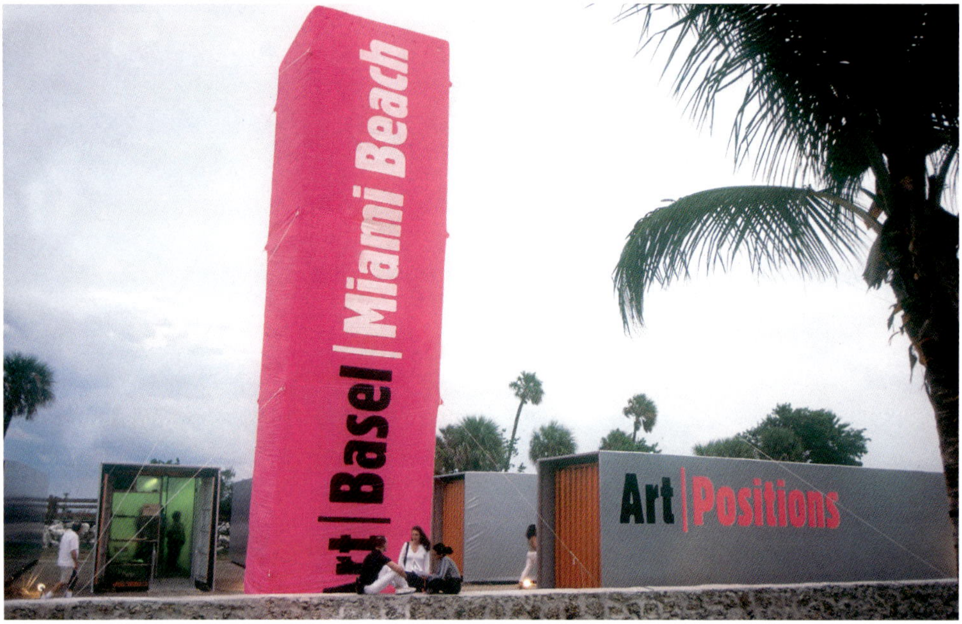

Art fairs

Art fairs, which gather work by different artists to show under one roof, usually only for a few days, with the primary objective of selling works, are a crucial component of the contemporary art market. They fall into two categories: gallery fairs (where a selection of galleries show edited highlights of works by artists whom they represent) and artist fairs (where artists show their own work). Even if you're not actively buying, they are an easy way to see the latest work causing a stir, often fresh from artists' studios, which both galleries and artists feel is worth showcasing on a public stage.

Use major international art fairs as an opportunity to soak up what's happening on the front lines of contemporary art

Fairs where galleries have stands fall into various tiers, depending on the calibre of the galleries. At the highest level are fairs where the major international players, the superstar or branded galleries from around the globe, show work by artists who command thousands (sometimes millions) for their works and who are favoured by leading international collectors. For the more humble art collector, rather than seeing these art fairs (the top echelons of which include Art Basel, Art Basel Miami Beach, The Armory Show, and Frieze) as a place to buy art, approach them as an unparalleled way to get right to the beating heart of the contemporary art world. It's mostly at the private parties and viewings held in the days before the fair is open to the public when the majority of the works are actually sold. And that's if the pieces are even for sale in the first place, for often these works have already found buyers; galleries will hang works as a quasi advertisement for the calibre, profile and range of talent they represent.

Such slightly curious subterfuge emanates from the complex relationship between pre-eminent private collectors and major galleries – the former don't really want to see works 'casually' before buying them; they want to be shown works in private that have been

The distinctive entrances to art fairs at Art Basel, Miami Beach (left) and The Armory Show (below).

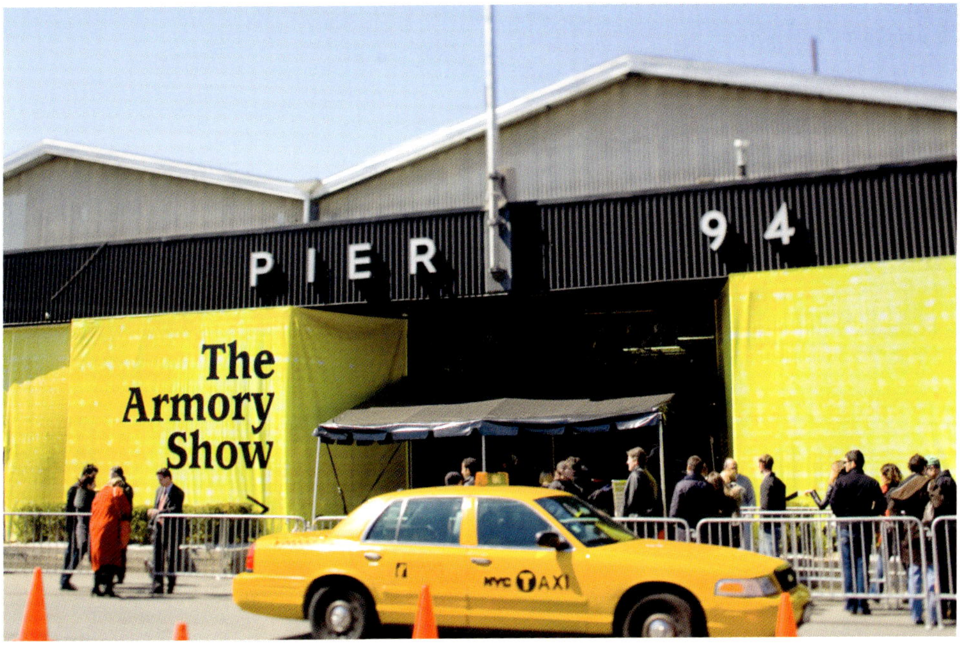

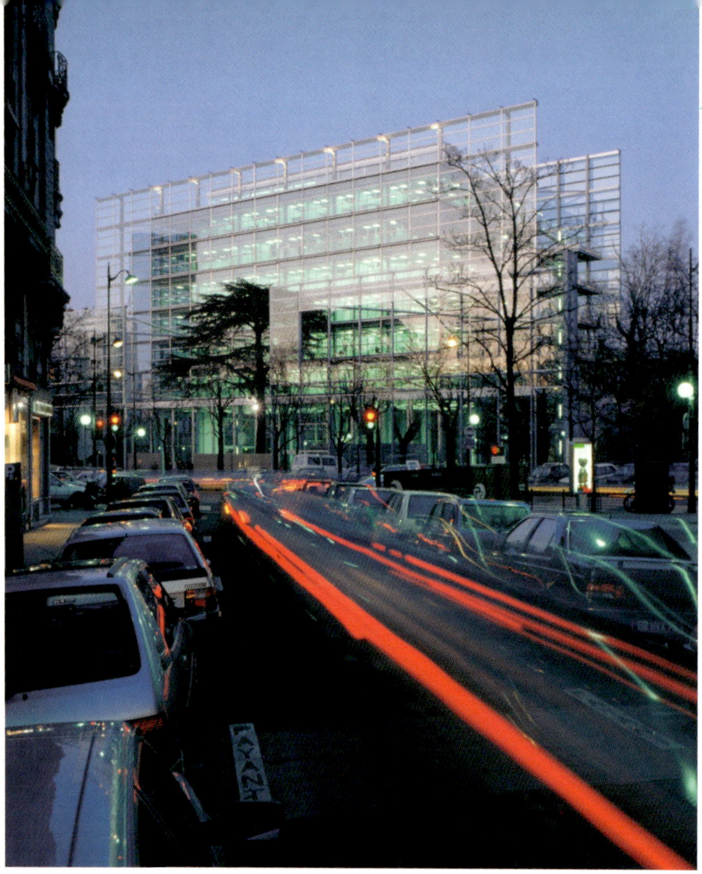

The Jean Nouvel designed Fondation Cartier, Paris (left) and the Kunst-Werke Institute for Contemporary Art, Berlin (right).

cherry-picked away from the 'hoi polloi'. Works by high-profile artists or hot new artists aren't openly sold by galleries, they are 'placed', a more strategic sales method where dealers inform a select few of their collectors about pieces which have become available to buy, or they simply tell collectors what they should buy to develop and enrich their personal collections.

The importance of understanding the operational exclusivity of the major art fairs makes it easier for art enthusiasts outside this exclusive coterie of collectors to re-calibrate their expectations of an international art fair. Don't necessarily approach these fairs with an eye for purchase, instead use them as a way to see new trends emerge, become familiar with the artists around whom there is a buzz, get a feel for the artists whose stars are rising, and refine your own tastes in an environment that's at the sophisticated epicentre of the art market. Prices will almost never be on show. Often if you even ask you'll be shot a soul-destroying look. Take it on the chin. Getting an exact answer from major gallerists can be like getting blood from a stone. In the main, this is not the environment for selling to a casual passer-by (though it's not wholly unheard of). But don't be intimidated. Have your own agenda. Look out for the artists who have pieces on show at several international galleries. Make a note of artists whose work you are drawn to. Be aware of the feel of the art as a whole – the mood it's tapping into, the styles that are recurrent. This way you can feed this knowledge and awareness into a sphere that's within your budget.

Don't see this as a knocking of your worth – far from it! Exploit the richness and range of art at these fairs and channel the experience, knowledge and understanding into the part of the art market that's relevant to you. Spot 'names' and you may find that they have produced multiples, studies, editions or limited-edition prints at a fraction of the cost of originals (available elsewhere). You'll soon have a keener eye for emerging artists who have taken a certain style that's in vogue and either run with it, developed it, subverted it or consciously rejected it. Make the major art fairs work for you.

Galleries gather under one roof for the London Art Fair (overleaf).

Don't necessarily approach these fairs with an eye for purchase, instead use them as a way to see new trends emerge, become familiar with the artists around whom there is a buzz ...

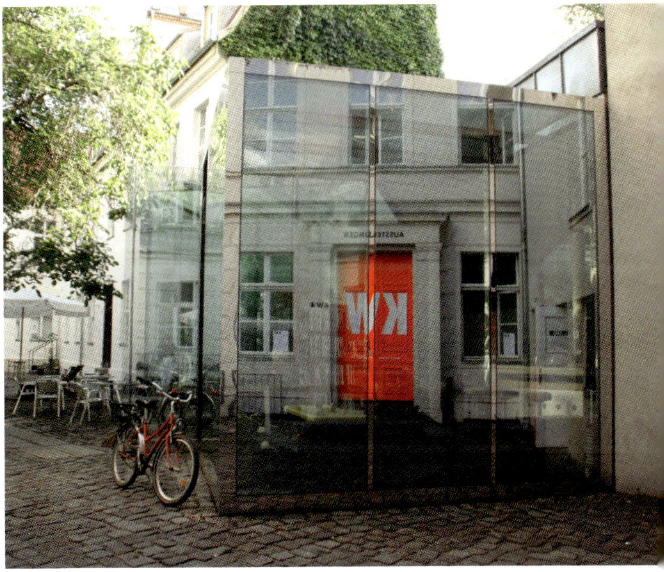

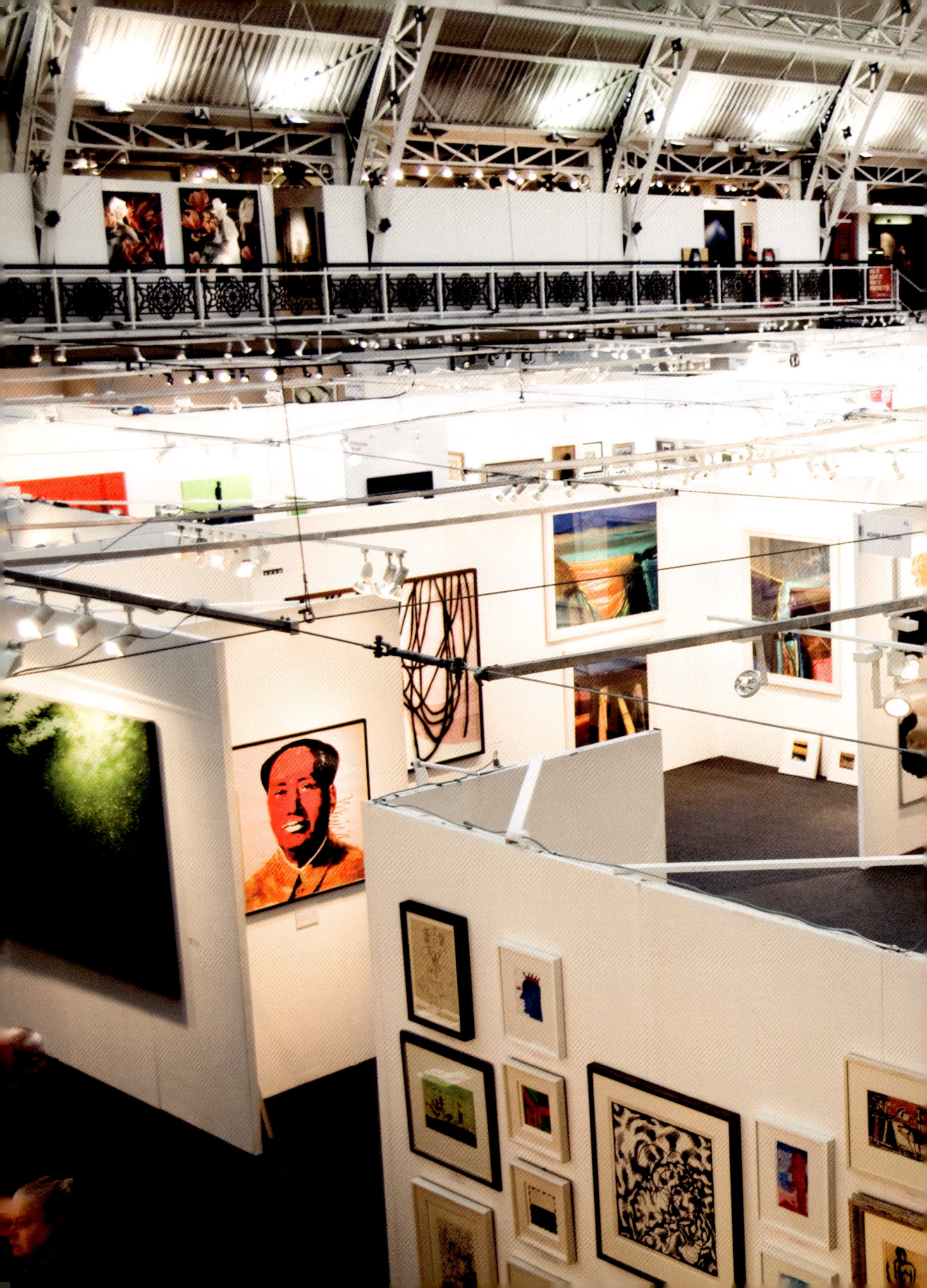

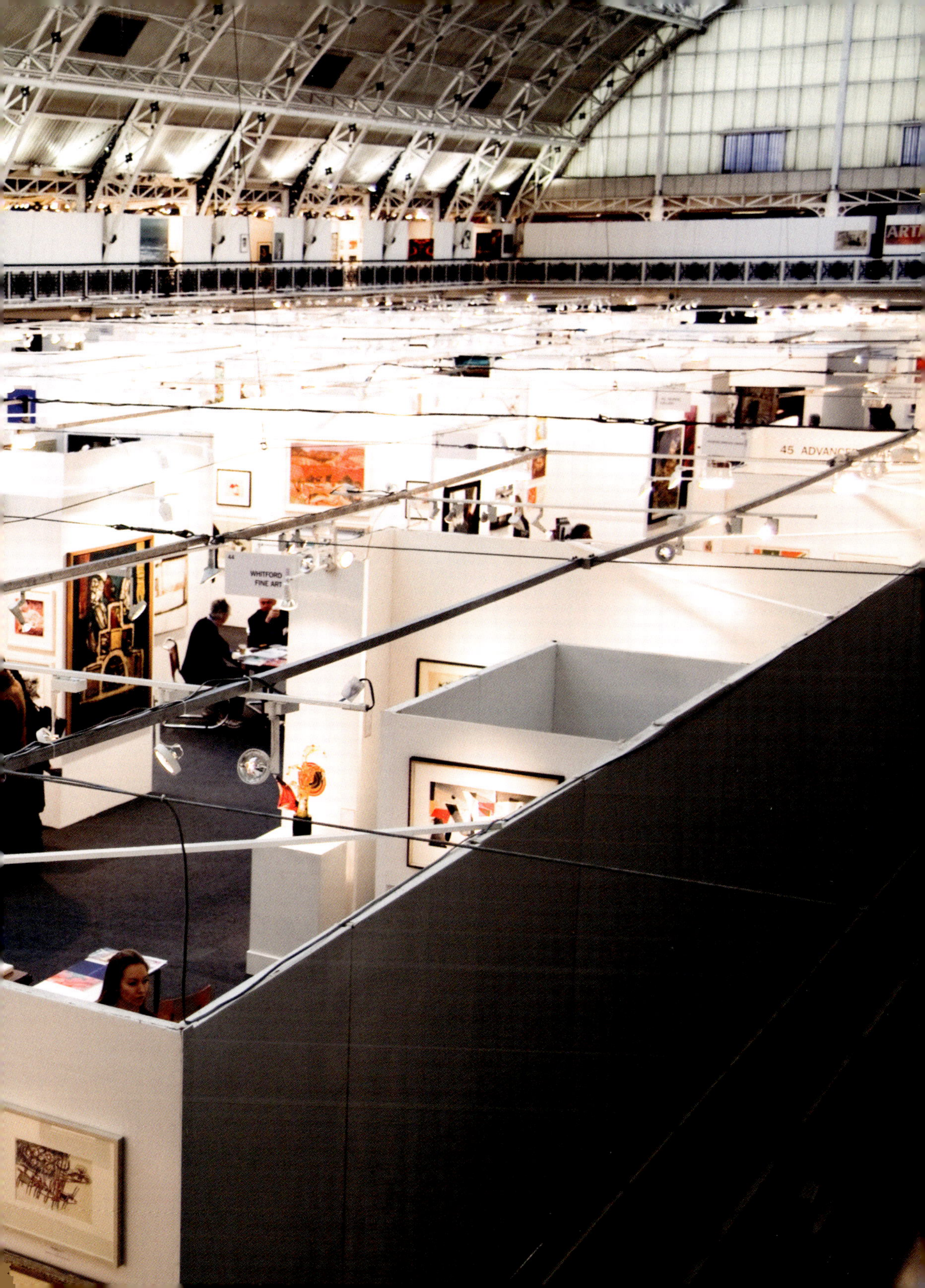
WHITFORD
FINE ART

It's also worth noting that commercial galleries in a city where an art fair is being held will have tailored their shows for a crowd humming with cultural energy. Artists exhibiting will be the ones galleries want to give a high-profile push to, so it's worth finding out about exhibition openings and making a note of who is showing. Have fun discovering new artists and galleries by taking advantage of the art world's hedonism and attending the private views – only a minority are as exclusive as they sound; most galleries happily welcome art lovers to opening nights (call before if you're nervous about dropping by), especially if they are potential buyers, plus a busy, buzzy opening night can only be a good thing for galleries – it makes both them and their artists look popular and in demand.

Use the smaller, satellite fairs to familiarise yourself with the landscape of emerging artists and galleries

Less intimidating and overwhelming are the smaller satellite art fairs that have grown up around the major fairs and which are, broadly speaking, more approachable and which actually sell work that a wider cross-section of art enthusiasts can consider investing in. Look for fairs which gather emerging galleries (ones that have been open for five years or so) like Basel off-shoot Liste; fairs which exclusively sell multiples or limited-edition prints (Christie's in London launched such a fair, Multiplied Arts, in October 2010 during Frieze week, for example); fairs where galleries show work by emerging artists; fairs that focus on the work of artists or galleries of that city; or fairs that promote the accessible pricing of their work (the Affordable Art Fairs, for example).

Find out as much as you can about each fair and keep that in mind when you are taking a panoramic view of the art. There will usually be artists and galleries vying for places at the fair, so find out what the criteria and stipulations for entry are to establish the calibre of the art you'll see (such information is usually available on the website). Find out if the organisers censor the artists who galleries select to exhibit (for example, do emerging artists have to be represented by a gallery? Must they have practiced for a certain amount of time?). Armed with knowledge of the fair's selection process, you'll be able to gauge the art's quality, price and style more accurately.

Use fairs to discover new galleries that you'd like to build relationships with

Keep a log of the galleries or artists exhibiting at the fairs by saving their catalogues and programmes (you can also usually find them online). Make a note of the galleries (or artists) showing work that you especially like, galleries where the quality of work stands out, or where the gallery owner is approachable and helpful and *sign up to their mailing lists*. It's up to you and you alone to pick out the handful of galleries from the hundreds that appeal to you. Even if you don't buy something there and then, it's an opportunity to broaden your knowledge of galleries – nationally and internationally, or even in an area of your home city that you're not familiar with.

Meet and speak with the artists

At an artist fair, chat with the artists; gain first-hand insight into their work, their inspiration, methods and interests, and find out more about the artists themselves. See how committed new artists are to their practice, and find out a bit more about the career trajectories of more established artists.

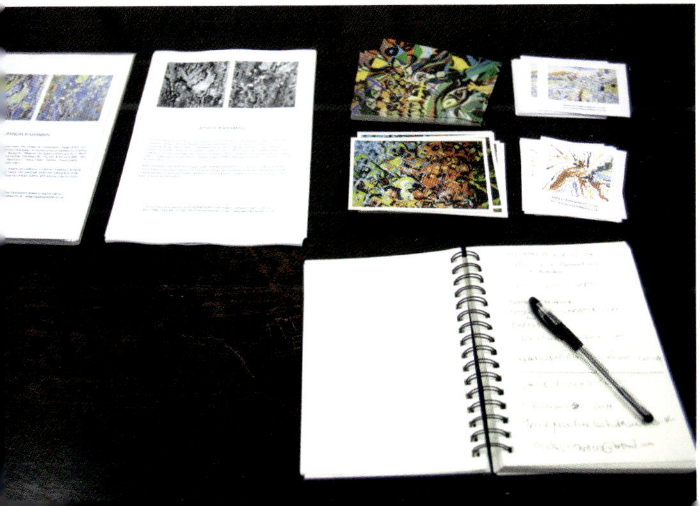

Make a note of galleries showing work that you like and sign up to their mailing lists.

Get connected

The best and easiest way to stay in the loop about art fairs, gallery openings and interesting artists to watch is by listening to the art chatter via newspapers, magazines, e-zines, gallery mailouts, blogs, subscriber art bulletins and social networking sites. Subscribe to online and print edition mailouts – make it so easy for yourself that after a while you don't even have to forage for information as news and tips automatically come to your front door or inbox. But choose with care: only subscribe to those whose style and approach you like – that last thing you want is to wade through something because you feel you have to.

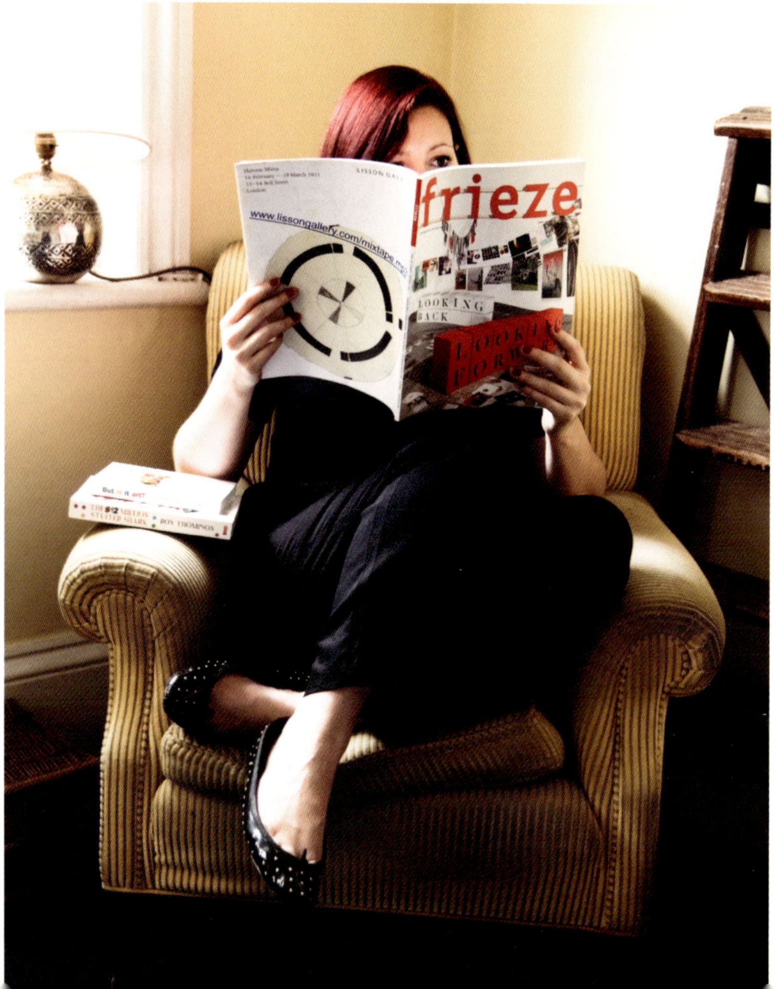

GOOD TO KNOW TIPS FOR GETTING CONNECTED

* Have at least one or two regular sources of international contemporary art news (magazines or online) from publications like *Frieze*, *The Art Newspaper*, *Art Forum*, *Art+Auction*, *Monopol*, *art*.es, *Connaissance des Arts*; and online sites and blogs like artdaily.com, artinfo.com, artnet.com and artworldsalon.com.
* Tailor your sources to your advantage: find *local* bloggers, newspapers, magazines and listings sites (the UK's ArtRabbit.com lists new UK gallery exhibitions and is in the process of expanding its reach to the rest of Europe, with Berlin already underway), and sign up for news from sources specialising in your specific art interest – be that animal or urban art.

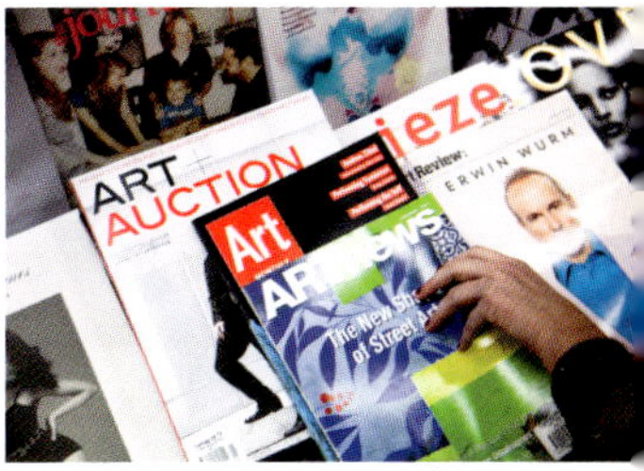

* Mix sources and styles of information: combine the emerging art-focussed publications with those that cover news about established artists, the irreverent with the serious, the witty with the wise, the practical with the more *avant-garde* and experimental.
* Don't feel overwhelmed: make casual scanning a habit and pick out the interesting and easy-to-digest bits.
* Expand your friend network on Facebook and the people you follow on Twitter to include a contemporary art community.
* Join art-oriented social networking sites: examples include New York algorithm-based www.art.sy, which analyses users' tastes and suggests galleries and artists they may like; the online community of London magazine www.art-review.com; German-originated www.independent-collectors.com, where collector-members exhibit their collections online; and the collector-gallery-artist hub that is www.saatchionline.com.

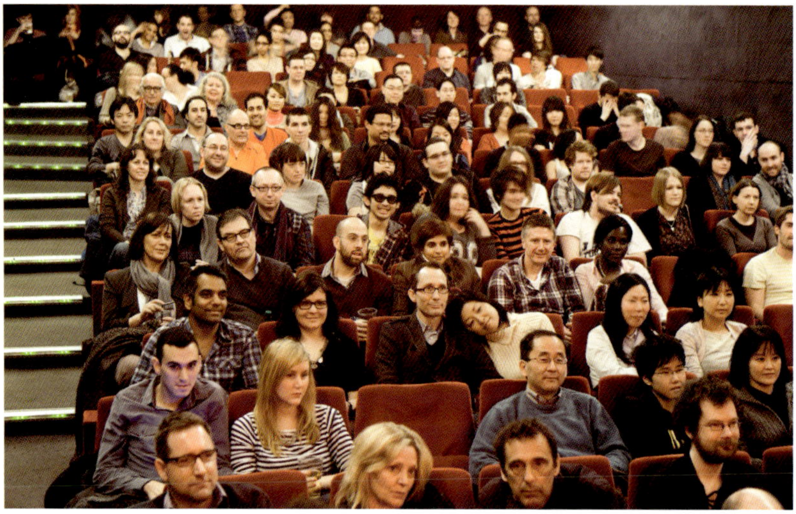

Art talks and courses

Most cultural institutions hold lunchtime, evening and weekend talks about art by curators, artists, critics, gallerists and collectors. They are an easy and rewarding way to enrich your understanding of art. Some are even free. It's worth signing up to receive email alerts from the institutions or cultural clubs that stage debates and lectures. Try to get on the mailing lists too so when there are talks that pique your interest you can book up. A few have specific contemporary art courses, and some offer collecting contemporary art courses (such as London's Whitechapel Gallery). They sell out fast, so be sure to book ahead.

Art society membership schemes

The membership schemes of our cultural institutions and art societies are a wonderful way of supporting the contemporary art world and gaining exclusive access to events and exhibitions. These societies aim to nurture future collectors, benefactors and patrons, and raise money to buy contemporary art for cultural institutions, to preserve existing collections or to support a particular artistic community.

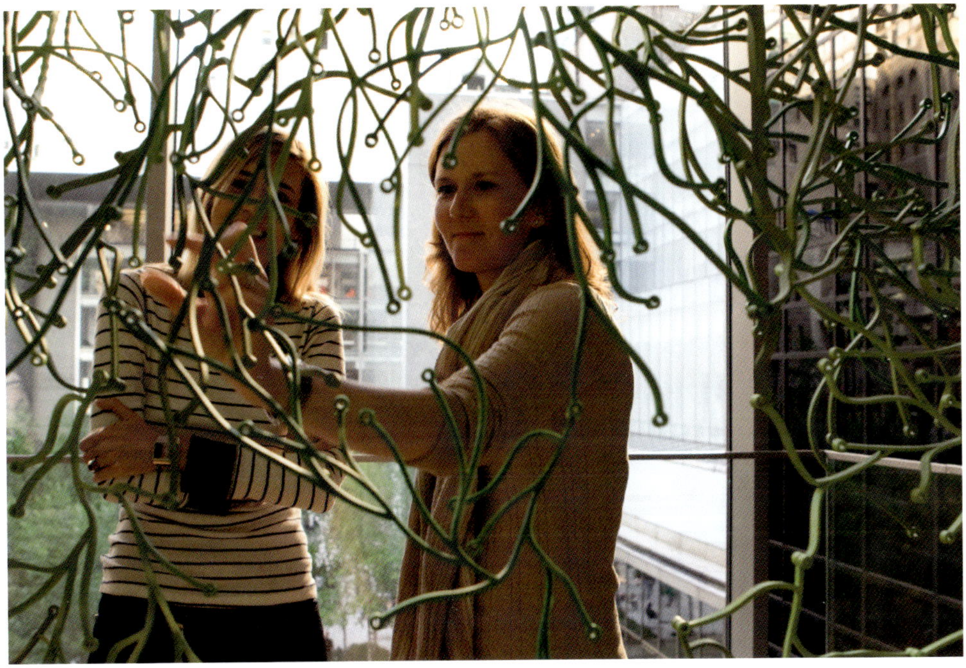

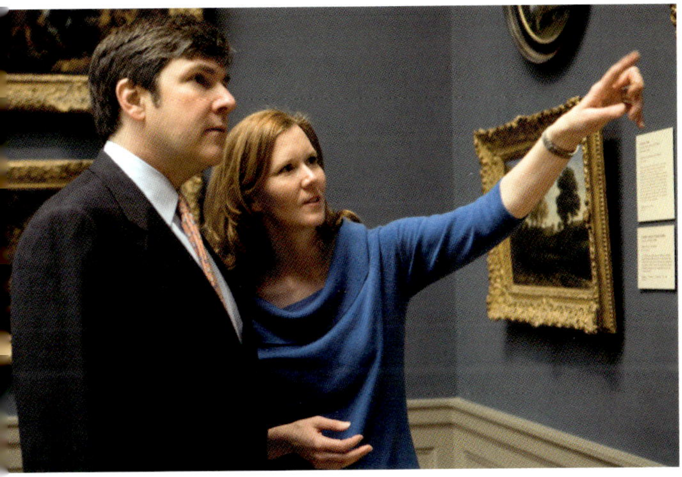

Guided tours by organisations such as Art Smart (www.artsmart.com) are an easy and rewarding way to enrich your understanding of art.

Membership can start from as little as £50/€60/$75 a year, but there are different levels of financial commitment, each of which offers greater privileges. Basic membership is likely to keep patrons abreast of local art news (exhibitions and so forth) and invite them to a range of events, including private viewings at major exhibitions and on curator-lead gallery tours (often including behind-the-scenes). A more generous donation will most likely lead to invitations to artist studios and artist-lead workshops, private and corporate collection visits, international trips, and intimate and exclusive parties and dinners with like-minded art enthusiasts, artists and collectors. The premium membership will often provide collectors with a go-to source of support – advising them on building their art collections.

You can usually find more information on the websites of various galleries, but it's also worth investigating independent art societies – for example, in the UK there's the Contemporary Art Society (www.contemporaryartsociety.org), the Art Fund (www.artfund.org) and Love Art (www.loveartlondon.com).

Build up a trusted network of galleries

Commercial galleries are the galleries that find, promote and sell art rather than simply displaying it, as would a public gallery. Research the galleries that sell work by artists that appeal to your taste and which operate within your budget (art fairs are a great place to do this, as mentioned earlier).

Look for galleries that are run by people who you feel you can approach and build a relationship with

The intimidation game in the art world is legendary, but don't be put off. There's an urban myth that gallerists on London's Cork Street (a chic art enclave) judge visitors by their shoes. Dress like you mean business and know what sort of relationship you'd like to have with that specific gallery. Talk to them about what you like, artists you admire, what gets you excited. If you are serious about buying they'll respond positively and may even help you build your collection, highlighting artists you might not have come across.

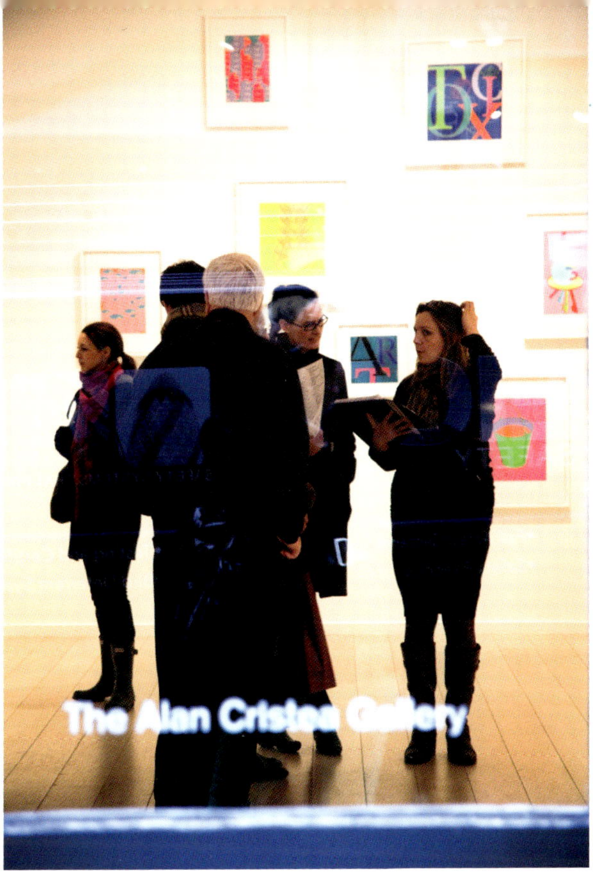

Develop a relationship with a gallery that can help make your collection the best it can be.

The art on display in galleries is only a fraction of what's available, so building a relationship with a gallerist can open up a whole new world beyond what meets the eye. It's also in their interest to nurture you as a collector – the relationship works both ways.

Don't be afraid of judging galleries as they judge you

Once you have started to get to know a gallery, be aware of how they nurture and look after their artists. Do they seem to be on the lookout for new talent and are they successful in their purpose? Look at the artists they represent and analyse their track record: have their artists gone on to forge successful careers? Do they encourage their artists to grow stylistically or merely to churn out work that sells? Make sure you're getting involved with a gallery that will help make your collection the best it can be.

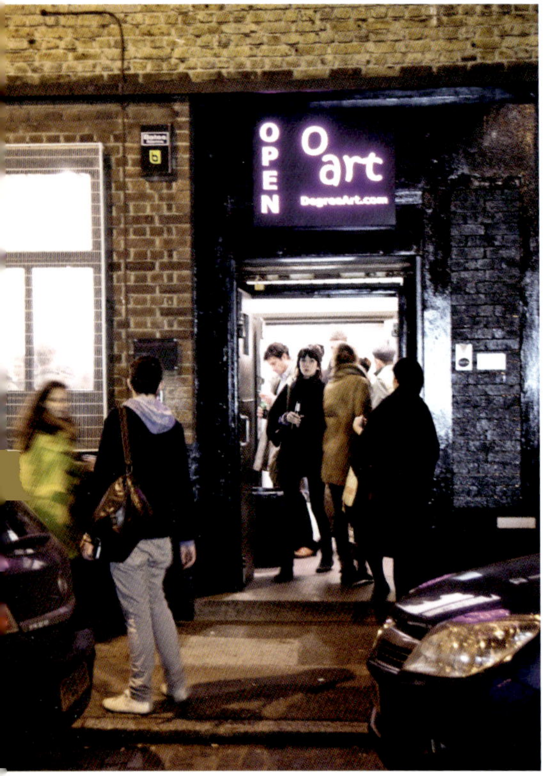

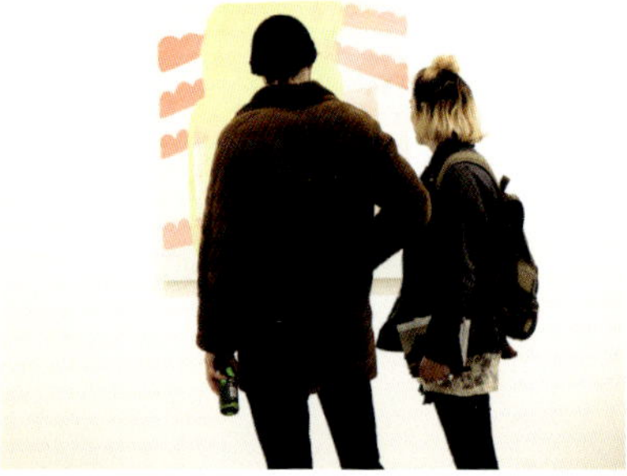

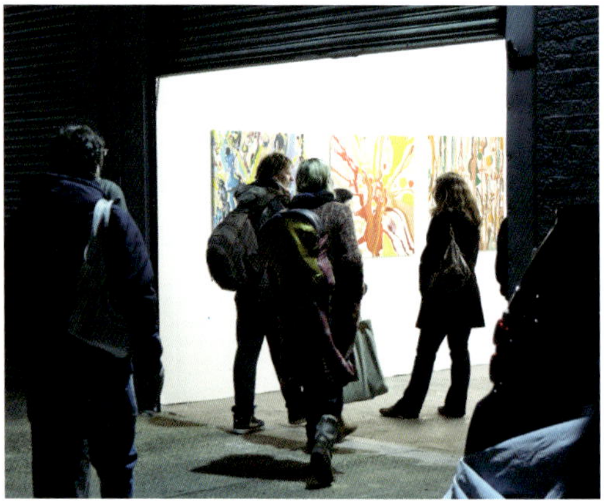

Have an active relationship with galleries

The easiest first step in building and maintaining a relationship with a gallery is to sign up to their mailing lists, and by then attending private views and openings. Here you'll meet artists and fellow collectors and begin to develop a relationship with gallery owners.

Use galleries as a springboard

Ask gallerists about any local contemporary art societies, groups, websites, bloggers, fairs and publications they would recommend. They will be plugged into the local art scene, so ask them to point you in the right direction.

Look out for multiple gallery open evenings

Many art-centric streets (with multiple galleries) have linked open days/evenings and vernissages (e.g. First Thursdays in New York City and on London's Vyner Street where a selection of galleries stays open late on the first Thursday of the month). This can be an easy and natural way to broaden your circles.

Art tours and trips

Take cultural weekends away. Don't limit your view of contemporary art world to that which is most readily accessible from where you live. Make an effort to explore art galleries, fairs and exhibitions abroad too. In the UK, organisations such as The Contemporary Art Society run trips abroad to view and buy art. If travelling on your own, research city hotels with strong art links like The Andaz and Le Meridian in London, New York's Ace Hotel and Gershwin Hotel, or the international Morgan Hotel Group, which has strong art connections. Such hotels make a great base as they are likely to have all practical art-related information at their fingertips. Look at links on the art magazine and art fair websites as they will often post details of hotels with art links and organisations that arrange trips.

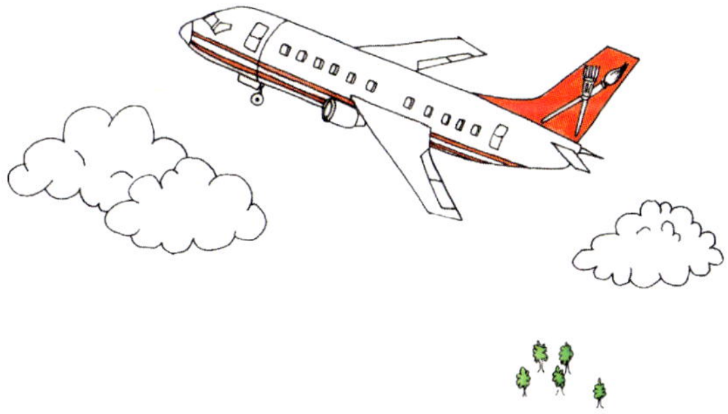

02

What to look for

What to look for

YOU CAN BUY some amazing work at attractive prices if you look out for the right things. Don't be put off by grand-scale pieces with prices in the hundreds of thousands, and headlines bleating out gazillion dollar auction records, because these are the news flashes that are relevant for a minority. But without the headlines and reviews it can be hard to know where to begin. Before you think about where and how to buy art, first think about *what*, not as in art by particular artists, but the different *types* of art.

Artist editions

One of the most accessible ways to invest in more affordable contemporary art is by buying artist editions, prints and multiples. These are a democratic way for artists to disseminate their work to a wider audience as by the very nature of being multiple versions of the same work, there are more of them. And because the artist can divide any initial outlay between the editions, individual editions cost less.

An artist at work at the Stroke Urban Art Fair.

Popularized in the post-Second World War period by artists including Andy Warhol (who made over 800), Roy Lichtenstein

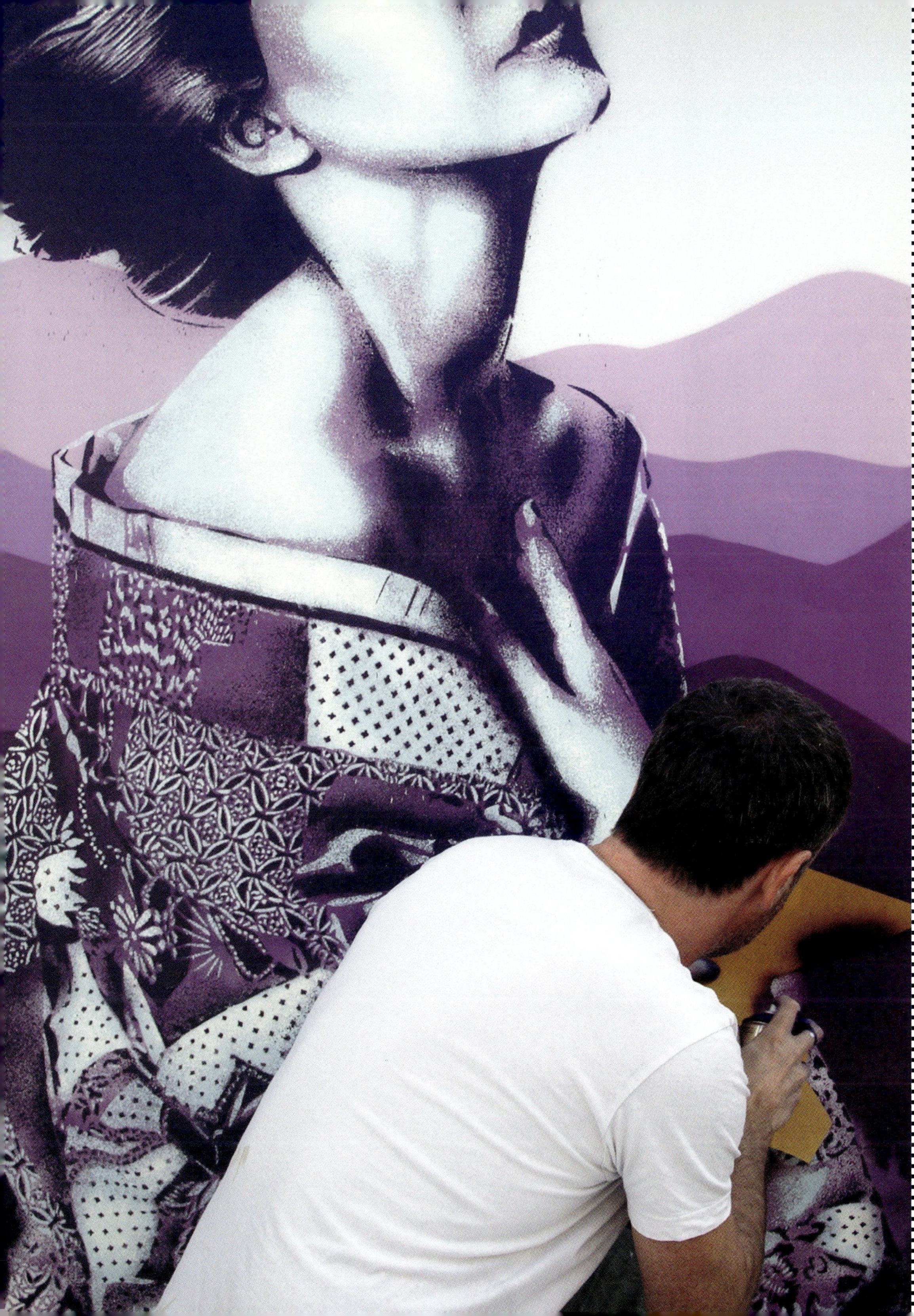

(who made over 350) and Joseph Beuys (who made over 600), prints on paper are a way of leaving a mark, a bit like a footprint; an artist creates a work from which several copies can be made – ink is pressed down onto a screen, blocked and only where it touches does it leave a mark. Techniques can vary, depending on whether the work is made by an intaglio process (carving into a surface as with etching, drypoint, aquatint or mezzotint) or blocking (where the print is taken from the raised points, or uncovered points on a surface, such as relief printing or silkscreen printing).

Prints are not reproductions of original works (like mass produced posters, for example), but are instead mimetic reproductions taken from a plate. Multiples differ slightly in that although many versions of the same still produced work, but each work is made unique by hand-finishing or similar techniques. Multiples will be very similar, but not identical.

An artist will work closely with a print studio in a collaborative process to produce a plate, from which a finite number of prints are created. The studio will advise the artists on the best methods and potential for creating the effect they want, but the creative vision of the process ultimately rests with the artist. The most interesting prints, of genuine significance, are those that make full use of printing processes to create a work that couldn't have been done any other way – i.e. that isn't simply a way to make many versions of a work but is genuinely the best method of producing that work. A respected press is The Paragon Press (www.paragonpress.co.uk), whose print collaborations are owned by museums and respected contemporary art collections around the world. Many print studios and foundries who produce works for mainstream galleries, public galleries and print publishers also run galleries themselves, such as UK-based Jealous Gallery (www.jealousgallery.com), which also holds an annual print prize for MA graduates of London art schools, or the internationally renowned CCA Galleries, www.ccagalleries.com (which work with Coriander Press).

Sculptural editions work in a similar way: an artist will work with a foundry (such as Stroud-based Pangolin, who have cast sculptures for artists including Damien Hirst, Marc Quinn, David Bailey and

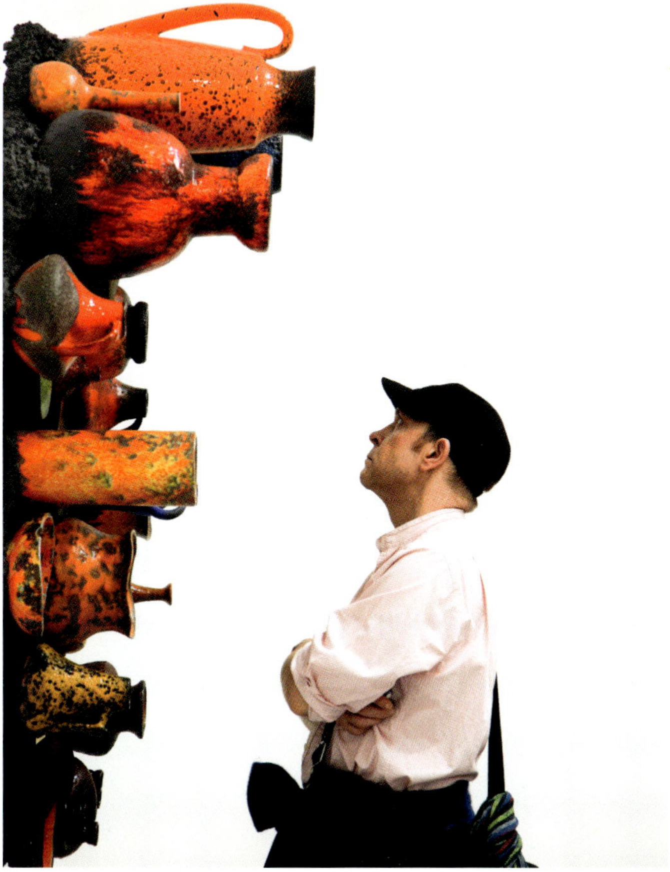

To gain access to and communicate and engage with the art world, you'll have to speak its language.

Antony Gormley, and who run a sculpture gallery in London: www.pangolinlondon.com). The foundry will work with an artist to produce sculptural editions to the artist's specifications.

Limited-edition runs of prints and multiples should be numbered showing what number in the edition it is (i.e. 1/100). Often (but not always) the prices rise incrementally as the run sells out – there can be a pre-published price, a published price that will then rise mid-sale, rise again just before the run sells out, and again when the edition has sold out. The smaller the edition run, the rarer and more exclusive the work.

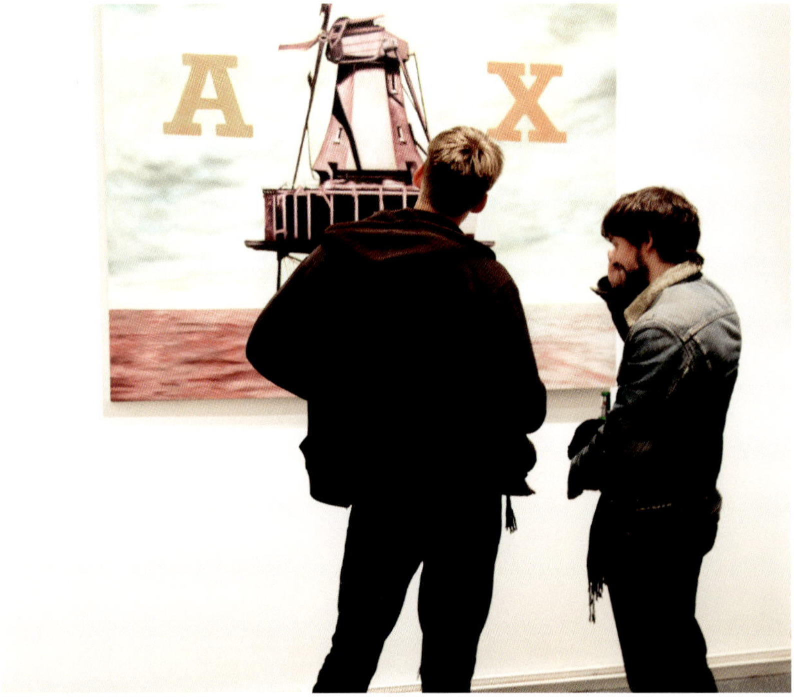

Because an edition of many means there is no uniqueness, even when the run has sold-out, a rise in price is less common than with an original, one-off work of art. There is a politicised nature to editions, a democracy in their non-exclusivity – they are not unique, they are designed to be owned by many, and to be attractively priced. But a rise in price is not unheard of – the popularity of a print or change in fortunes of an artist can raise the value of an edition. When artist Mark Wallinger's created his nine-foot-tall piece *Ghost* – a negative image of a George Stubbs horse that looks like an apparition of a unicorn – he also, in collaboration with The Whitechapel Gallery, produced a domestically scaled (51.1 cm x 42.9 cm or 17 in x 20 in) silkscreen print edition of 500. The nine-foot original is now held in the Tate Collection, the artist won the Turner Prize in 2007 and one of the editions, initially priced in 2001 at several hundred pounds, was sold at auction in 2011 for£1,700/€2,000/$2,700.

Advantages of editions

* Priced lower than one-of-a-kind works of art.
* Because there are multiple copies, this means you can often think about your purchase for a little longer without fear someone else will snap it up. If they do, it's fine – you can both have one!
* A chance to buy work by big name artists at more reasonable prices.
* An affordable way to take a gamble on a new artist.
* A way to support artists, and arts and charitable institutions that often produce prints to raise money.
* Domestically scaled: unlike grand-scale pieces, editions are usually easy to accommodate in a domestic setting.
* Prints are a recognised artistic process and can increase in value just as with originals.

Galleries exclusively selling prints are especially popular in the current economic climate. The Multiple Store (www.themultiplestore.org) works with artists including Fiona Banner and Anya Gallaccio; Counter Editions (www.countereditions.com) make prints for leading UK public galleries including Tate and The Hayward Gallery by artists including Michael Landy and Jake and Dinos Chapman; Cereal Art's roster of artists includes David Shrigley and Takashi Murakami (www.cerealart.com), while Other Criteria (www.othercriteria.com), part-owned by Damien Hirst, makes print editions of works by established and emerging international contemporary artists including Harland Miller and Peter Doig.

There is a politicised nature to editions, a democracy in their non-exclusivity – they are not unique, they are designed to be owned by many, and to be attractively priced.

GOOD TO KNOW BUYING PRINTS

* Check the print method: speak to the gallerist about the artist's choice of print method, whether it is a computer-printed edition, or made by a more hands-on process and why this is (it could be for colour quality, archival properties etc – it's good to know what the priorities and concerns of the artist are).
* Look for works which use the technicalities of a particular printing method because that is the best way of realising the vision of the artist (i.e. that the work isn't made purely as a commercial enterprise).
* Check the limit of the limited edition; exclusivity adds value.
* Buying near the end of the sale of a limited edition means you know how popular the edition run is because of how quickly it has sold (which will affect the resale value).
* Buying early (lower numbered editions) means the print will usually be more valuable when the run has sold out (a reward for having taken a gamble early in the sale).
* Collecting the same edition number for different prints can be an interesting quirk, especially if buying works by the same artist.
* For the same reason (that it's an interesting quirk), significant numbers can add value (i.e. 1/100, 50/100, 100/100).
* Artists' proofs (a working proof or test print) are highly prized – look for the AP or P symbol instead of a number. Prints marked with HC (Hors de Commerce) come directly from the artist and are unnumbered prints for the artist to give away.

* Check the artist signature. Some editions have numbered and signed versions, and others are just numbered. If there is no signature, ask if this can be done.
* Ask for a certificate of authenticity, which gives the details of title, dimensions, medium, production method and release date, and which should be signed by the artist and have confirmation that the edition size will not be exceeded or added to. Once an edition has sold out, that's it: no more should be produced. Printing plates or images should be destroyed at the end of the print run by the artist or publisher (if they haven't worn out) so the edition run cannot be added to.
* Be wary of mass reproductions: printing methods like offset lithography (the method used for most magazines, newspapers, posters and books) aren't the same as original prints.

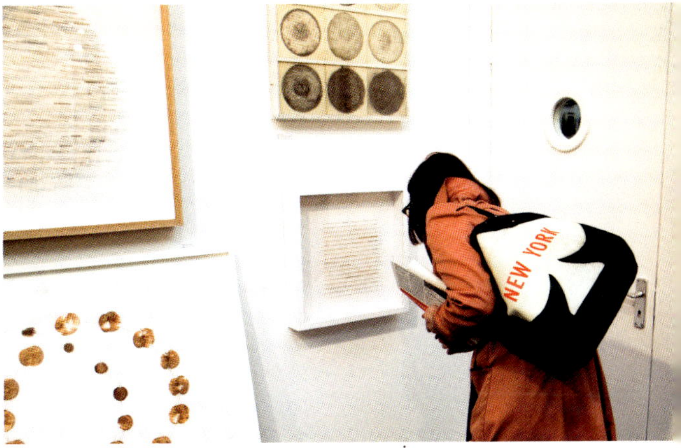

Original work by emerging artists

'Emerging' art is the buzz-word of the moment, implying excitement, potential, optimism, hope and promise of something great. Although a fairly nebulous term, emerging artists are essentially those at an early stage of their career but who are perceived to be going somewhere – by building up a cohesive, well-received and well-regarded body of work, and who people are talking excitedly about. They are usually young, but not exclusively (age shouldn't really be a factor in determining an emerging artist. However, the excitement and novelty of youth often plays in their favour).

An artwork from a graduate show at the Royal College of Art catches the viewer's eye.

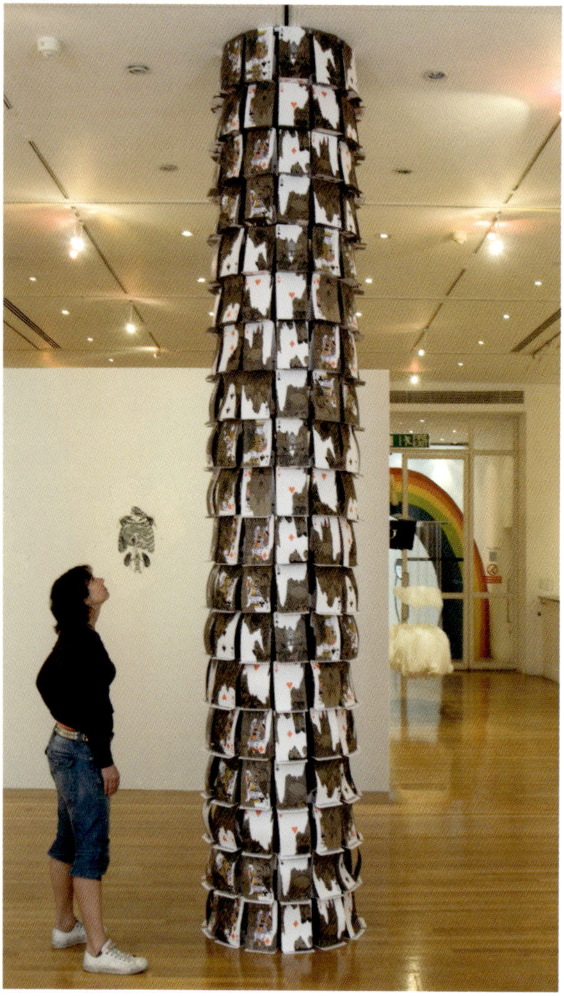

Sadly the term is rambunctiously over-used, a label often slapped on to any new artist who wants to be seen (usually by the gallery promoting them) as a name to watch. The best advice for negotiating the slippery terrain is to think about the source (usually a gallery) and make sure it's one whose opinion you trust. The label should definitely be taken with a pinch of salt and interpreted as a personal opinion, rather than a statement of fact that an artist is on the up or a signifier of art world cache and glamour. At the end of the day, success is ultimately a lottery – being spotted by the right people, capturing the zeitgeist, or

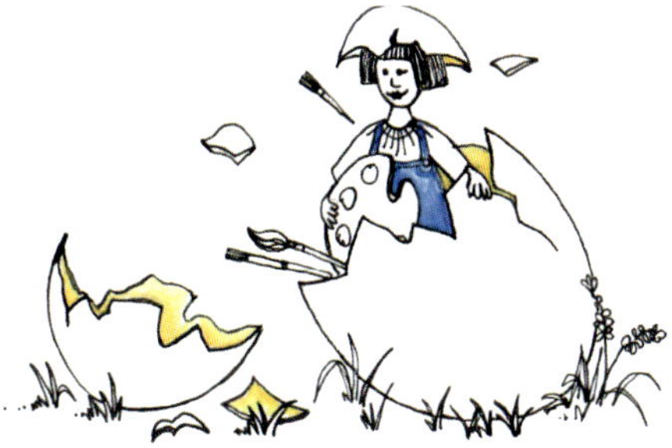

GOOD TO CONSIDER EMERGING ARTISTS

* Investing in an emerging artist near the start of their career is an ethical investment – you are supporting them not only financially, but emotionally at a crucial point.
* Look for a clear, easily identifiable, fresh style, and unique identity.
* Look a cohesive body of work that makes an impact as a whole – is there a dominant or overarching theme that unites the work?
* Look for artists who show commitment to their craft – for example, by having done an MA.
* Don't be seduced and impressed by shock tactics – analyse whether it is shock for shock's sake and whether its impact has longevity.
* Assess the quality of production (of both ideas and materials and the time put into individual works).
* A certificate of authenticity is not usually necessary for an original work of art (as with editions). Proof of purchase (such as a receipt) should be enough.

striking the right social or political note for the time – and only a few emerging artists will go on to become more established. If you can, speak with the artist yourself (or the gallerist) and talk to them about their ideas and methods to see if they are someone you believe in. You can then judge whether you think they are an emerging artist.

Taken in good faith, and confidently evaluated on your own terms, emerging art can be a great way to buy work at the start of an artist's career before prices escalate.

A good way to keep your eye on the most promising crop of emerging artists is to look at the group shows and prizes that gather artists from multiple arts schools, who have usually been nominated by a tutor, selected by a curator and judged by a panel of artists, critics and curators. In the UK alone there are several highly respected prizes that have come to be seen as major platforms for launching the careers of emerging artists, including: New Contemporaries (www.newcontemporaries.org.uk), the Catlin guide and the Catlin Art Prize (www.artcatlin.com); the Jerwood Drawing Prize (www.jerwoodvisualarts.com); the London university-based Future Map (www.futuremap.arts.ac.uk); curators Catriona Warren, Robert Dingle and Kay Saatchi's Anticipation Prize at Selfridges; and the Saatchi gallery/Channel 4 prize, New Sensations (www.saatchi-gallery.co.uk/4ns). Similar art prizes can be found internationally, gathering art graduates from various regions. They are a great way of seeing the crème de la crème of graduates.

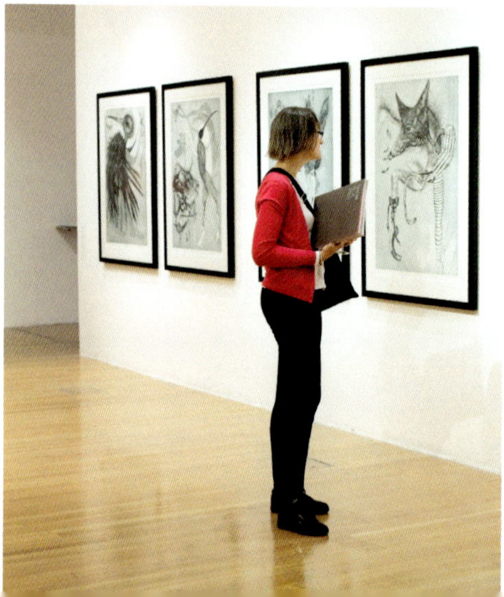

Sketches, studies and drawings

Unfinished or draft sketches, usually in pencil, chalk or ink, are original works that are often keenly priced. They may not be as polished as the finished article, but can nevertheless capture the spirit of a piece or the style of an artist and enable you to invest in works by established artists at attractive prices.

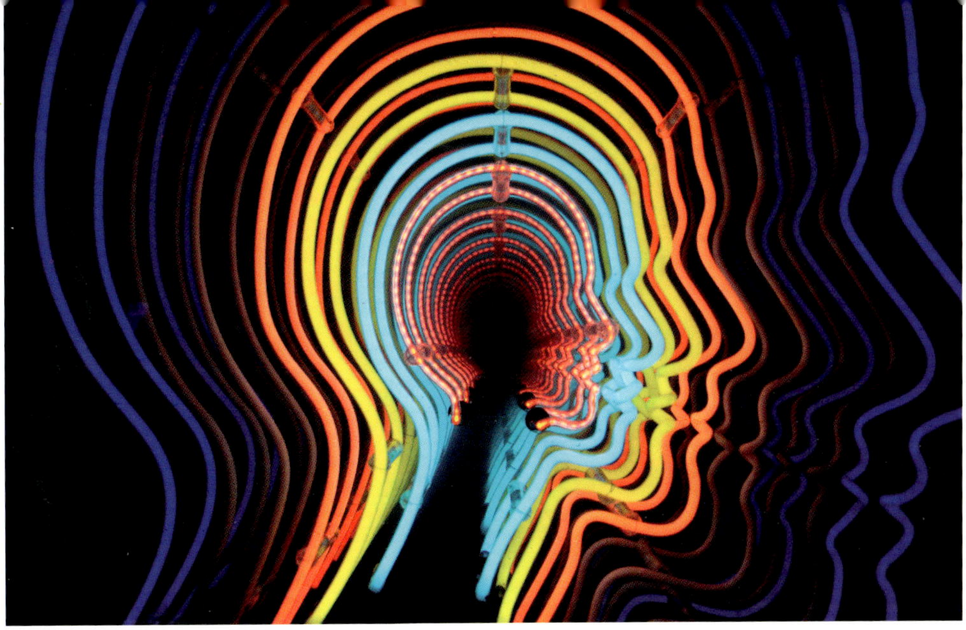

Alternative art

Certain categories of contemporary art fall outside the usual strictures of the art world, such as outsider art (art by self-taught artists, or those with mental health issues), kinetic art (motion art), digital art, and urban art (also known as street art, guerrilla art, or graffiti art). Newer or non-traditional art forms are always treated with a degree of wary tolerance, but it's worth remembering that the advent of photography brought with it cries that it was the death knell for painting. Don't dismiss these 'other' ways of producing art – be open-minded.

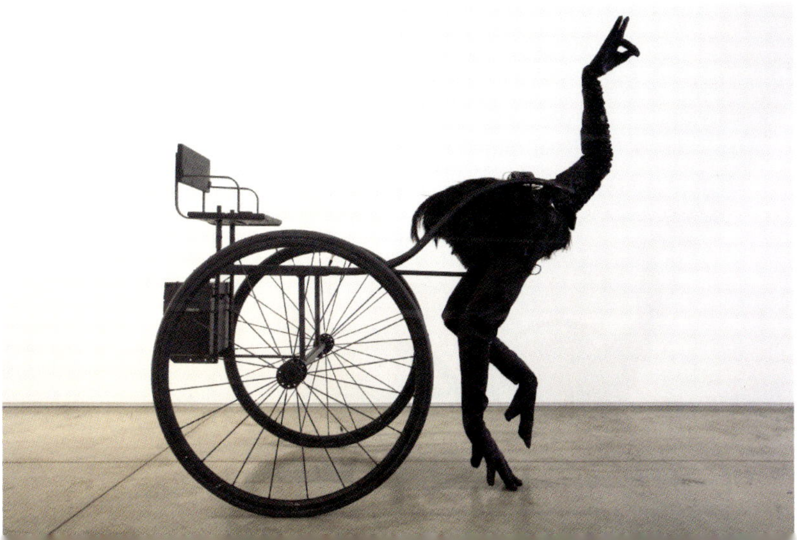

Moving art at the Kinetica Art Fair (left and above).

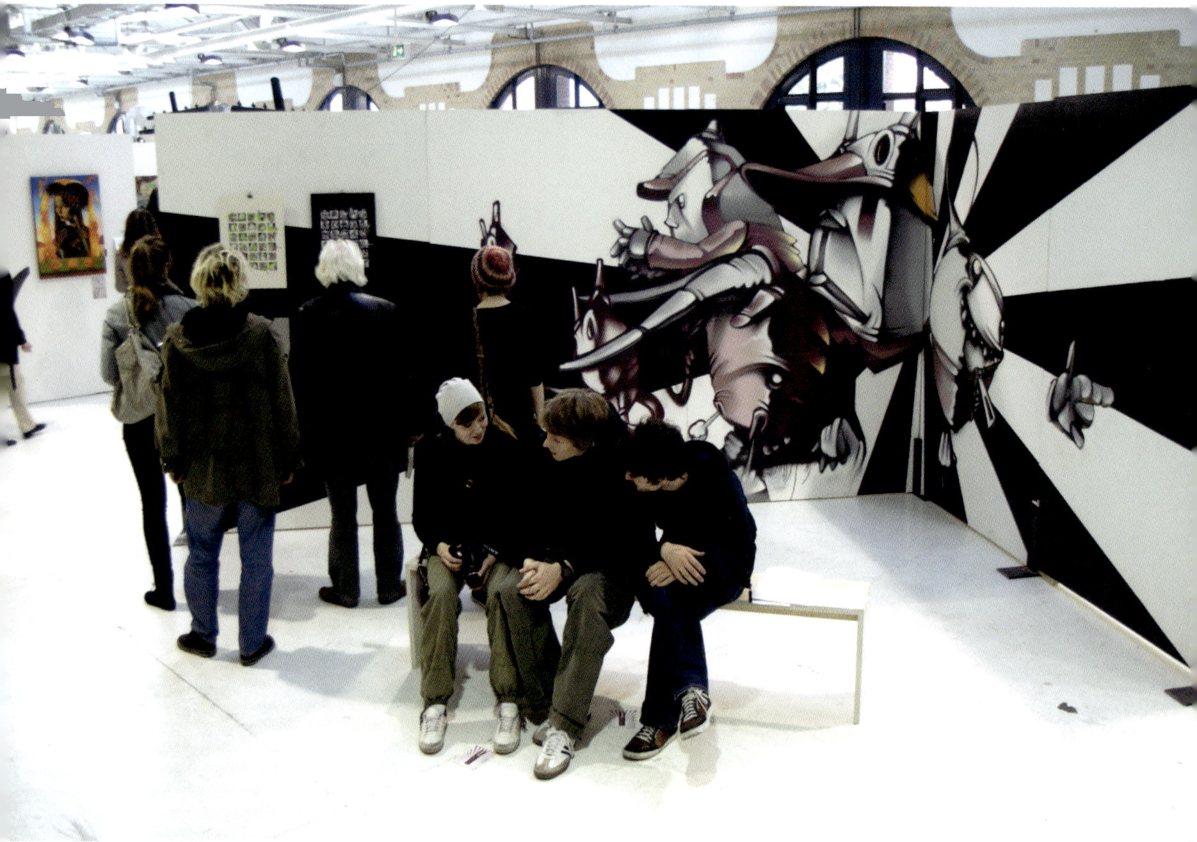

Artworks
from the Stroke
Urban Art Fair.

Watch out for alternative movements, those that challenge or provoke the accepted order of things.

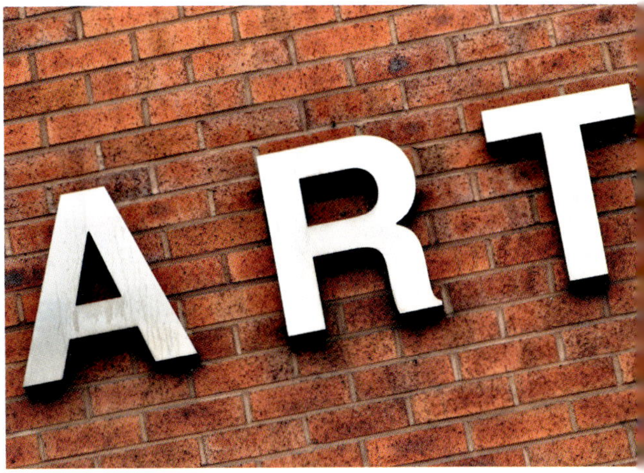

Urban art is such a recent phenomenon – it has only just been accepted by the art world and officially blessed through gallery shows art fairs and reviews. The anarchism of its nature means it is underground, alternative, against the system, outside art's usual parameters, and street artists usually have pseudonyms. However, street artists like Banksy, Invader Shepard Fairey and Pure Evil are examples of street artists who have become established artists – sold in galleries and at auction for high prices. It's a valuable lesson to learn – watch out for alternative movements, those that challenge or provoke the accepted order of things. The Lazarides gallery first promoted UK artist Banksy, and continues to sell art with an alternative edge via the off-shoot gallery The Outsiders www.theoutsiders.net.

Digital

Because of technological advances, digital art, made using digital technology and covering a wide range of art where digital processing is significant in the creation and production, is increasingly popular. From David Hockney's 'paintings' on his iPad (printed as limited editions) to Tracey Emin's 'Photodiary on Blackberry', a giclee print which sold at Christie's in 2010 for £4,750/€5,500/$7,600, the potentials are varied and limitless. If an image is a digital artwork, check to see if it is a limited-edition run (the same rules apply as with conventional prints) and whether the original digital file has been deleted. Be wary of digital reproductions of original works which will have little or no investment potential.

Sculpture

Sculpture can be anything that is *carved*, where material is chipped away to leave a form (such as wood, marble, alabaster, limestone, granite etc); *modelled* from a pliable substance like wax or clay; cast by pouring molten plastic, clay or metal into a mould and then cooling and setting it before removing the cast; or made using *assemblage*, where a sculpture is made of various parts of structures joined together or from found objects.

There is often a misconception that sculpture is exclusively expensive, and that it is huge and problematic to display. This simply isn't true. Admittedly, traditional bronze and silver sculpture can be

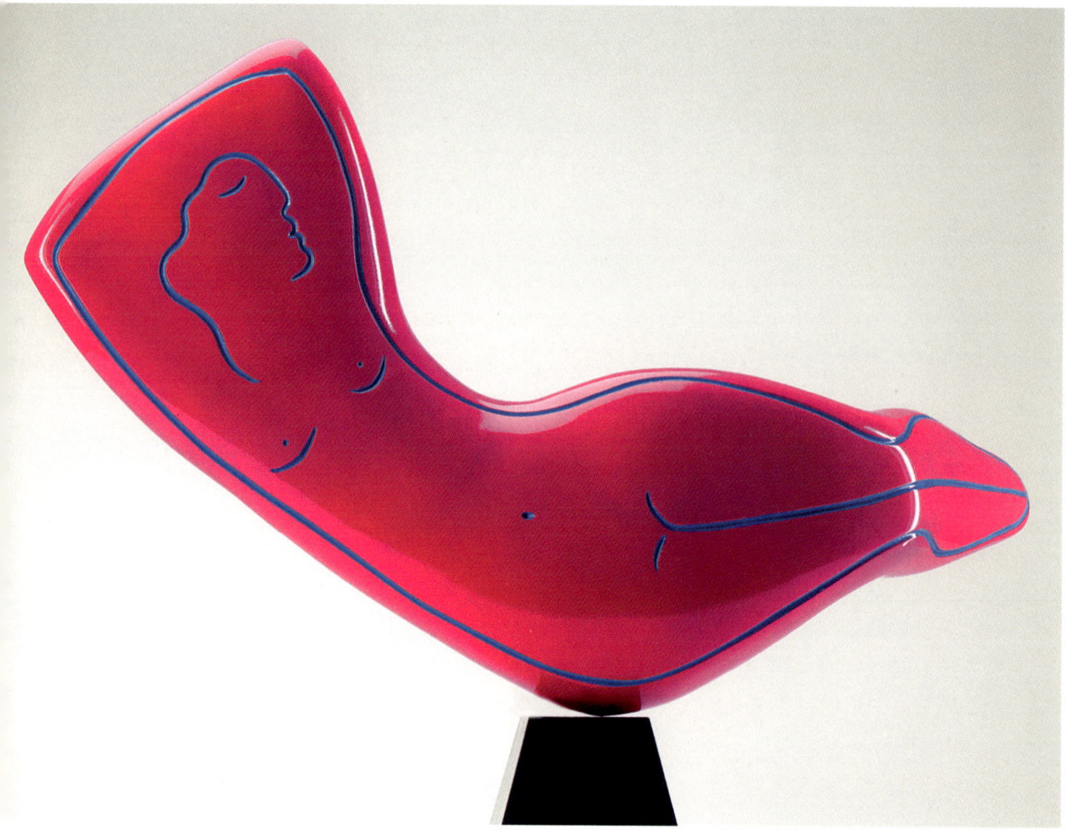

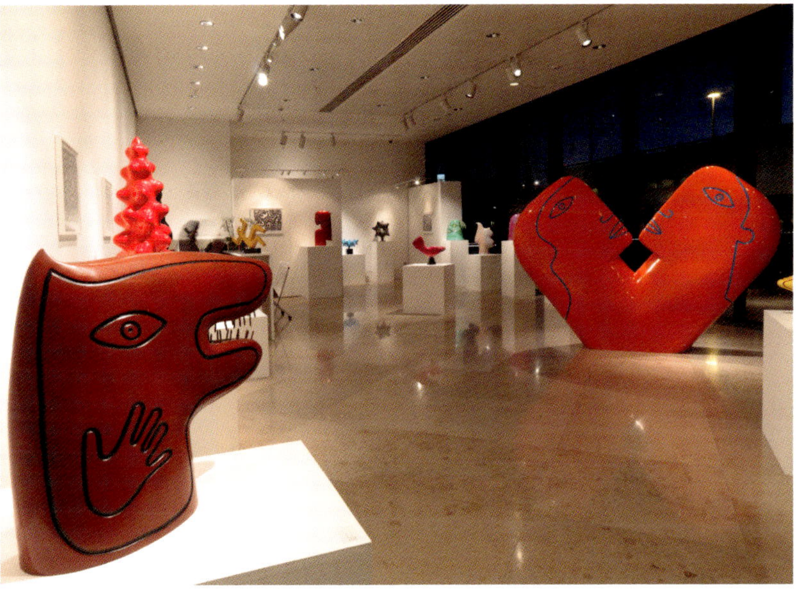

Bold sculpture at Pangolin Gallery, London (far left and left) and the Royal College of Art (below).

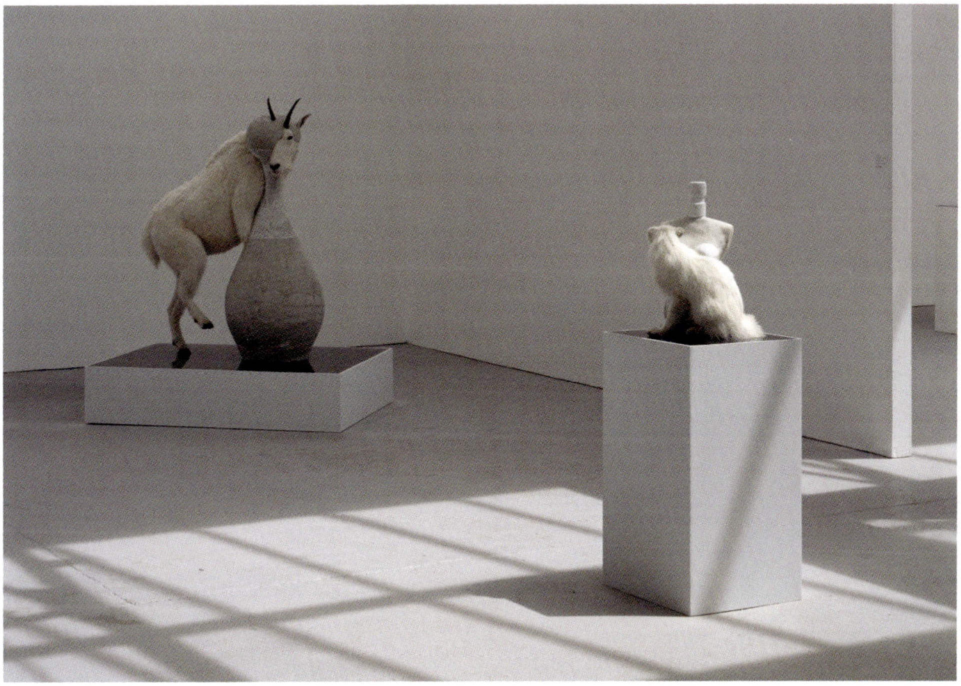

pricey because of both the cost of materials and the nature of production, in that the cast and production process has to be outsourced to a foundry, however, sculpture is also often made in editions, which brings down the price, and can also be made from more affordable materials – ceramic, wood, plastic or glass, or found objects for example.

GOOD TO CONSIDER BUYING SCULPTURE

* Don't be afraid of it – it's like other forms of art, just three-dimensional.
* Consider scale – smaller pieces can easily be displayed in a domestic setting, on a desk or mantelpiece for example. Artist jewellery can even be considered sculpture.
* Tactility – the touch and feel of sculpture can add to its appeal. Its three-dimensionality means it invades personal space and can be more involving to interact with.
* Sculpture is often more durable – it is usually less affected by variations in light and heat.
* Consider outside spaces as possible places to display sculpture (but remember you may need a protective finish and to wax them to maintain the colour and protect against the harsher vagaries of the elements).
* Check the provenance of the piece – i.e. where it has been made – by asking the gallerist or artist. Outsourcing to cheap production in places like the Far East can diminish the value.
* There can often be an inherent material worth to the piece which can affect the price (with gold, for example).
* It can be slightly more difficult to transport after purchase.

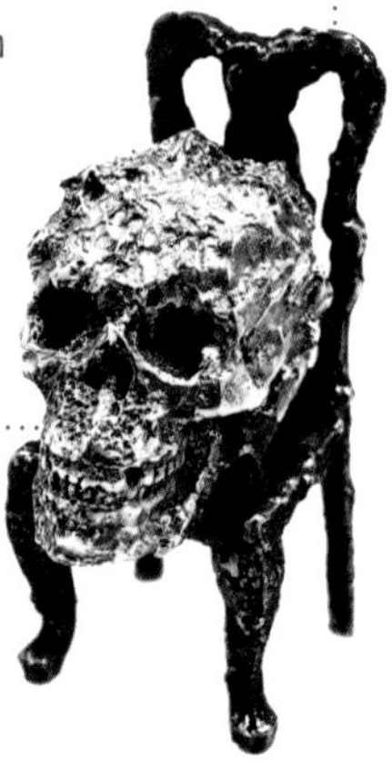

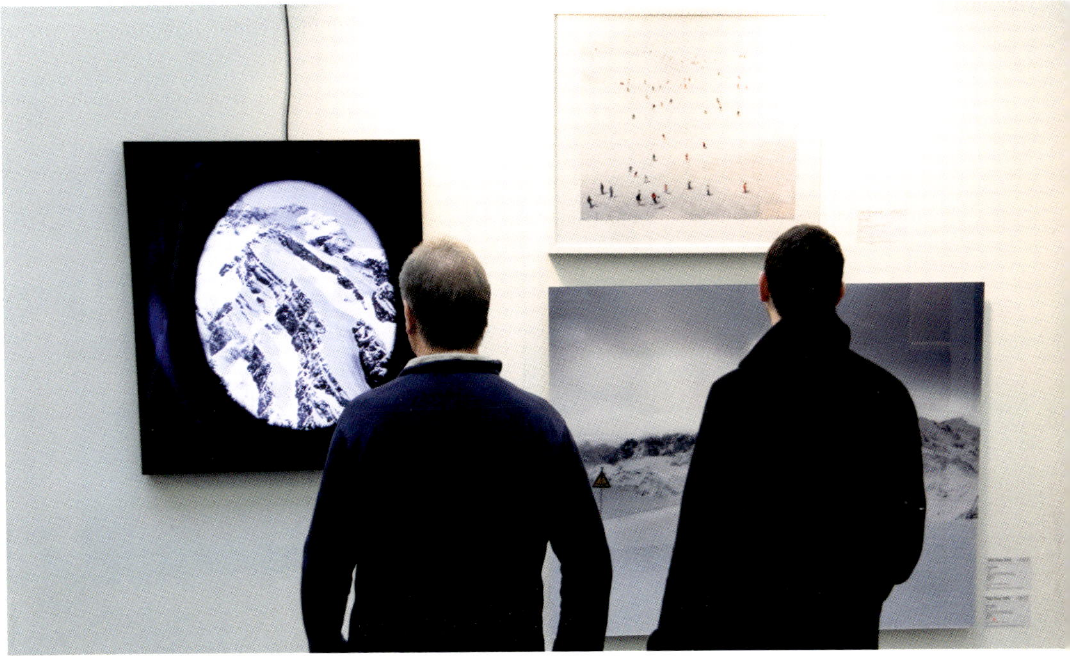

Photography

There are many different elements to consider when looking at a photographic art work: the way the image is captured (digital or film, for example); whether it is a colour print or black-and-white; the print process (chemicals in a darkroom, laser technology, computer printers, Polaroid transfer, or by using gelatin silver or platinum salts); the paper used; and the time frame when the picture was printed (modern prints are the production of an image long after the original was taken, while a vintage print was made within five years of the image being taken).

As the methods vary, so do opinions on the quality, longevity of the print and visual impact. There are schools, for example, who think that an inkjet printer (or giclee print) is an inferior method of printing because the print has been run off a computer-driven printer rather than hand created. However, the inks used often have more advanced archival properties than regular c-type prints (the generic name for a

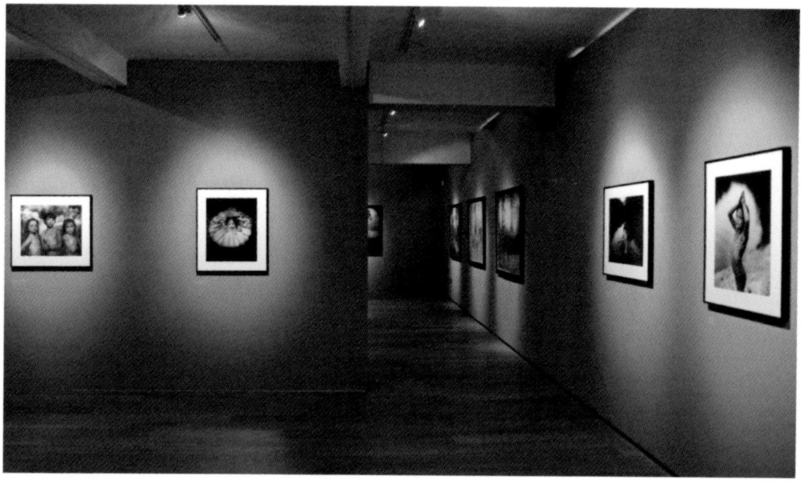

modern colour photograph print) which makes them popular with both artists and collectors. Digital printing (not to be confused with digital reproduction), meanwhile, allows for much more detailed manipulation of an image (on a computer). Gelatin silver printing is the most common form of black-and-white printing, while platinum or palladium prints, which can produce more subtle and complex tones and have a longer life expectancy, will be more expensive.

It certainly can seem complex and confusing. The best way to make sense of it all is to assess on a case-by-case basis and ask questions – talk to the gallery, printmakers or artists themselves about why certain production and printing methods have been used. Is it aesthetic or for convenience, for example? Many artists prefer working in a certain way, with certain materials and it's good to know these specifics. It'll help you understand how the piece has been created, and the thought that's behind it. Work out not only what the artist's priorities are, but also your own – what it is that you most like in the quality, look and feel of a work. What is important to you? Is it that the artist themselves made the print, or is it enough that theirs was the eye that captured the image in the first place, or is it more important that the inks have the best archival properties? Ask questions and come to your own decision.

Craft

Craft, which can cover artistic creativity expressed in all manner of materials and disciplines from ceramics to weaving to patchwork, has a tricky relationship with contemporary art. Many traditional craft-makers would not consider themselves contemporary artists, but those with an *avant garde* thrust often do – one can think of Tracey Emin's patchwork quilts or Grayson Perry's pots or tapestries. Often, because of the utilitarian or functional purpose of craft, it is not considered contemporary art, but there are no hard and fast rules. In general, when it comes to craft, look beyond functionality for pieces that provoke or inspire an impassioned, perhaps politicised, dialogue and which are exhibited as contemporary art. It's also worth looking at the websites of respected crafts councils for their approved lists of artists and fairs.

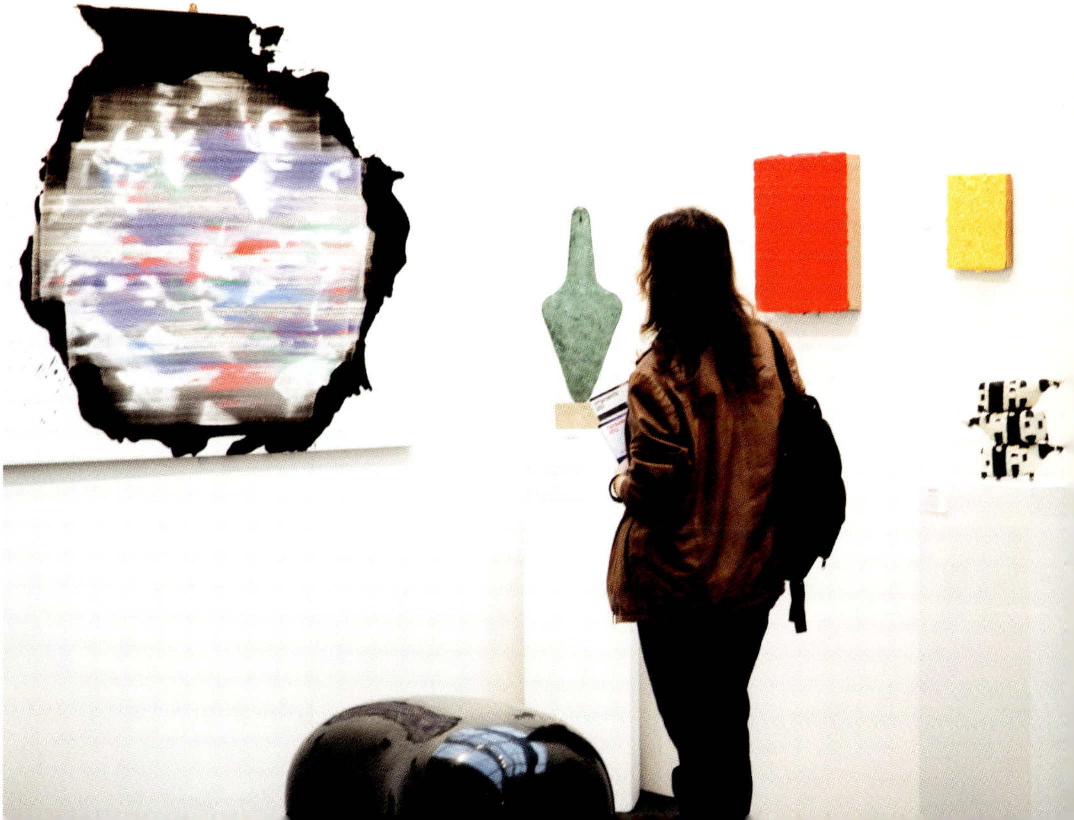

Other considerations

Appreciation

Before you buy a piece of art, make sure you have given enough time and attention to appreciating it – many a regrettable purchase has been bought on impulse, under pressure, or in a rush. The best purchases will be those pieces you have actively engaged with and have carefully considered.

GOOD TO KNOW APPRECIATING ART

* Take your time: give yourself time to think about the piece, and time to gauge your reactions.
* Relax: give the artwork space, and give yourself space to interact with it on an emotional level, on its own terms without the stresses of the day clouding your reactions. Let your reactions slowly bubble to the surface of your consciousness.
* Think about the conversation you are having with the artwork. Is it one that you could live with, and will keep you interested for years to come?
* There are no rights and wrongs. Appreciation and buying is a mix of instinct, passion and personal taste.

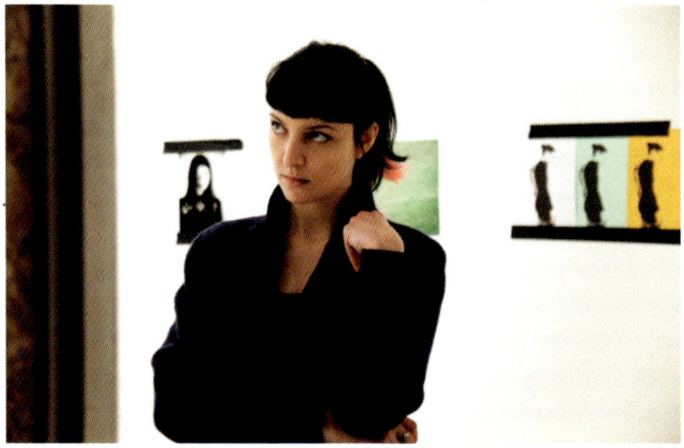

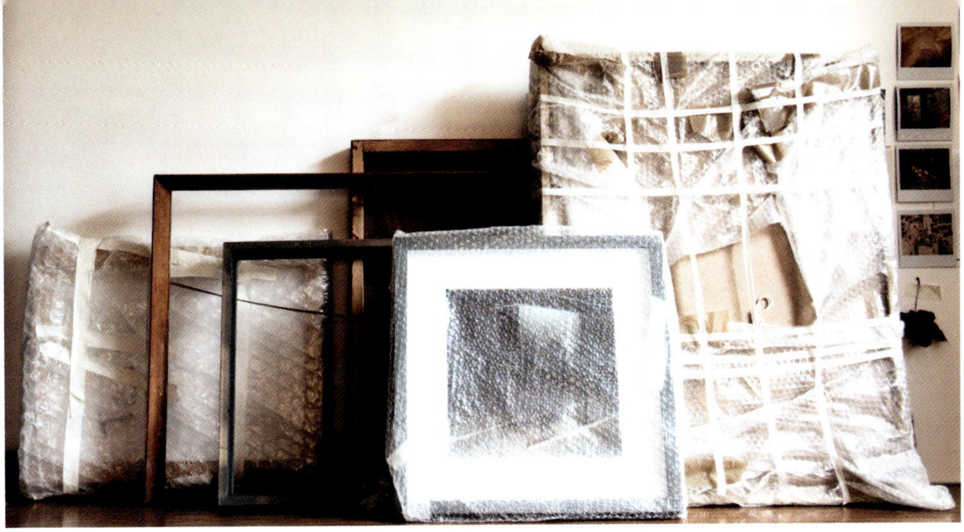

Framing

Framing is a vital part of the process of buying a work of art (that's not three-dimensional) both from an aesthetic and preservation point of view.

Considerations

* Ask about the framing of the artwork for sale – if sold as framed, ask why it was framed like that (was it an artist stipulation?) and where it was framed. You want to be sure it was done by a reputable framers and not on the cheap.
* Galleries and artists may have a special deal or relationship with a framers (especially if they are framing in bulk) so that might bring down the price for a framed version of the work as opposed to getting it framed yourself.
* Don't be afraid of re-framing. Charles Saatchi is a famous re-framer of works he buys (much to many artists' chagrin). Have the courage of your convictions – you are the one who has to live with it.
* Monitor the packaging or the artwork: whether rolled or put in an envelope, make sure the work arrives with you as perfectly as you saw it hanging in the gallery – the preservation of an artwork begins the moment it is made.
* Expect to pay upwards of £100/€120/$160 for a good frame (simple timber) – much less may mean cheap materials and poor workmanship.
* A great frame, which presents a work optimally, can add value to a work.

GOOD TO KNOW FRAMING

Discuss with your framer the requirements and needs of your artwork before you start. Alongside deadline, environment in which it is to be hung and budget, think about the artwork's needs:

Aesthetic

* Open your mind to the transforming power of a frame. Be visionary – a frame can completely change a picture, bringing it to life and drawing out specific elements of its character. You want the frame to show off the artwork to its best advantage.
* Consider mounts – when they suit a work, mounts can add gravitas, a luxurious feel and increased scale to a work. Ask for 100% cotton boards which are free from the impurities that can damage the artwork over time. Check that the mounts are cut straight.
* Not all works *need* framing – for example, many people choose to hang canvases without frames, and oil on canvas isn't usually covered by glass as the varnish applied to the paint is considered sufficient protection.

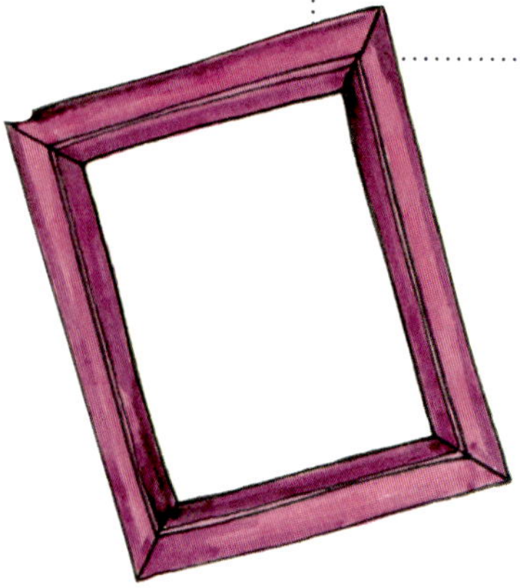

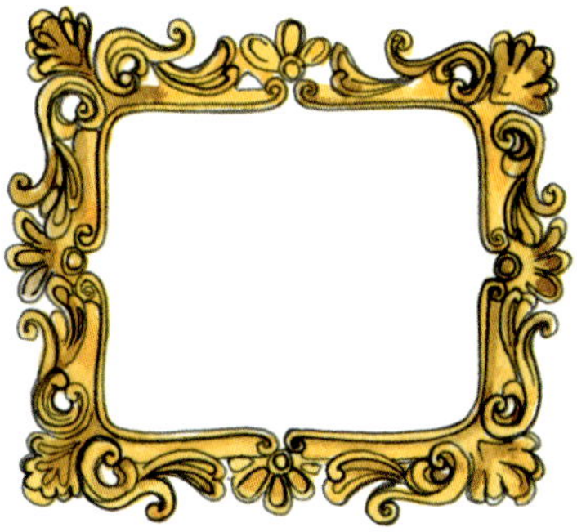

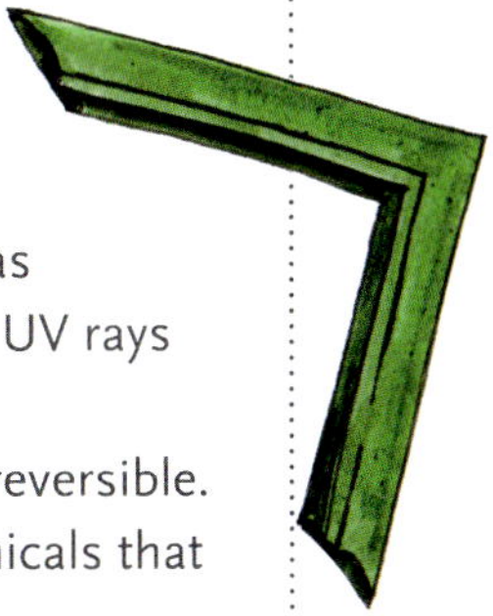

Preservation

✱ Ultra-violet filters in glazing will protect (as much as possible) art from fading by removing 80-90% of the UV rays – a good idea for bright rooms. UV light can cause discolouration, fading or yellowing. The process is irreversible.

✱ Avoid MDF frames and others which contain chemicals that may seep into the work and distort the colours.

✱ Never have any artwork glued to a back – it can damage the quality and diminish the value of the work.

✱ Check the corners – they need to be neat and firmly joined.

Protection

✱ Perspex glass with UV filters is a good idea if the work needs to be shipped, transported, or regularly moved around – it's both lighter and any shattering won't damage the artwork as glass would.

✱ Non-reflective glass will stop light bouncing off so you can see it in a bright room.

✱ Check whether the medium demands special requirements – for example, loose pigments (charcoal, chalk or pastels) can cause static build up and may be best-suited to laminate glass.

✱ With photo corners, never have four corners inserted. Paper needs to breathe and moves with minor temperature changes, so too much rigidity and tension may cause the work to tear.

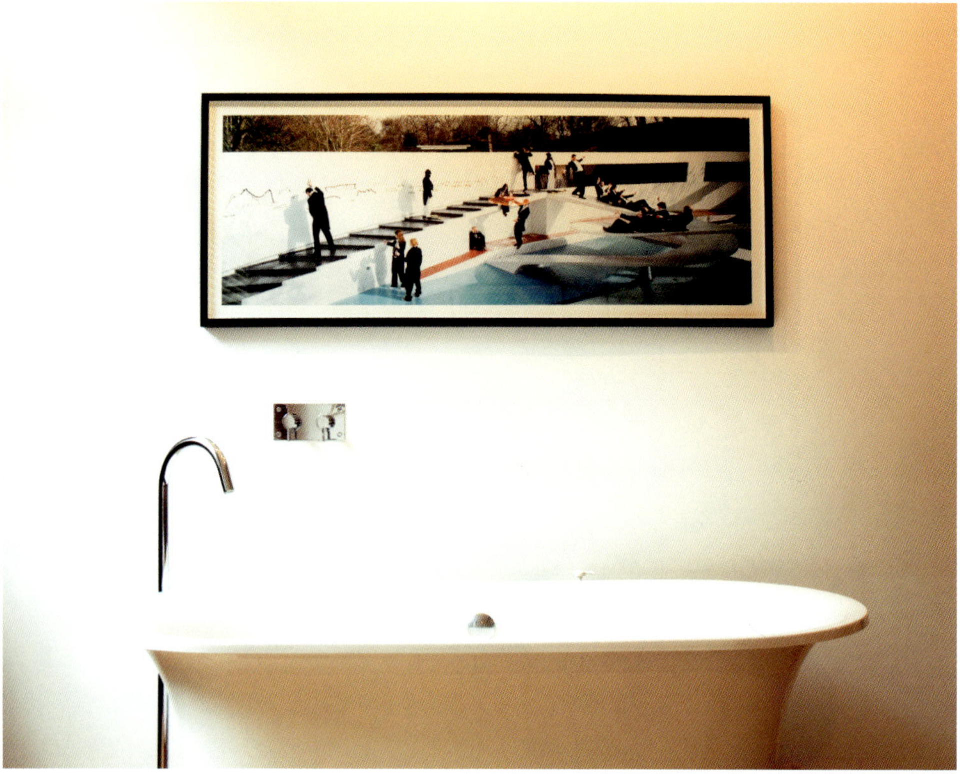

Hanging and conservation

Don't

* Hang works on paper in direct sunlight or spotlights.
* Hang works in damp or humid spaces – for example, bathrooms, basements or on un-insulated external walls.
* Hang works above a radiator or open fireplace (especially if the materials are heat sensitive).
* Hang pictures in rooms that have been freshly painted or re-carpeted because of potential chemical damage from fumes. Wait several weeks (or until the smell has gone).

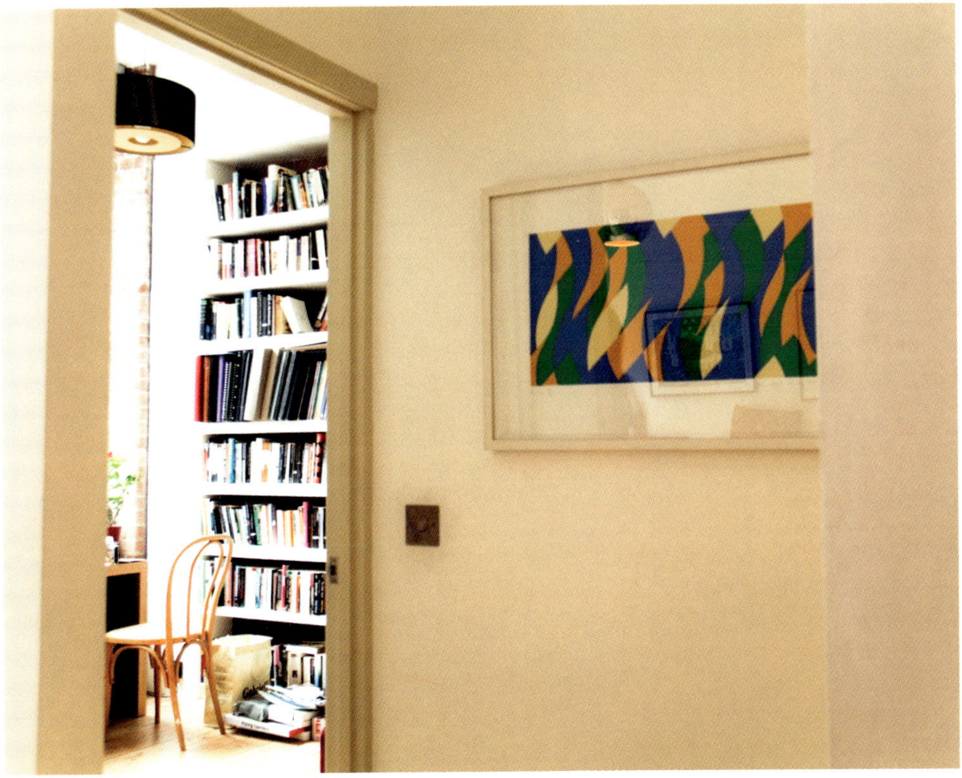

Do

* Add frame bumpers to the back of the frame – ideally a frame should not hang flush with the wall – because air should be allowed to circulate between the frame and the wall.
* Rotate the position of your collection every six months – you'll reduce the chance of any light damage.

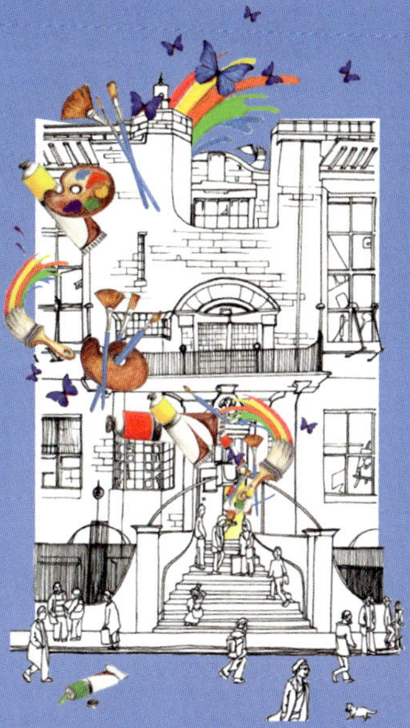

03
Where and how to buy art

Where and how to buy art

BUYING A PIECE OF ART is more than a financial transaction – it is emotional, richly complex, and can be the start of a two-way (often more) relationship that can be nurtured and developed, where gallerist, collector and artist work together to push style, taste, interest in and appetite for art.

Buying a work of art can seem like an infuriatingly convoluted (not to mention intimidating) process; it can be hard to understand the reasons behind pricing and negotiations, and it's often not as simple as paying and taking the work away with you then and there (because of factors like transportation, display, framing, etc). Be prepared for things to take a little while, but don't let this put you off. This complexity is part of what makes the experience so unique and special. In buying an original work of art you are also buying into a relationship with an artist; buying a print from a print studio is to engage with an intricate process by a skilled art practitioner; buying from a gallery can be the start of a long, nurturing relationship with a dealer who will keep an eye out for pieces you'll love; and as you continue to buy you'll be building a collection whose overall shape will be significantly changed and influenced by each new addition.

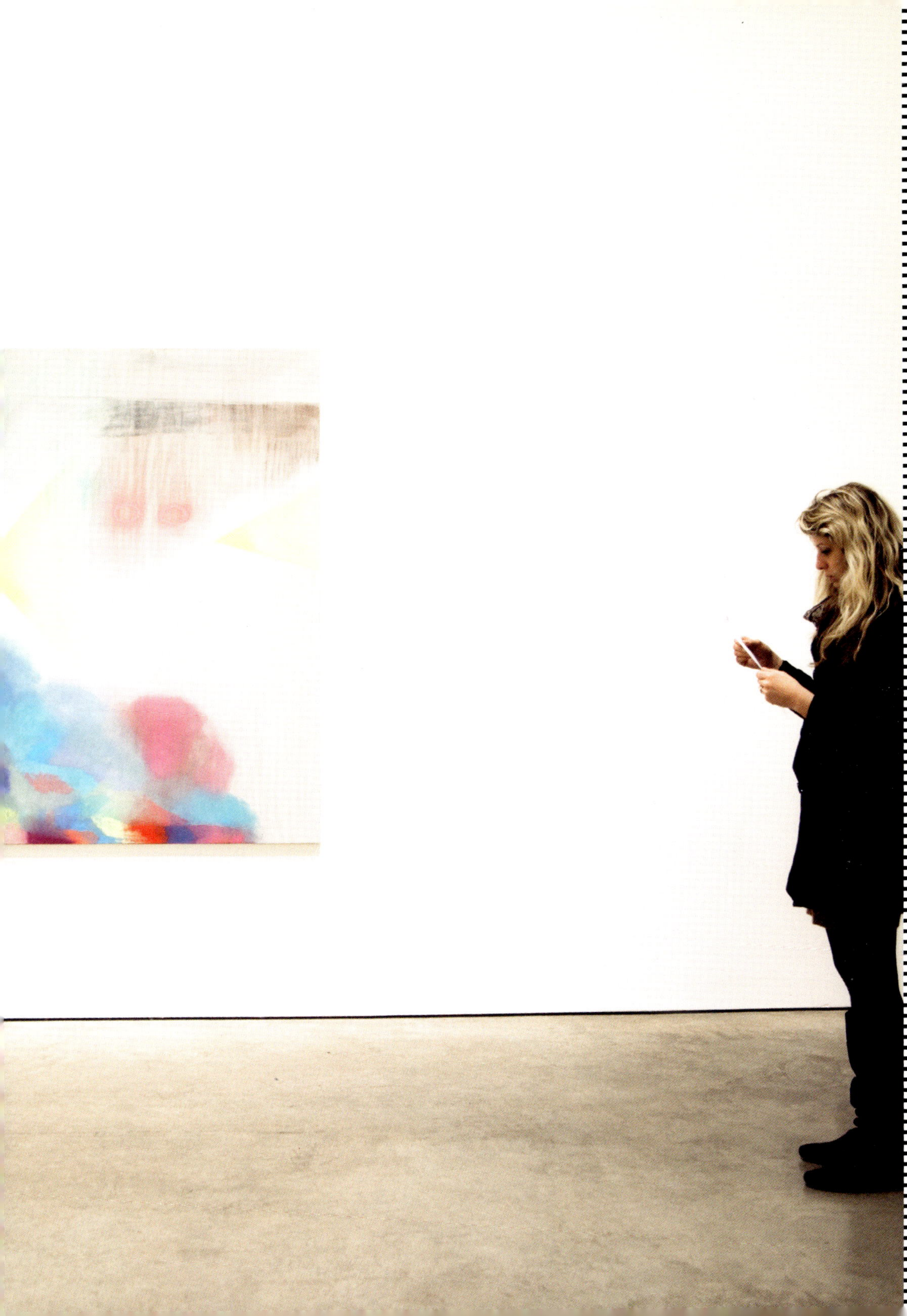

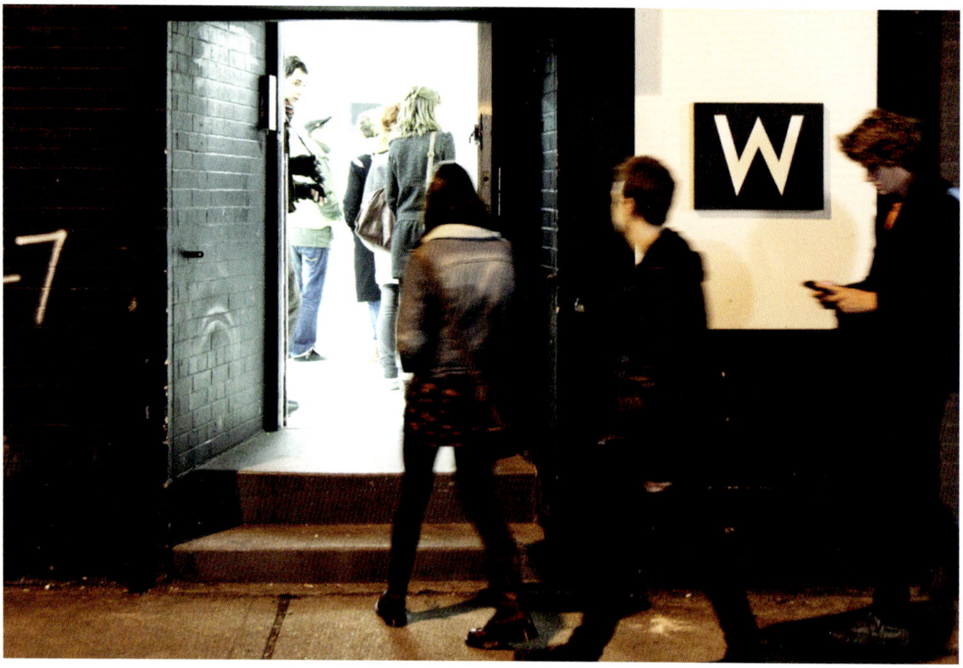

People gather for an evening vernissage.

The first sale of an artwork, from the artist to an initial buyer (be that via the artist's studio or in an exhibition) is called the "primary market". Here the price is established for the first time and a transaction made. Any subsequent sale of that same work means that it has entered the "secondary market" – which is usually via private dealers or auction houses. For major pieces of art, the price on the secondary market is of enormous significance as it validates the 'risk' of the first sale.

There are myriad ways to buy art, from galleries to dealing with the artists directly. And with the pros and cons of each comes a slightly different set of etiquettes and elements to be taken into consideration, alongside the general points which remain relevant across the board. The following sections explain how each of the various buying options work, and give a checklist-style buyers' guide that will help you navigate the landscape of where and how to buy art.

GENERAL TIPS FOR BUYING

* Buy art that you love. Don't underestimate the power of your taste and judgement to add personal value to a work; buying for investment alone is a dangerous game.
* There is no such thing as a 'must-have' (whatever you are told) – never feel pressured into buying. Take your time to think, appreciate and consider on your terms.
* Ask questions. Engage the gallerist or artist in a conversation about the art and express any particular interests (style, artist, etc).
* Research the artist. See what prizes they have won, where they've had shows (and who with if they were group shows) and which galleries show their work.
* Assess the calibre of the platform where the artwork is being sold – whether this is via an online gallery, art fair, public museum or auction sale, and use this to help evaluate the quality and price of the work.

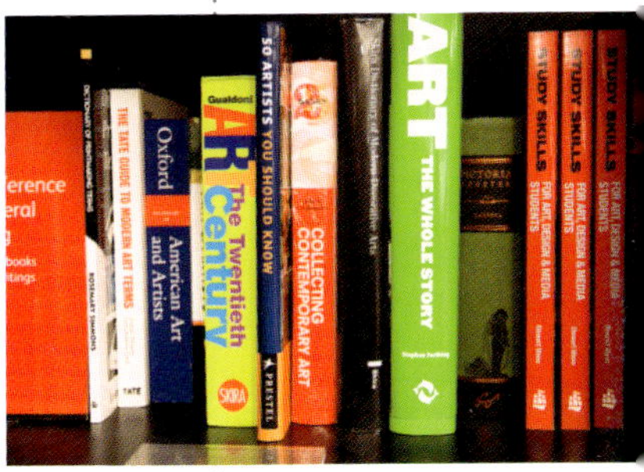

* Check the date, provenance and quality of work (be wary of buying substandard work by a respected artist).
* Check the artist signature and ask for a certificate of authenticity for editions –a if there is no signature, ask if this can be done.
* Buy with confidence. Find out as much as you can about the artist and their work and make sure you invest in something that you are proud to own.

Public art galleries

A good place to start buying contemporary art editions is from contemporary art institutes and museums. From the KW Institute for Contemporary Art in Berlin and Paris's Fondation Cartier to the New Museum in New York or London's Whitechapel Gallery, most contemporary art public galleries sell fantastic limited-edition artworks that have been produced by internationally celebrated artists for the institutions to sell as a way of fundraising. What's great about these as a starting place is that you can trust these museums to produce works by artists who are worth investing in. It's a great way to start building your collection with confidence.

You'll also usually be able to find these prints online in the shop section as well as in the gallery shop, so it's a wonderful way to shop internationally for art with confidence from the comfort of your home. Limited-edition prints and print portfolios (which collect carefully selected prints by a variety of artists) give collectors unparalleled access to works of a high quality, selected by internationally respected curators. Prints can be linked to specific exhibitions, or can be launched alongside summer shows or in time for Christmas. It's also worth looking at any artist-designed *objects*, from decorative trophies to tea towels, which might have been made for a gallery – they are a quirkily affordable way to invest in an artist.

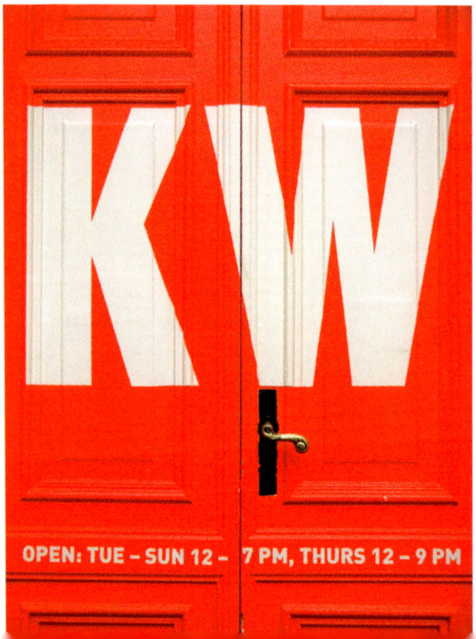

The distinctive orange doors of the Kunst-Werke Institute for Contemporary Art, Berlin.

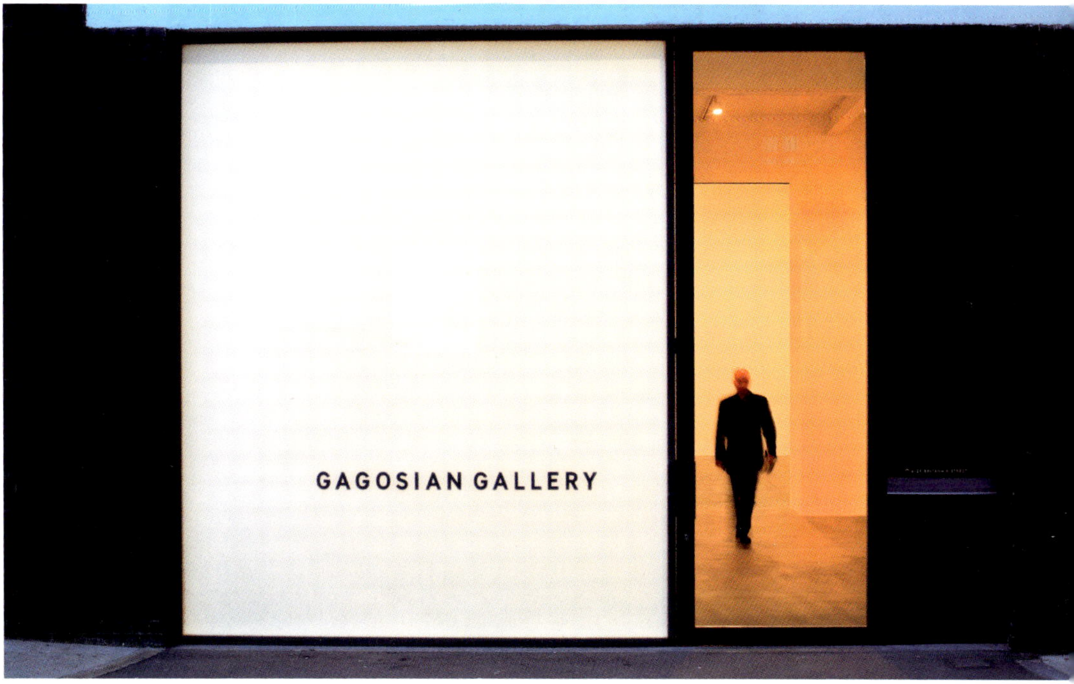

Commercial art galleries

Gagosian Gallery, London.

Most successful artists will be represented by a commercial gallery (often several internationally), that puts on shows for them, promotes their work, introduces their work to collectors, and acts as a mentor, helping to develop not just their career but their work too. There is not usually a formal contract; the relationship works on trust. You might see work by one artist sold by multiple galleries – although an artist is represented by one gallery, they will be able to show their work in other galleries too, provided their representational gallery is kept informed.

A gallery's reputation rests upon the artists it represents. That a gallery has represented artists who have gone on to become successful gives credence to new artists it chooses to represent. When a gallery with a strong reputation chooses to represent a new artist, this automatically adds to that artist's credibility.

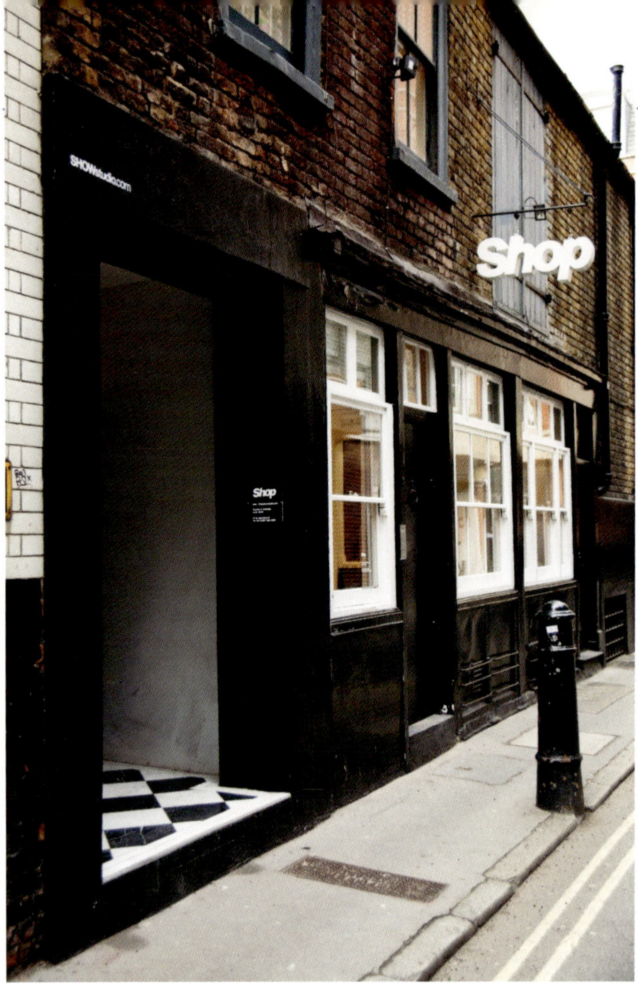

Showstudio, Bruton Place, London.

Stepping into a gallery is often an extremely intimidating experience – intentionally so. The echoing space, reign of silence, harsh lighting, absence of people and the lone gallery assistant either completely ignoring you or scrutinising your every move creates a subliminal message saying 'you're not eligible to be here'. Whether that ineligibility is because of budget, knowledge, art-world caché or whether you are wearing the wrong shoes, we've all been there and felt thoroughly inadequate, so fear not. Galleries have a mode of operation, that's all, and it's just a matter of getting your head round it, and understanding your place in that framework (whether you are in a gallery to buy, appreciate or out of curiosity). Once you can do that it's easier to feel more confident.

Know exactly why you are going in to a gallery and you'll feel more confident.

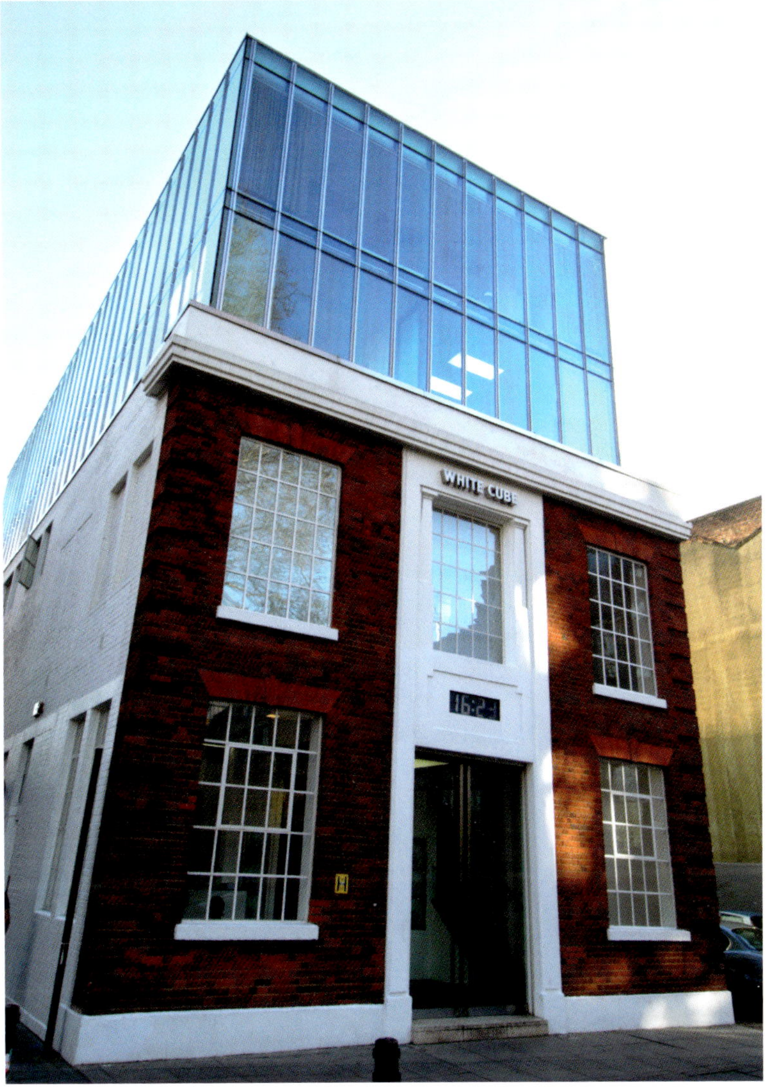

White Cube, London.

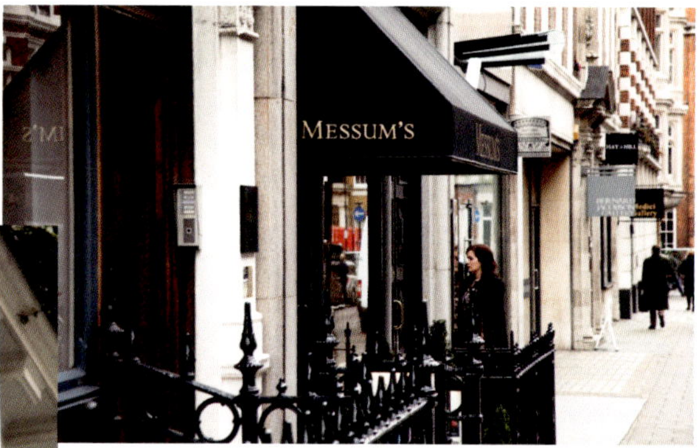

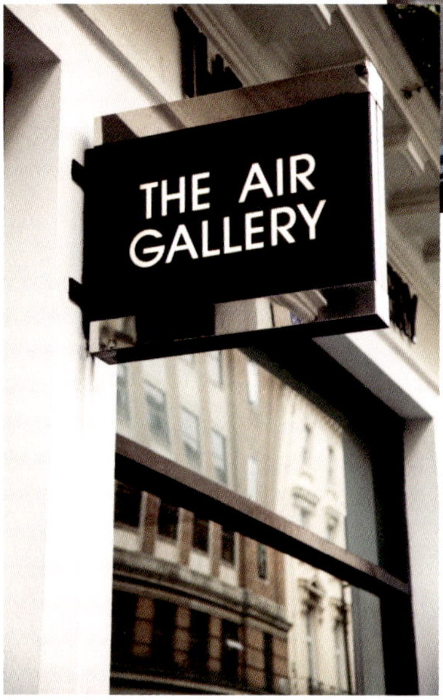

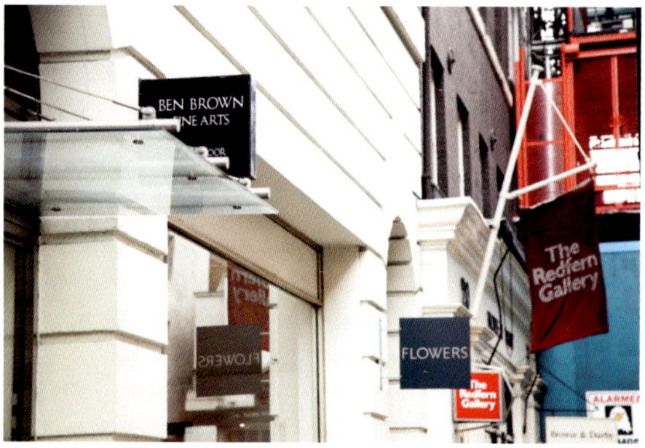

Major galleries with international reputations

At the top of the commercial gallery hierarchy are the branded galleries with international reputations, often with multiple galleries in various cities, that represent artists who are international household names; whose work is held in museum collections, bought by world-renowned collectors, whose exhibitions are reviewed by national and international art critics, and are the subject of in-depth features. These gallerists and dealers *themselves* will often be household names – Larry Gagosian and Jay Jopling, for example. The majority of the work in these galleries will not only be sold for crazy money, but 'placed' with specific collectors who are eventually likely to donate to a public gallery, or whose collection actively shapes the contemporary art

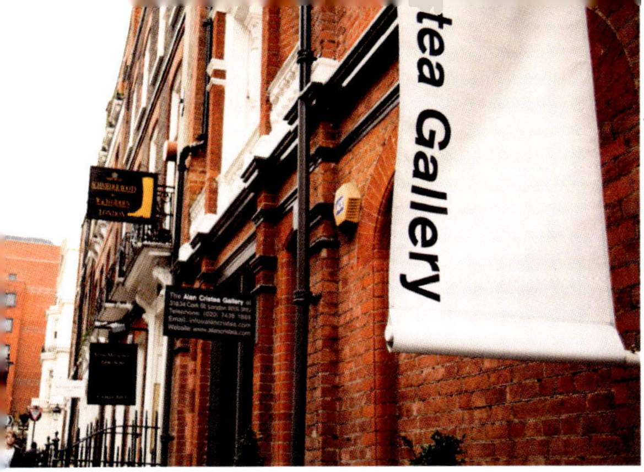

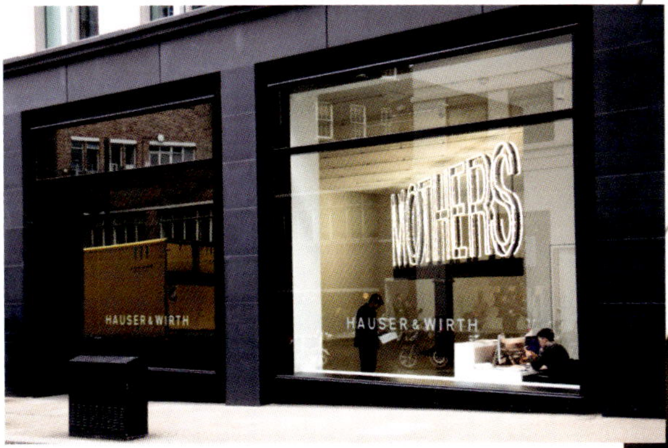

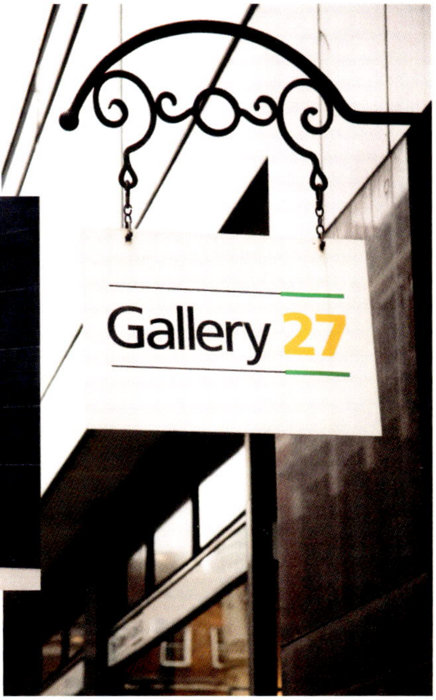

landscape. For the more modest art collector, visiting these galleries is likely to be about appreciating innovative work by the 'hot' names rather than buying. Occasionally, however, these galleries will sell limited-edition prints by the big name artists they represent, which is an affordable way to invest in work by a globally established artist.

Mainstream commercial galleries

These galleries represent artists with an established reputation and tend to be in big cities with a strong contemporary art culture such as New York, London or Berlin. They will have a presence at major art fairs and their exhibitions are often covered in the media. They will represent roughly 25 artists to whom they'll give one or two shows a year, sometimes alongside one another. These galleries are likely to be, to a degree, less intimidating spaces as they'll be operating with a wider cross-section of buyers, and collectors who like to shop around. Galleries usually take a 50% cut of the sale value of a work of art, so they fix their prices accordingly (although successful artists usually negotiate a better deal for themselves). This may sound extortionate, but gallery representation in itself adds value to artists' work through their reputation, connections, body of collectors, mentoring of artists and the promotional activities, and they have to cover their costs. The gallery's faith in an artist validates that artist within the art world, as their work is seen to have been judged by discerning, knowledgeable and experienced insiders.

High street galleries

These galleries are inevitably the highest in number, most varied in location and most accessible for the fledgling collector. Yet, strangely, these are almost the trickiest place to discern how and what contemporary art to buy. The works are readily available, are often more affordable, and are likely to be exhibited in a far less intimidating place than the white cube spaces of the mainstream

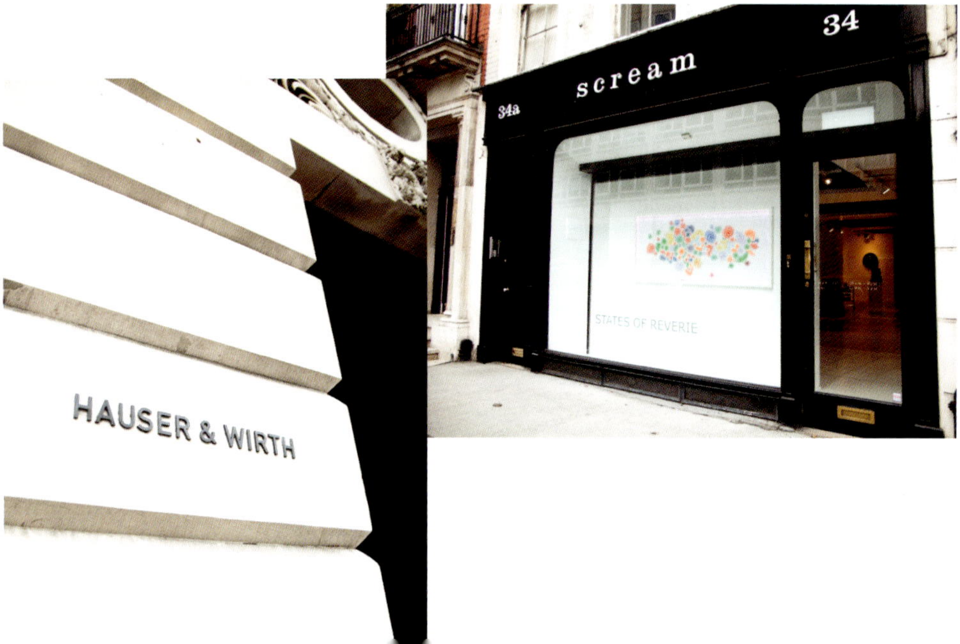

Scream, on Bruton Street and Hauser & Wirth, Piccadilly, London.

and stellar galleries. Yet the quality of the works can vary to a much greater degree. Look out for local reviews, and shows by artists who are beginning to make a name for themselves. Without the critical eye of reviewers and the same degree of art world scrutiny, the gallerist's judgement stands in isolation. So, ask questions. Find out about the artists' history – how long they have been practicing, where they have shown, and how often and where they exhibit. Such knowledge can add to your appreciation of a work, help establish how the work has been priced and give you an idea of where the artist is in their career.

Keep an eye on galleries that have a proven track record of representing emerging artists who have gone on to make a name for themselves. As an artist's career accelerates and they become more established (and their prices rise) an artist is likely to move up the gallery chain to be represented by a bigger gallery providing a broader platform for their work to be seen and appreciated. Artists may start out showing in one of these smaller, more off-beat (and off the beaten track) galleries with an eclectic show schedule and possibly more experimental, unruly art, but there will come a point when that gallery can no longer give the artist either the best possible space, exposure or resources for their work, so an artist will move up the gallery chain. This is a natural and accepted course of events, so it's good to become familiar with the 'feeder' galleries – those smaller outlets that have an eye for emerging talent and nurture and develop it so that the artist then graduates to show in higher profile galleries. Buying art *before* the artist 'makes it' (and their prices have skyrocketed) is a rewarding investment.

Gallery spaces

In cities with major contemporary art cultural hubs, you will find gallery spaces in prime locations that are hired out for exhibitions. Sometimes these will be taken by mainstream galleries when they want a more central location for a special show. Independent dealers will often hire the space for themed exhibitions – artists from a particular country, for example, or touring exhibitions.

Gallery spaces will often be hired by an artist, or a group of artists, without representation – who stage what's (sometimes rather unfairly) known as a 'vanity show'. Buying the work of unrepresented artists is taking more of a gamble on a work of art because it hasn't been given the 'blessing' of the art world through a gallery's selection, and while there isn't a dealer to raise prices, they are still likely to be elevated because of the overheads involved in hiring the gallery space. August tends to be a prime time for these shows – when the art market is slow and galleries reduce their hire costs.

Make sure you know the nature of the show you're viewing. It will help to establish the basis upon which to evaluate the quality, price and caliber.

Not for profit art galleries

These are an invaluable component of the gallery landscape. The 'not for profit' ethos promotes artists' creative development and experimentation, provides an exhibition platform for emerging artists, and shifts the focus away from the commercial. These galleries are a beating heart of creativity, the engine rooms of the art world, generating an energy for genre-breaking styles and ideas. It's here that you'll discover artists before they have made their names, which makes them fertile ground for collectors looking for exciting new artists to invest in.

Many not for profit galleries are artist-run or have rotating committees made up of artists, and support themselves through project-funding or self-funding. Often the gallery is more of a gallery-cum-studio space, from where they organise talks, workshops and events to help their funding. The website www.nonprofitgallery.com doesn't just list not for profit galleries worldwide, it also explains why each was set up and how it was run, these elements being as vital to the gallery concept as the art for which it provides a platform.

Although these galleries have an active de-emphasis on the commercial aspect of selling art in favour of a focus on the production of experimental art by dynamic artists keen to push boundaries, their fundraising schemes can be an exciting and unusual way of

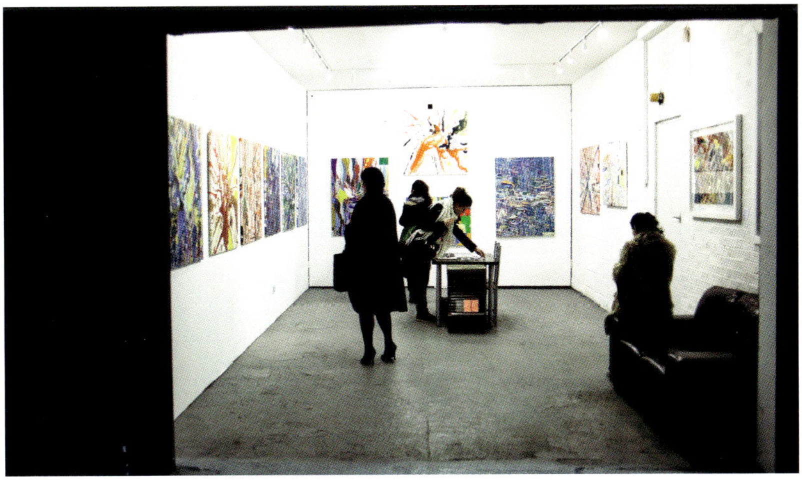

A gallery in an unconventional space.

supporting the ideas and aims of the organisation. Many put together print portfolios, a limited-edition collection of prints by selected artists often by successful artists for whom the studio was a vital springboard for launching their career. This can be an exhilarating way to invest in a selection of artists you're not familiar with, whilst simultaneously supporting the collective. Examples of UK galleries include: Matt's Gallery (www.mattsgallery.org), Cubitt (www.cubittartists.org.uk) and Studio Voltaire (www.studiovoltaire.org), while Artists Space in New York (www.artistsspace.org) has in the past received portfolio donations from artists including John Baldessari and Cindy Sherman. East London's The Drawing Room (www.drawingroom.org.uk) stages a biennial silent auction, with work donated by over 200 established and emerging artists, sold to support their drawing-focused initiatives, programmes and exhibitions.

The 'not for profit' ethos promotes artists' creative development and experimentation, provides an exhibition platform for emerging artists, and shifts the focus away from the commercial.

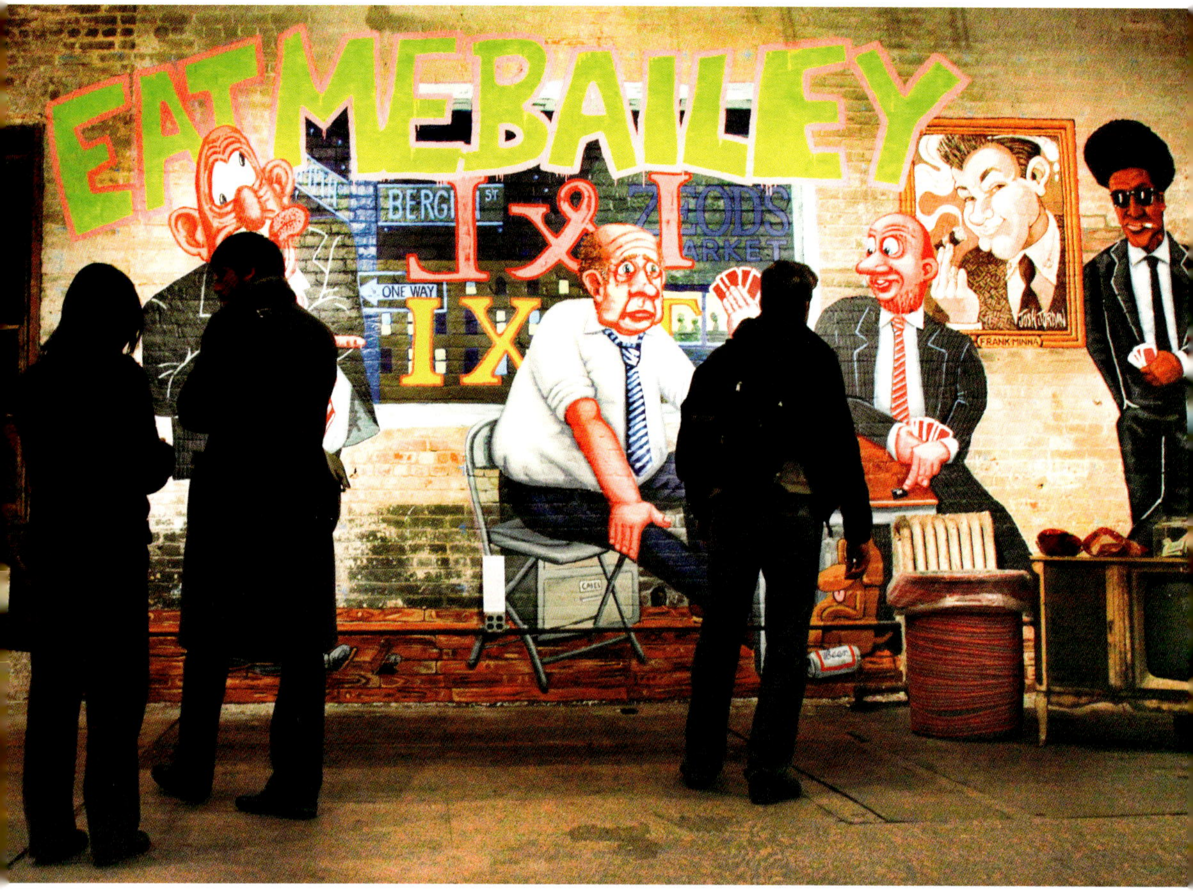

Pop-up galleries often take place in unusual spaces.

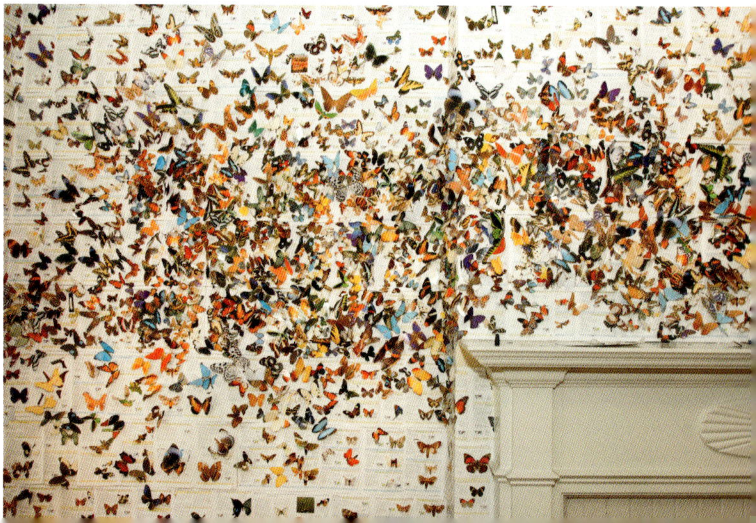

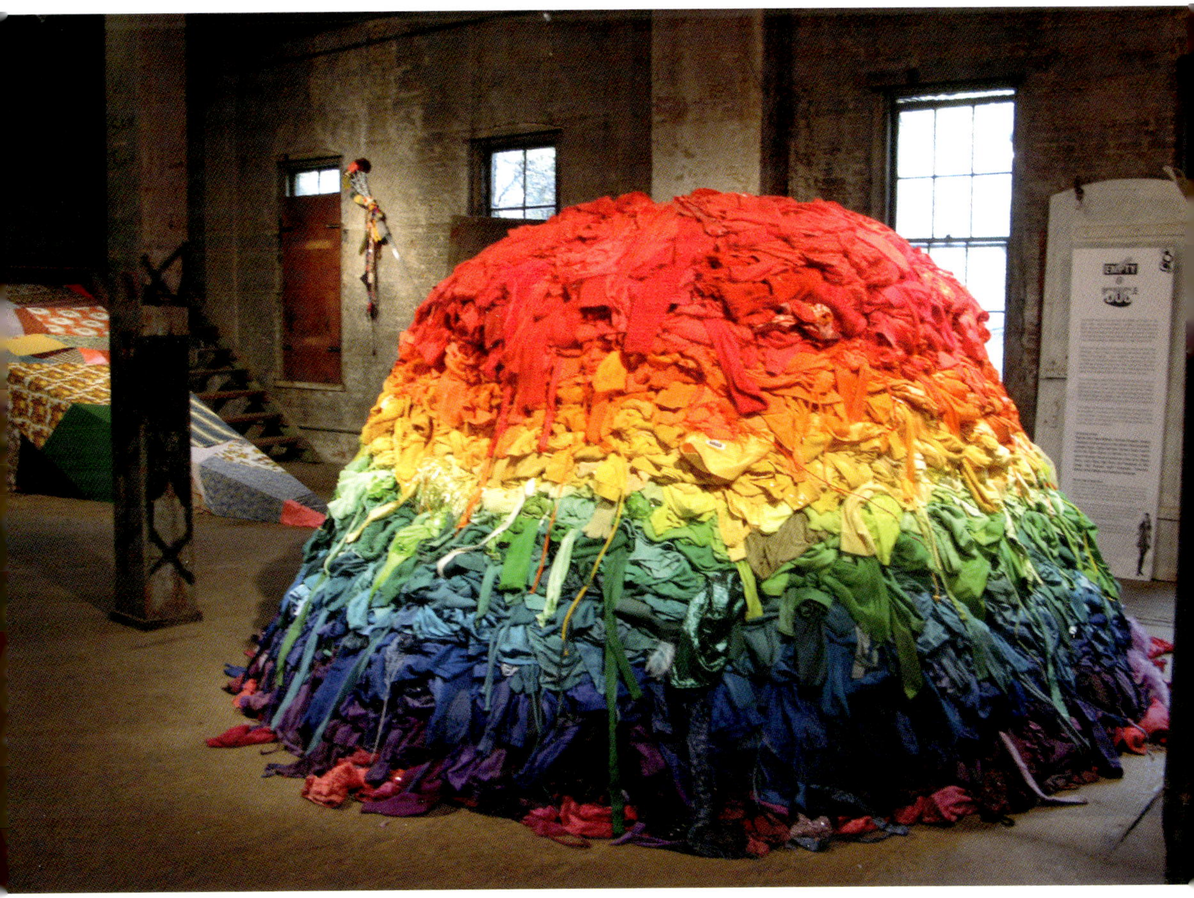

Pop-up galleries

Pop-up is another buzz word of the moment; there's a real excitement (for both consumer and organiser) in staging temporary events in unusual spaces – think disused factories, warehouse spaces or former metro stations. The novelty of location, daring, short timeframe, and challenges of a strange exhibition space add to the creative frisson of a new show plus it can be an opportunity to actively interact with and reinvigorate the creativity of a local community. The short-term nature of the project means there aren't the overheads, the

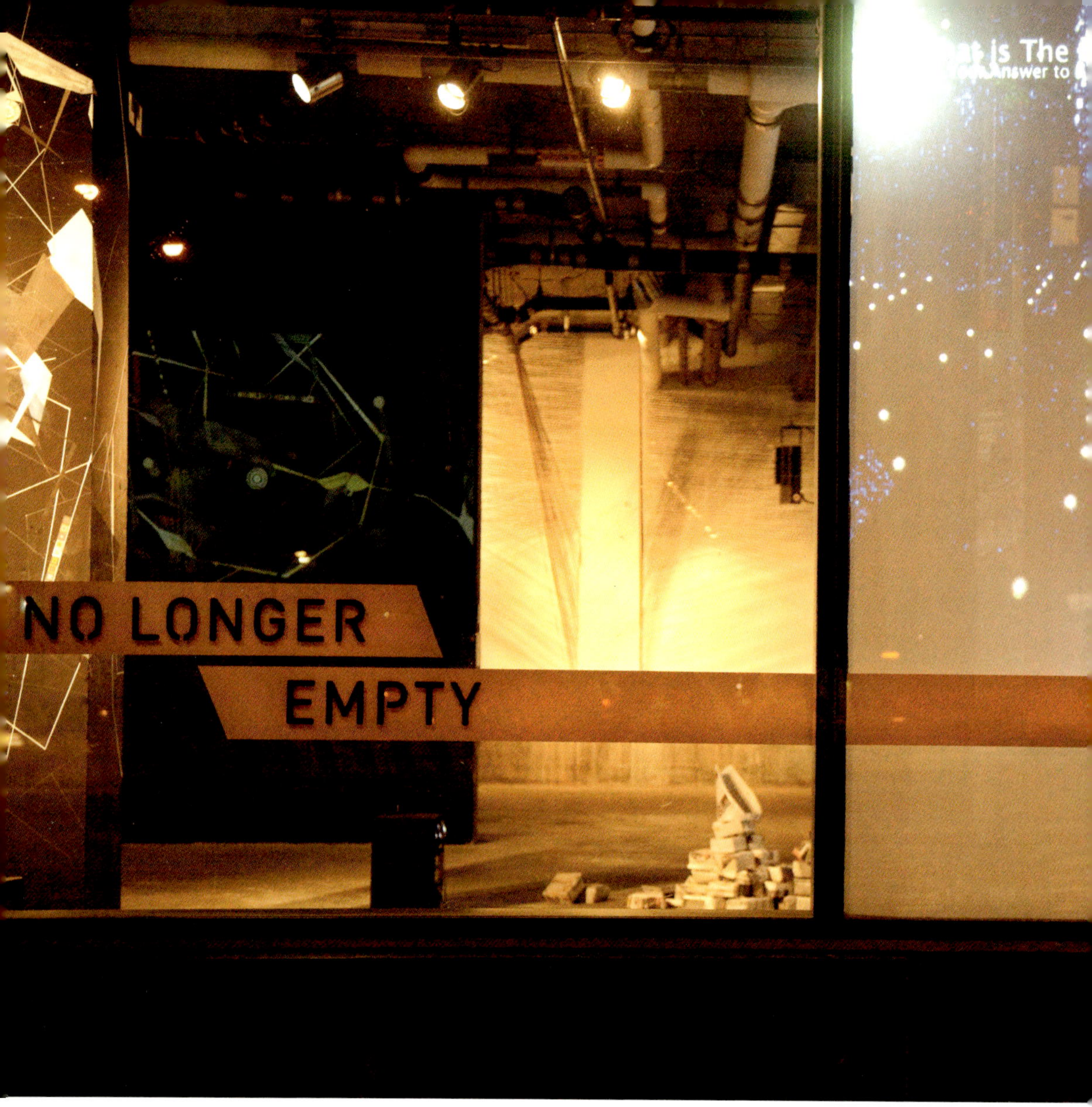

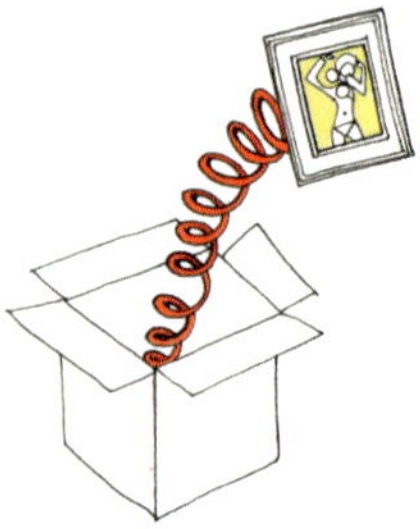

bureaucracy, and the long-term costs – which can bring the prices of art on sale down. There are now groups whose sole purpose is to "reconfigure the art space as a public sphere in the urban context" such as NYC group No Longer Empty (www.nolongerempty.org). In harsh economic times, a cool pop-up gallery can add to the real

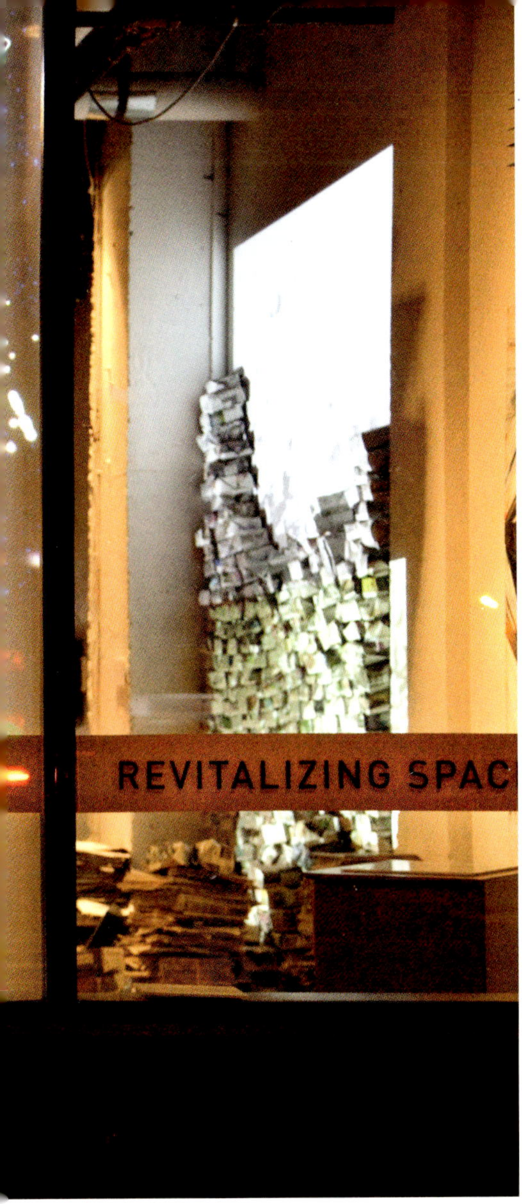

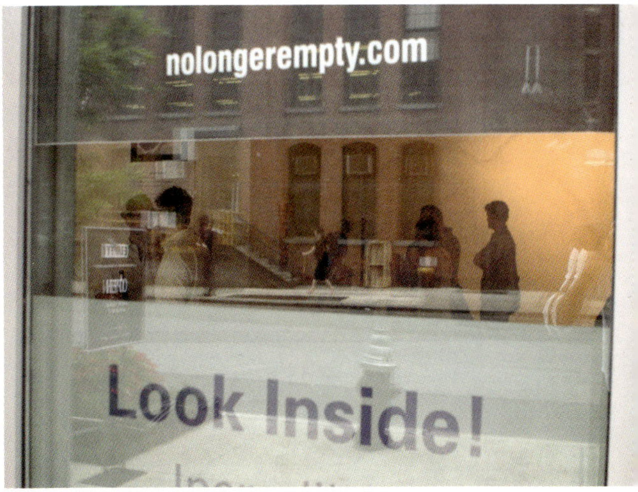

estate desirability, so spaces are let for a low fee or for free. As a result, galleries can become a permanently roving pop-up concept: Berlin-based gallery Helmrinderknecht (www.helmrinderknecht.com) left their permanent gallery space in the spring of 2011 to focus solely on pop-up projects – not just in Berlin, but internationally.

Dealers

As an addendum, it is worth mentioning the linguistic differences between the terms gallerist and dealer. From their gallery space, a gallerist is someone who deals with artists directly, who nurtures selected artists, and who programmes shows throughout the year. A dealer is an umbrella term that also includes those who sell art but don't necessarily have a space; they may work with artists directly, but will usually work on the secondary market – i.e. brokering deals that take place after the first sale. They can also be known as art consultants or advisors. Some find the term 'dealer' derogatory, others find the term 'gallerist' too prissy.

GOOD TO KNOW
ESTABLISHING A GALLERY'S CREDENTIALS

* Length of time it has been open or dealing – five years goes some way to establishing a gallery's staying power.
* A clear and informative website.
* A carefully selected, curated list of artists (how many depends on the gallery's size and genre, but an overwhelmingly high number may suggest a lack of discernment and support for individual artists).
* A portfolio of representing or having represented successful artists.
* Participation and presence at reputable art fairs.
* Write-ups in the press (the gallery themselves or their artists).
* Customer testimonials (not just on their own website or promotional material).

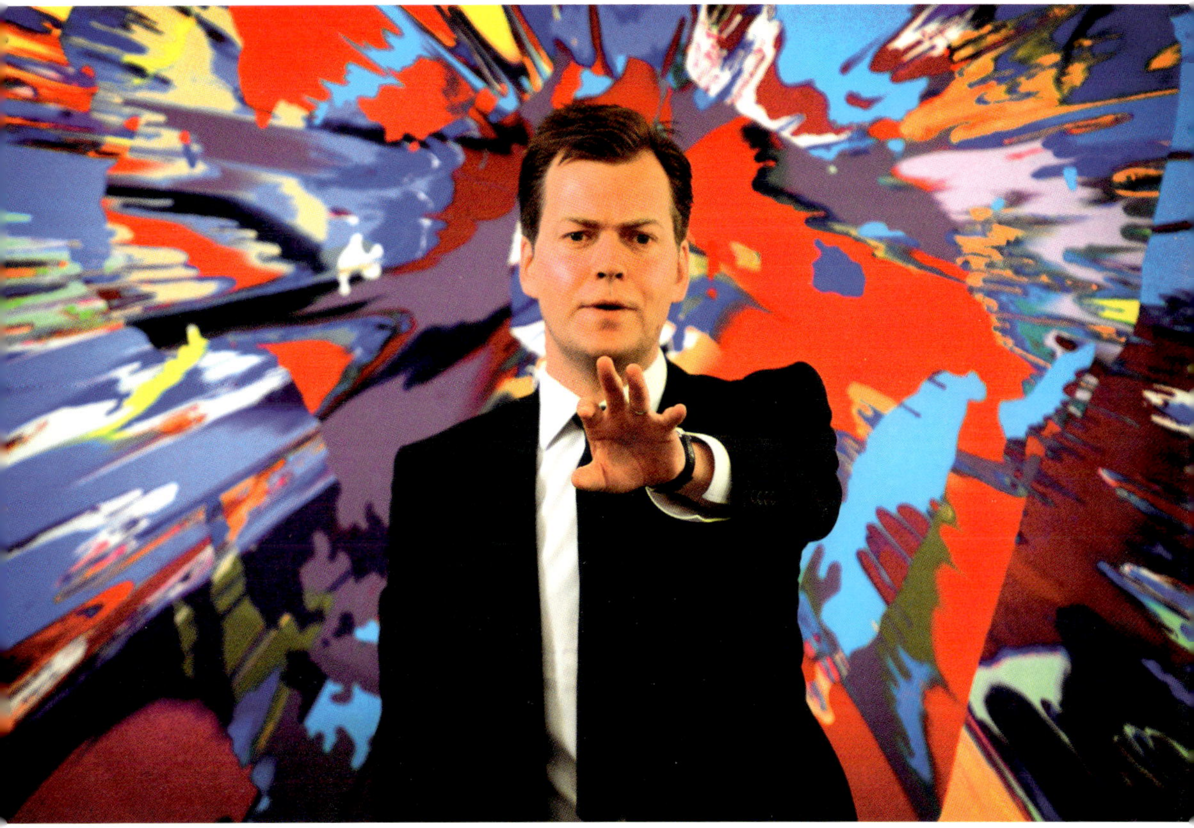

Buying at Auction

An auctioneer in action.

Contemporary art auctions can be electrifying – the buzz, the pace, the uncertainty, the mystery, the anticipation and the tension can create a livewire atmosphere that's invigorating, captivating and thrilling – almost like a theatrical performance.

An auction is a forum for secondary market sales where buyers, dealers, critics and bystanders gather before the auctioneer's platform. As each lot is called, its image is projected onto a screen with the starting bid (always lower than the pre-published estimate) in various currencies. If the work isn't on public display in the auction house, it may be brought out for viewing while the bidding is in progress. As the bidding starts, the bids increase at various increments at the auctioneer's discretion (percentage relevant to the estimate of the work). The screen projection notes the bidding rises, which can come from the floor, internet or telephones, or the absentee bid if one has been submitted. The auctioneer continues taking bids until bidders drop out and a final price has been reached, at which point he or she sharply smacks the gavel down, signalling the end of the lot sale. The bidder number is noted and the sale moves on to the next lot.

The hammer price is subject to a levy of around 20%, called the buyer's premium, which goes to the auction house as a fee for conducting the sale. The final price can be presented on record as either the hammer price or with the premium, but which it is should be made clear. The 'real' price of the work is without the premium added, i.e. the net sum that went to the seller directly.

Lots can be viewed in the showrooms and online before the sale. These are open to all and free. After the event, sale prices go down on public record – viewable on the auction house websites and on other sites including Artnet.com and Artprice.com. For this reason, prices at auction are incredibly important – they are a way of measuring a particular artist's worth beyond the riskier and more unstable primary market.

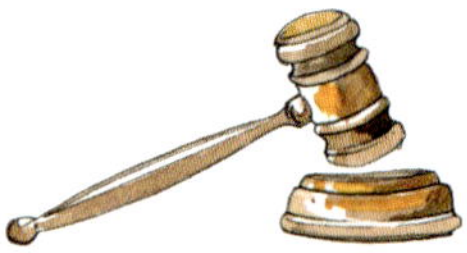

Buyer bidding methods

(subject to variation, but as a guide):

In person: by registering 30 minutes before the sale begins.

Absentee: by registering 24 hours in advance. A maximum bid is conveyed to the auction house, which is the most that the buyer is willing to pay.

Telephone bids: must be arranged at least 24 hours in advance and for which the estimated sale price of the work should be above a certain amount.

Online: Some auction houses make their auctions available to view live online, and pre-registered bidders can bid via this method.

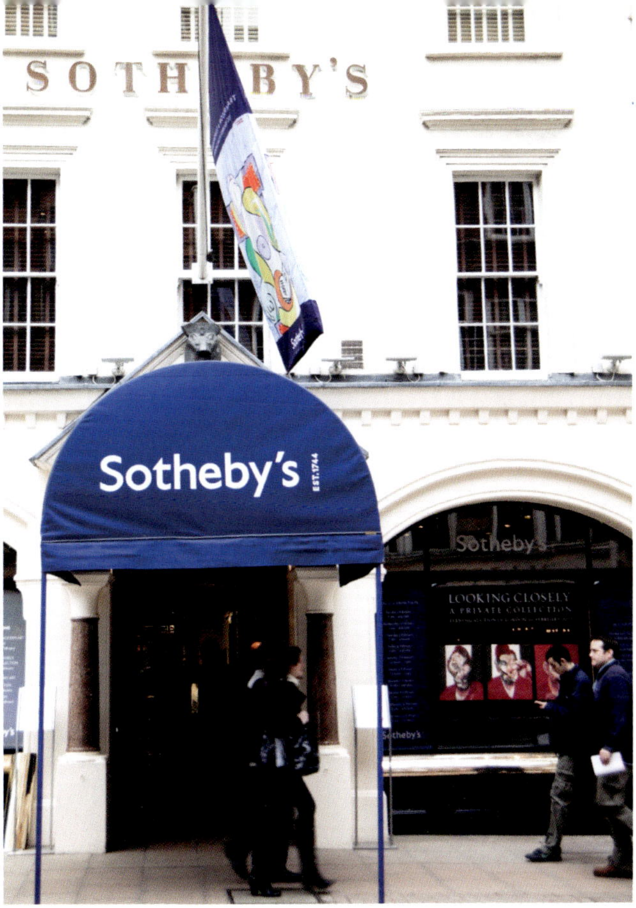

Sotheby's on New Bond Street, London.

Major auction houses

With auction houses all over the world, Christie's and Sotheby's are the big guns, controlling most of the major contemporary art market. Philips de Pury specialise in contemporary art, with a not inconsiderable focus on 'wet-paint art' – art so new it captures the freshness of contemporary. Each of these auction houses holds major contemporary art evening sales in New York (February/March, May and November) and London (February, June and October). These sales are fascinating procedures. The auction houses will have nurtured collectors and noted all enquiries before the sale. If there is any sense that a work won't make its reserve price, or if the buyers aren't 'right', a piece may be withdrawn, although this is not ideal – either for the auction house (who are left vulnerable to assumptions

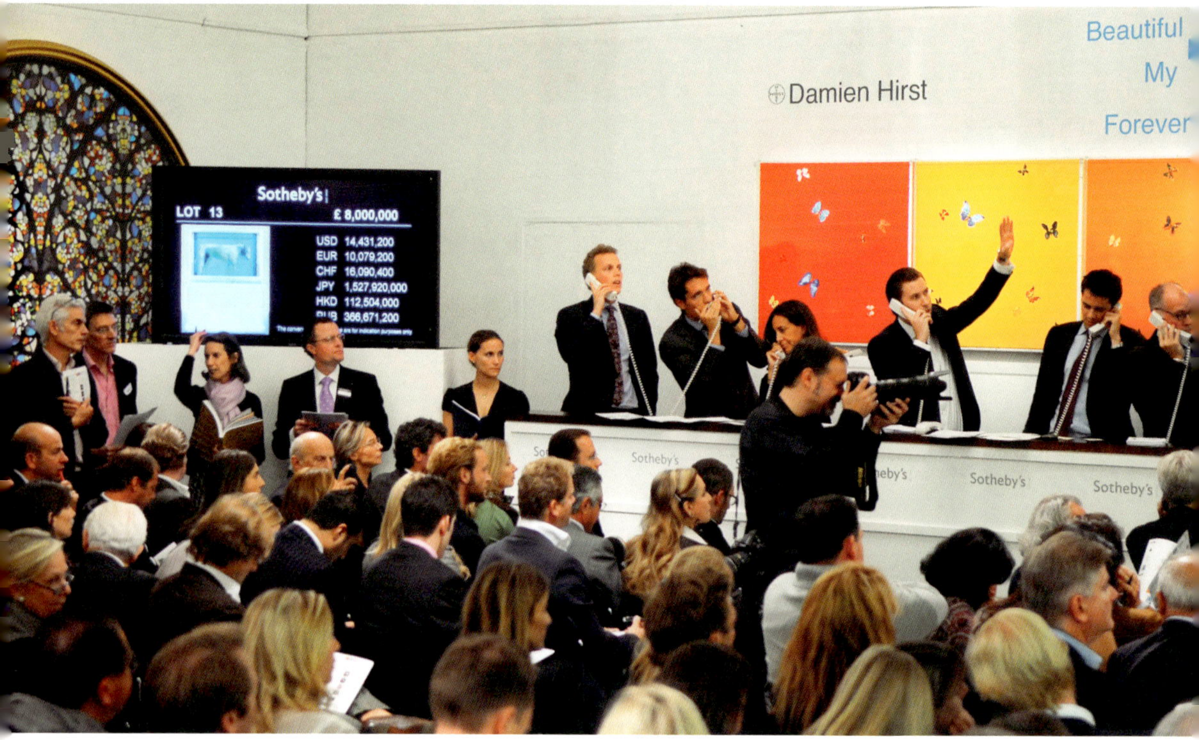

that they can't find the right kind of buyer), the artist (whose value, or at least the value of that particular work, is called into question), or the seller (who doesn't make a sale).

Being aware of major international auctions keeps you in the know when it comes to the artists, styles and genres which are popular and commanding high prices – these influences will inevitably trickle down to the more attractively priced echelons of the art market.

Second tier and regional auction houses

Auction houses including Bloomsbury in London, Rome and New York (www.bloomsburyauction.com); Van Ham Kunstauktionen in Cologne (www.van-ham.com); Germann Auktionshaus, Zurich

GOOD TO KNOW
ACCESSIBLE SALES AT MAJOR AUCTION HOUSES

Don't completely dismiss major auction houses as being too expensive. Look out for:

* Day sales: more affordable sales tend to take place during the day, rather than the evening, when the major, headline-making auctions are held.
* Themed sales: these gather art around a particular theme or motif.
* Print sales: Sotheby's have auctions that concentrate on prints or multiples (where you'll find, for example, plenty of prints between £500/€580/$800 and £3,000/€3,500/$5,000, including the buyer's premium). These sales will feature artists with an established market.
* Local/foreign offices: these regional offices (in cities like Rome or Amsterdam rather than London or New York) have smaller, less publicised contemporary art auctions with less competition for lots, meaning lower hammer prices.

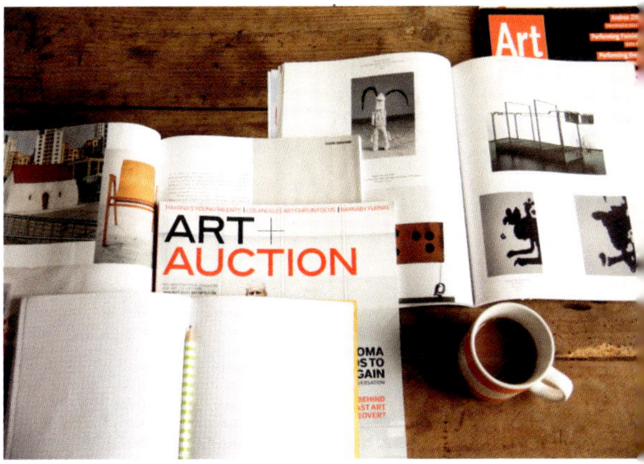

GOOD TO KNOW
BUYING AT AUCTION

* Build a relationship with one of the experts at an auction house who specialises in the kind of art you are interested in buying. As you develop this relationship they may give you the heads up about work you might like and warn you of problems with lots.

Due Diligence

* Look at the work before bidding on it. Lots are usually available for viewing by the public up to a week before the auction. Talk to the auction house staff about the work.
* Ask for a condition report on the work from the auction house before the sale.
* Check the provenance of the work, i.e. who is putting it up for sale and ask how many times it has been put up for auction in the past. Consider whether a work has been traded between dealers to make money, or the impact of it having sold below its estimate in the past. A good provenance (having been part of an important collection or been passed through a respected auction house) can add value to a work.
* Check the auction house's role in a sale. Does the auction house have a stake in the work? And is the person advising you on a work also advising the seller? This may cause a conflict of interest.
* Check when the work was last up for sale – use Artnet.com to verify independently.

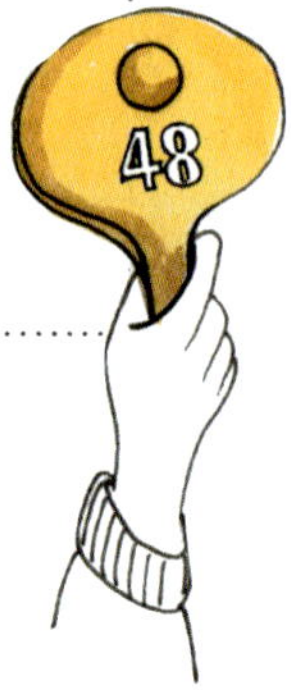

Bidding

* Bid with confidence and a cool, sober head.
* Don't come in too early. See how the bidding is shaping up and who else is interested. Wait for early bidding to die down and jump in when it's just the serious collectors left in the game.
* Jump bids. If you want to rattle a determined opponent, jump bid with a decisive, bold leap up a couple of increments.
* Know your limit. Don't get caught up in the heat of the moment and over bid what the work is worth or how much you are happy to pay.

Hidden Costs

* Factor in the buyer's premium to the final sale price before you start bidding. Details should be in the back of the auction catalogue, but it's worth knowing that there will usually be an extra 20–25% levied on to the hammer price of the work.
* Check if there is an artist's resale price (droit de suite – a fee that is payable to living artists). This will often be indicated by a coded symbol like a diamond. An artist's resale price can be around 4% for works between €1000/£850/$1,350 and €50,000/£45,000/$67,000.
* Check for other potential hidden costs like import duty, VAT, and transport and fees for late collection, which can mount up significantly.

Post Sale

* Ask about unsold lots. In the days following an auction there are usually a couple of days' trading, precipitated by dealers trying to strike a bargain. If there is something you are particularly interested in, phone up and see if the seller will accept an offer (who may prefer that it sold to a collector rather than a dealer).

(www.germannauktionen.ch); and Artcurial, Paris (www.artcurial.com), can be less intimidating, have more attractive estimates and have house sales (those prompted by death, debt and divorce) with unexpected gems, and less high-stake competition for lots. They are prime ground to strike a real bargain. It's tricky to keep tabs on all local auction houses, so focus on your area, sign up to their contemporary art bulletins, and, if you can, establish a relationship with the contemporary art experts there so they will alert you to relevant and unexpected contemporary art lots when they come up.

Online auctions

You may miss the drama, tension, rhythm and pace of a live action auction, but the ease, global reach and extended bidding timeframe of online auctions has its appeal. Nearly all online auction houses will have an online presence, allowing online bidding alongside the live bidding. From arts hub Artnet's online auction section (www.artnet.com/auctions) to bidding emporium eBay's art section (there are over two million works for sale at any one time, most for less than $300/£190/€220), there's a whole world of online bidding potential, with international auction house hubs like Live Auctioneers (www.liveauctioneers.com) collating auctions across the world. If you can, it's best to see before you buy, especially if you are parting with a sizeable sum of cash. With eBay, prices are low and the risk high – there's no regulation, and the potential for scams and misrepresentation is rife. You can't ask for condition reports as you would with a structured, regulated auctioneer. Even art experts run the risk of being duped. In October 2010 a former trainee of Tracey Emin's was jailed for 16 months after selling at least 11 forgeries of her work for £26,000/€30,000/$42,000 on eBay.

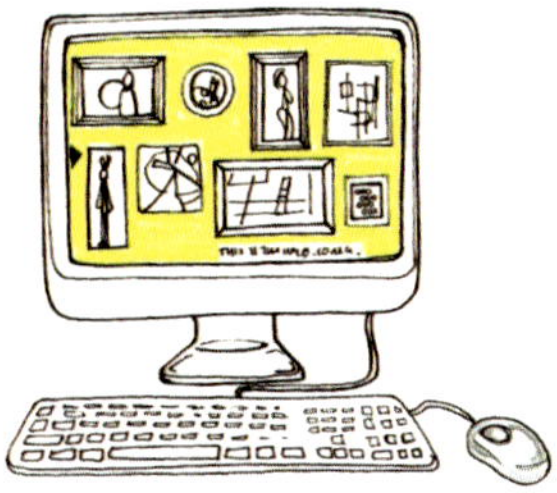

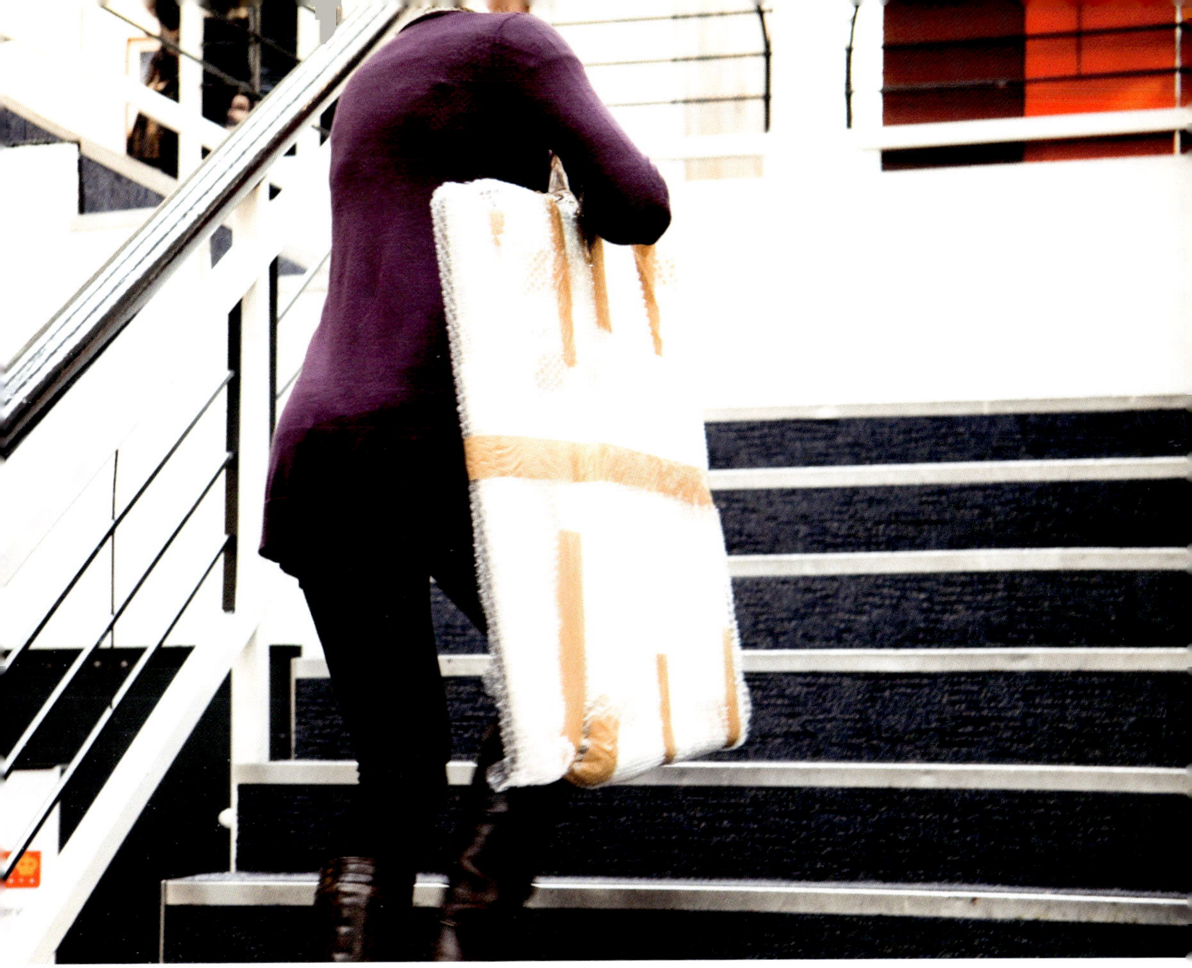

Art Fairs

Approach fairs with a mixture of enthusiasm and cynicism. Art fairs are a wonderful opportunity to discover a wide and diverse range of art from galleries all over the world. But there's a subversive school of thought that argues that fairs are art supermarkets for the super rich. WW Gallery (www.wilsonwilliamsgallery.com) have staged their Art Star Superstore at fairs, presenting works of art in the manner of a supermarket with aisles full of stacked, plastic-wrapped paintings to be bought from a checkout. This may be satirical, but it's worth bearing in mind. Don't hold the fairs on too much of a pedestal; they may not be shopping malls, per se, but they're not a *million* miles away either.

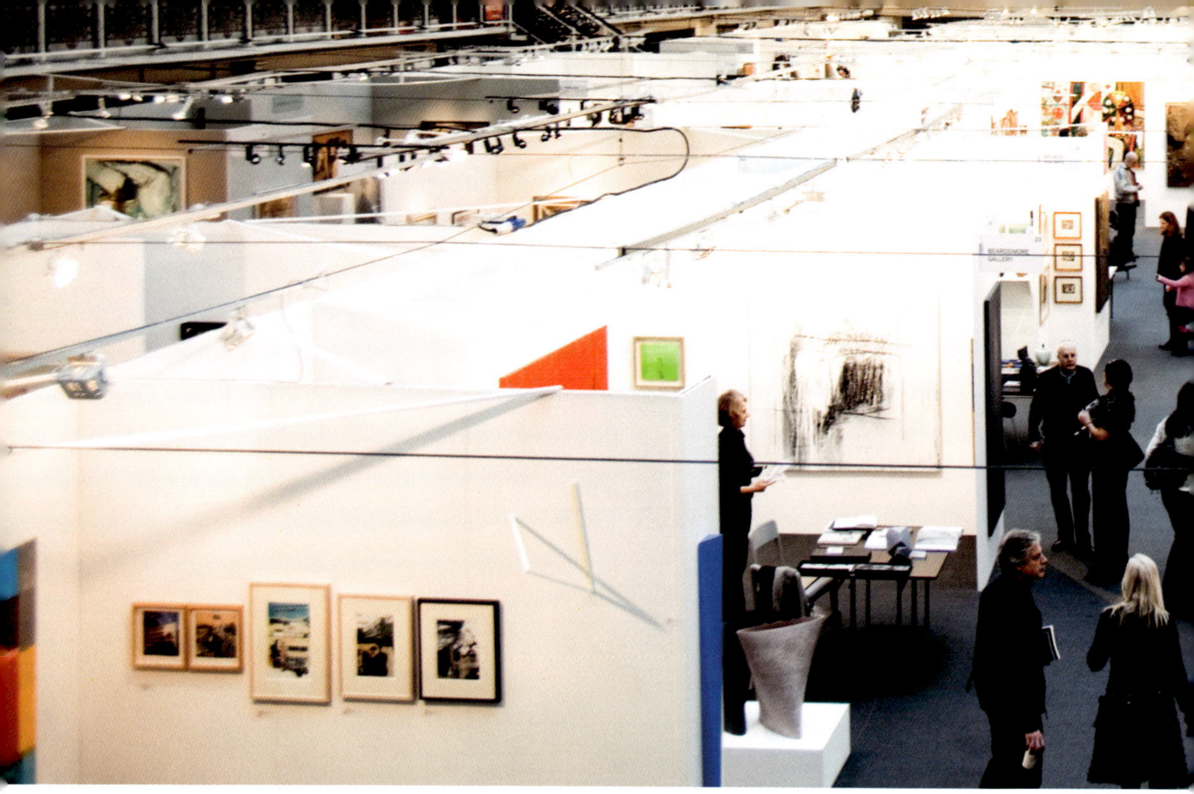

GOOD TO KNOW
FAIRS

* Look for the satellite fairs of the major art fairs (The Armory Show in New York, Art Basel and Frieze et al). The smaller fairs like Scope, Liste and Volta are more affordable and less overwhelming (see listing in the Art Diary section).
* Sign up for talks and tours of the fairs. Check the fair programme online in advance.
* Look out for the special sections – artists' projects, special exhibitions etc – because this can be where you'll find the most exciting and experimental work, which is often the most affordable.
* Be aware of the exhibition criteria for participating galleries – it will help to establish the level of art you're looking at.

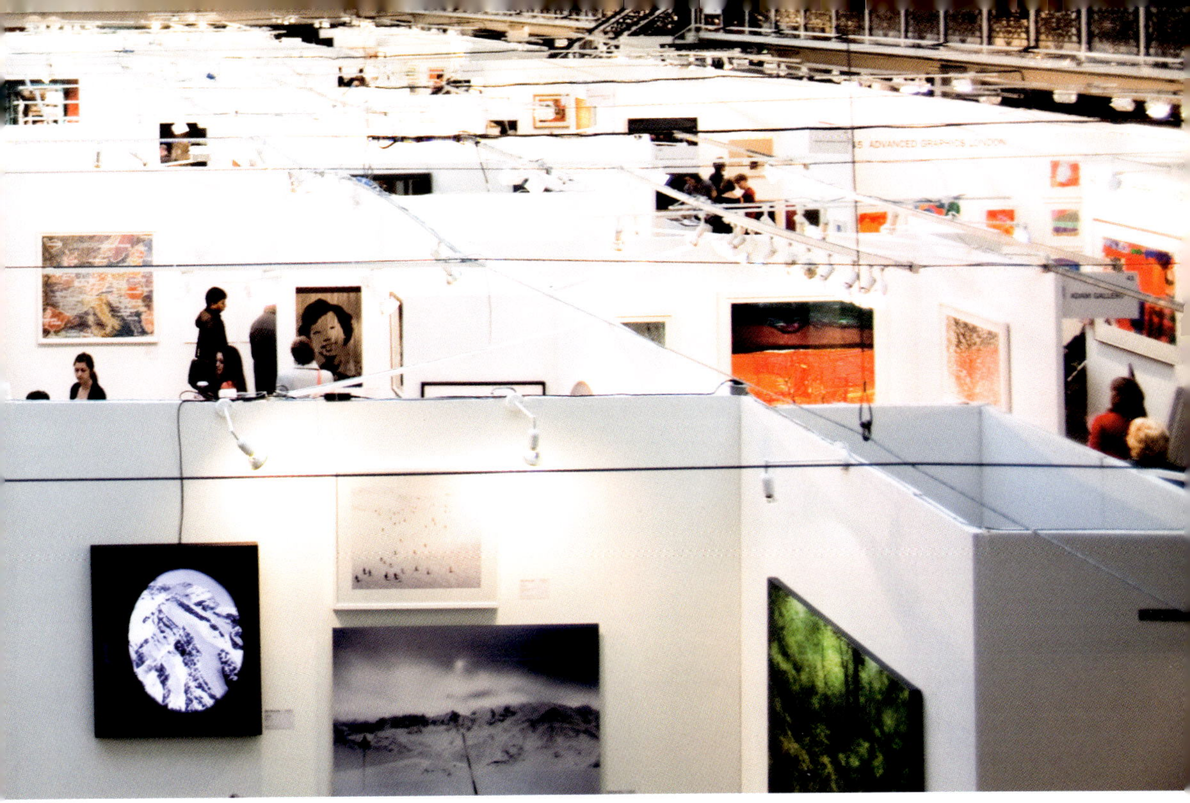

* Talk to the gallerists: ask about the work you are interested in to gain a greater understanding. At the more accessible art fairs ticket prices won't always be displayed. This encourages people to engage in conversation with the gallery owner.
* Use fairs not only to discover new artists but also to build relationships with new international galleries. Sign up for the mailing lists of the galleries whose work you like and use the fair as a starting point to build relationships. Tell the gallerist which artists you like and ask to be kept updated on new exhibitions by that artist.

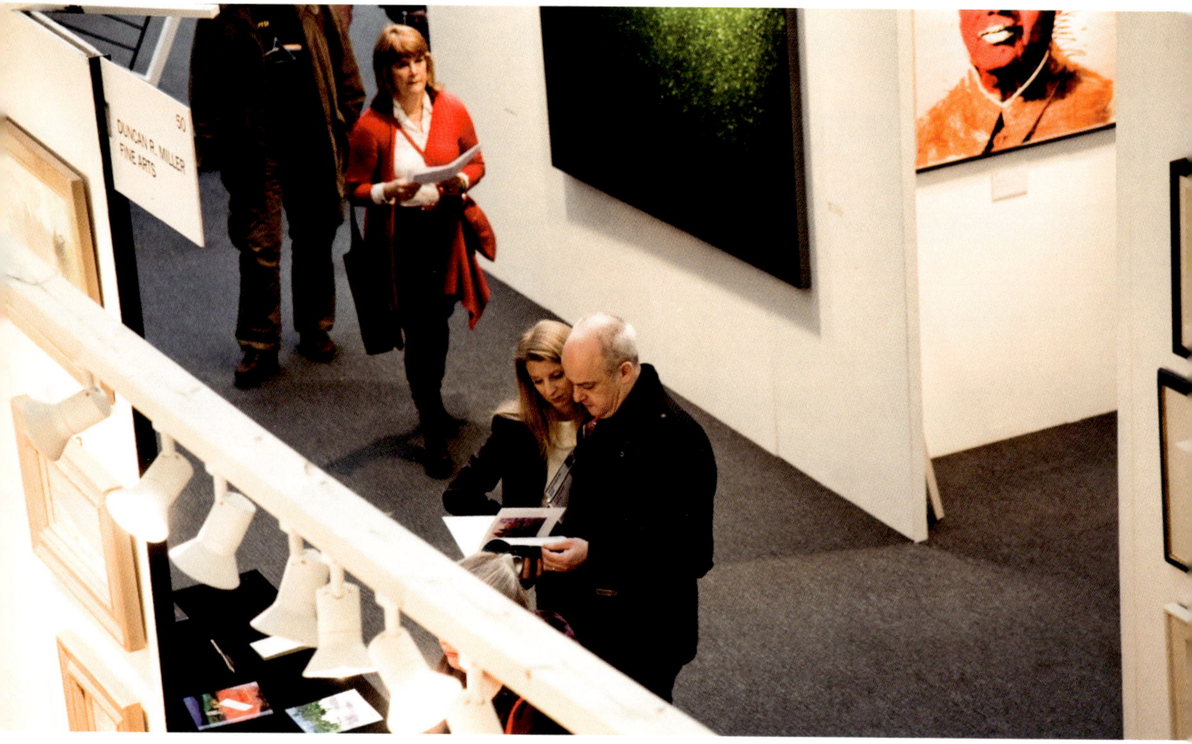

TIPS

* Plot a route round the fair – this way you can be sure you'll see as much as you can and won't leave out whole sections.
* Take regular breaks – fairs can be large, sprawling and overwhelming; it's physically tiring to wander around them, but, more importantly, it can be mentally tiring to take in all the new information and images. Take advantage of the cafés to rest and re-fuel!
* Visit early in the day to avoid crowds.
* Visit several times – usually a ticket will allow re-entry, so take advantage of this. With each visit, work your way around the fair in a new route; you'll see different works if you approach the stands from different directions.
* At the end of the fair, gallery owners can be more open to price negotiation.

Artists directly

One of the best things about buying contemporary art is that you're buying the work of artists who are alive, who are reacting to the same global events, preoccupations and concerns as you are, and who are producing new work that's constantly evolving, changing and taking a new direction. Rather than there being a wholly conclusive evaluation of their complete oeuvre, the appreciation and understanding of their ever-evolving body of work is constantly changing.

Open studios, artists' collective shows and fairs and artists' websites are just a few of the ways that collectors can buy art directly from artists. There's something special about buying directly from an artist – something intimate, unique and personal – especially if it involves going to their studio and seeing firsthand how and where they work. It's an opportunity to get to know the story behind a work, straight from the artist's mouth, understand more fully the creative process, and find out a little bit about the artist as a person.

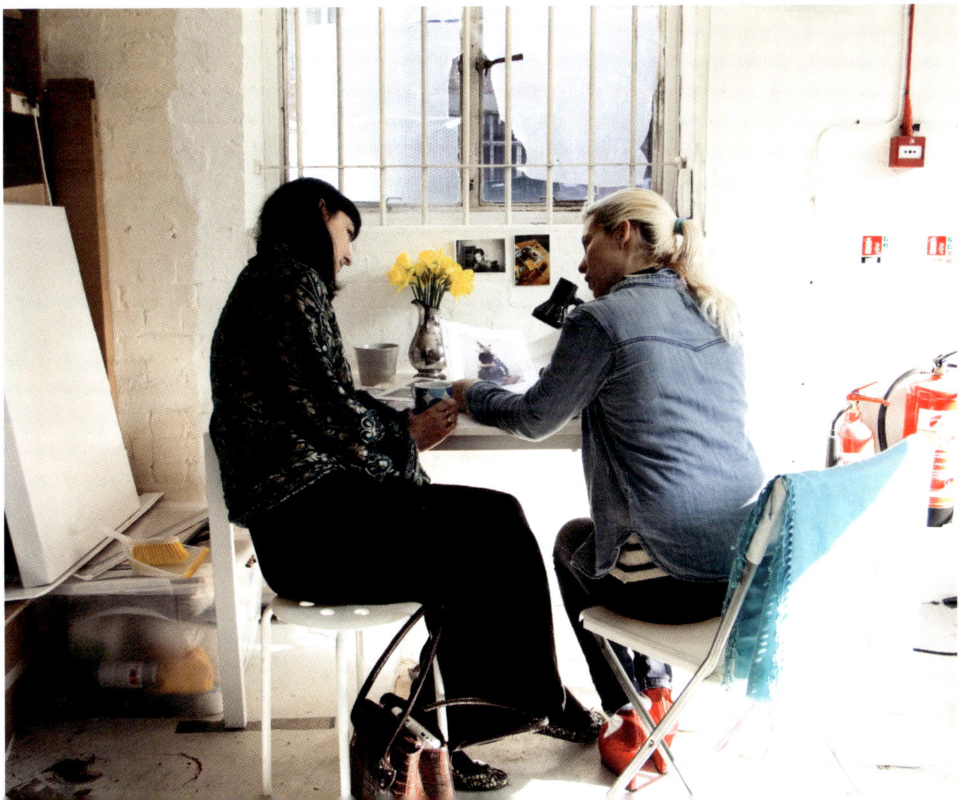

Don't be afraid to contact artists directly, either via their websites (both emerging and established artists sell directly from their websites; at her online gallery www.emininternational.com, Tracey Emin sells limited-edition prints from as little as £275/€320/$440) or by talking to them at fairs and private views. Be up front about how much you like their work and ask them about it. Ask them who else's work they admire and whose work they have bought themselves. This can be an original and interesting way to discover new artists who work using similar ideas, styles or politics. Ask if you can commission work which they will create especially for you.

Advantages of buying from artists directly

✱ Engaging directly with the producer and creator of the work is a more intimate and special experience than dealing via an intermediary, and can cut out the cost of a middle man.
✱ Entering into a discourse with an artist can mean a greater understanding of each piece, and how they live and work.
✱ Building a personal relationship with an artist can open up possibilities for commissioning work.
✱ Knowing the artist personally can increase the emotional value of a work to you, the collector.
✱ If the artist is not VAT registered, you may not be paying added tax as you would when buying from a gallery.
✱ You can specially commission pieces.

Disadvantages of buying from artists directly

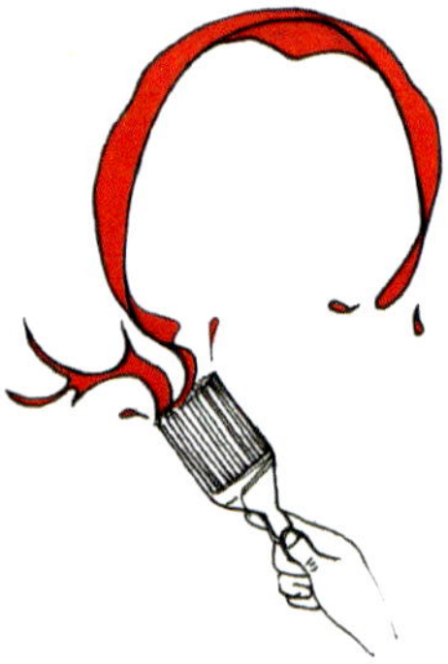

✱ Artists may have a delusional idea of the value of their work as they are more emotionally attached to it and are often not sufficiently distanced from it to negotiate on a business level. Their prices may therefore be inflated.
✱ The buying process can be more protracted and less organised than going through an official business system.

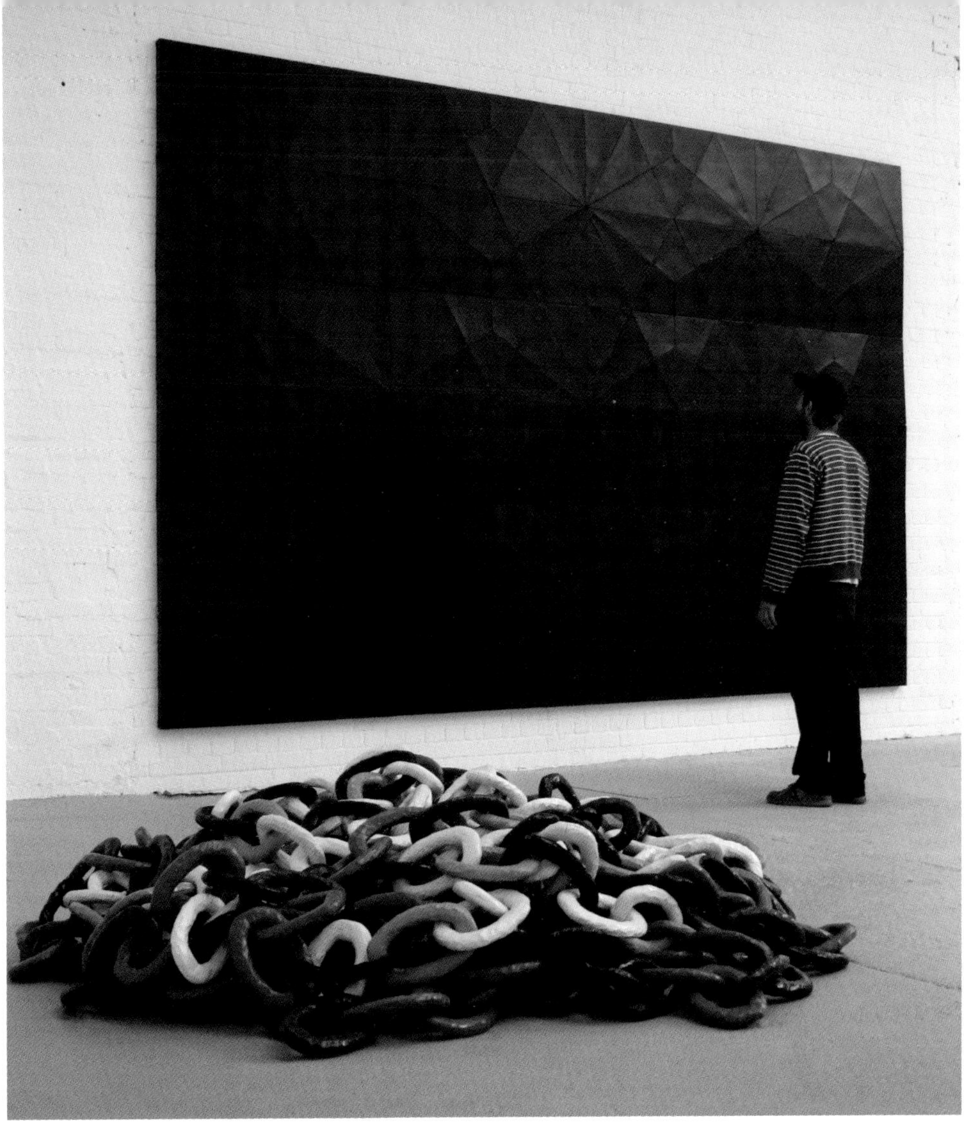

Graduate shows

A graduate show.

Degree shows, which are usually held in the summer months, exhibit work by recent graduates from art schools, and are a glorious way to buy work by artists at more affordable prices. Sign up for the mailing lists of the most prestigious schools, establish yourself as a collector, and try to go to one of the preview evenings. Since the vast majority of students will be unrepresented, it's a chance to decide for yourself who the stars of tomorrow will be and contribute to their future success by investing in them early. Talk to the students; get a sense of who their influences are, how they work and their creative process. See if they have shadowed or studied under an eminent artist. Their personal story can influence your appreciation of their work and help you to decide whether they are doing something truly interesting and original. If you like their work, take their details and get in touch.

GOOD TO KNOW
DEGREE SHOWS

* As with emerging artists (see chapter What to Look For), look out for a striking style and a cohesive body of work.
* Take into consideration the calibre of the art school: students from more internationally renowned schools (The Slade School of Fine Arts, London; University of Art and Design, Helsinki; Parsons, the New School, New York) have already gone through a rigorous selection process, and were seen to show the most promise of their intake. Although, that said, it's by no means the case that the most prestigious schools will universally produce the best artists.
* Ask whether the artist has been approached about gallery representation: it's not necessarily an automatic indicator of their perceived potential, as developments may ensue post show, but the best students are likely to have been singled out at an early stage by gallerists.
* Look out for work that's made using high-quality materials and sophisticated or interesting techniques.

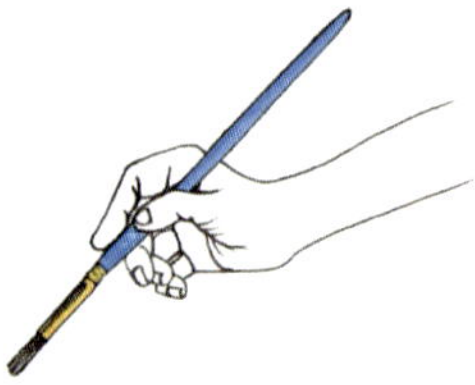

Buying Online

Buying art online can unnerve many art collectors, but, like so much in life, the art world is developing, broadening, diversifying and expanding through online platforms and social media. The internet is opening up the art world (at least certain aspects) to a more level playing field, especially for new gallerists, emerging artists and artists selling directly to collectors. There are enormous advantages to online galleries, galleries with an online presence, online art fairs and auction sites and buying from artists' own sites, although there are particular elements to be aware of when making purchases.

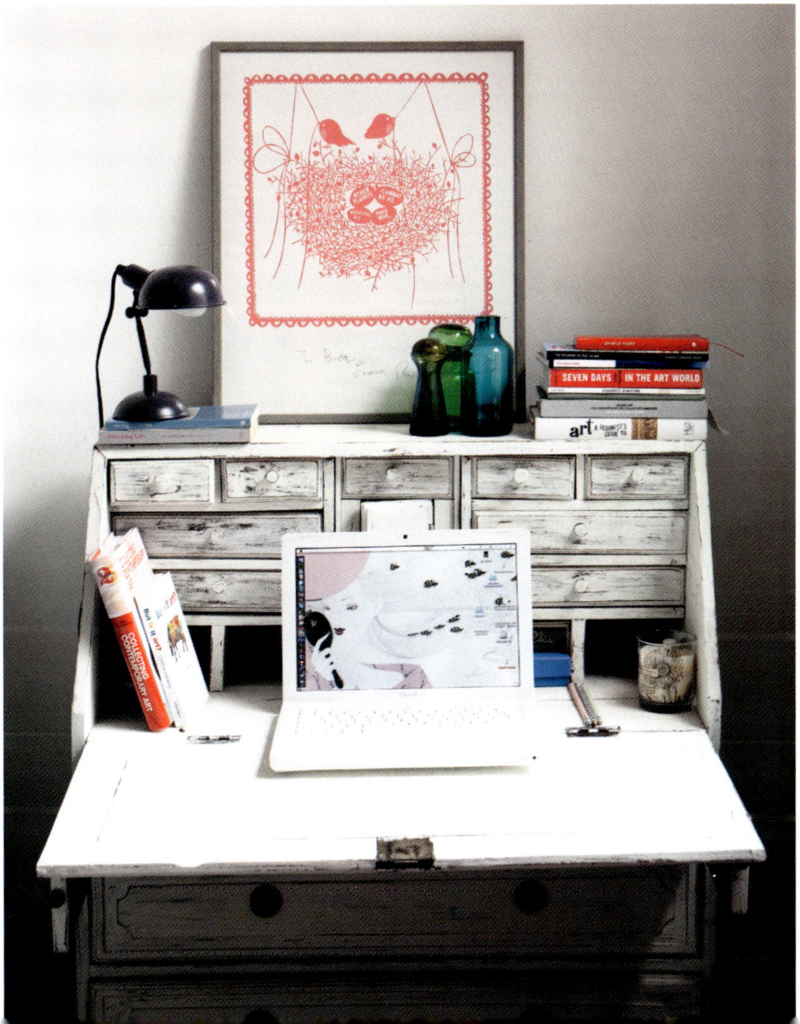

Advantages of buying online

* A gallery's site can help determine its credibility, with show histories, artist CVs and portfolios. It's the perfect starting point for doing a background check on galleries.
* Browsing an online gallery allows you to bypass the often intimidating experience of wandering round a physical gallery, and peruse the art from the comfort of your own home.
* By looking at a variety of artists' works online you can build confidence in your taste, develop a discourse on the artists you like and why, so you can discuss your likes and dislikes with confidence.
* Access to international artists through online galleries located all over the world, and via art social networking sites, allows for an easy introduction to a broader spectrum of artists.
* Prices at exclusively online galleries are often lower as there will be fewer gallery overheads.
* Online galleries often have a 360-degree approach to interacting with the art market. Buyer feedback, online communities and links to press reviews are more readily available.
* You can usually compare prices by the same artists at different galleries.
* You can go back and look at a work again, uninhibited by the prospect of a gallery assistant watching you.

Disadvantages of buying online

* There's no real replacement for the physical visual impact of actually seeing a work of art in the flesh. Colour quality and tones vary depending on computer programs and it can be difficult to gain a sense of scale, while subtle nuances – the layering of paint, the way light reflects, muted shades, the interaction between media in collage and composite work – can be missed.
* Bold colours, simple shapes and graphic designs stand out while scrolling down the page. What looks good on a computer screen may not look as good on a wall in a domestic setting.

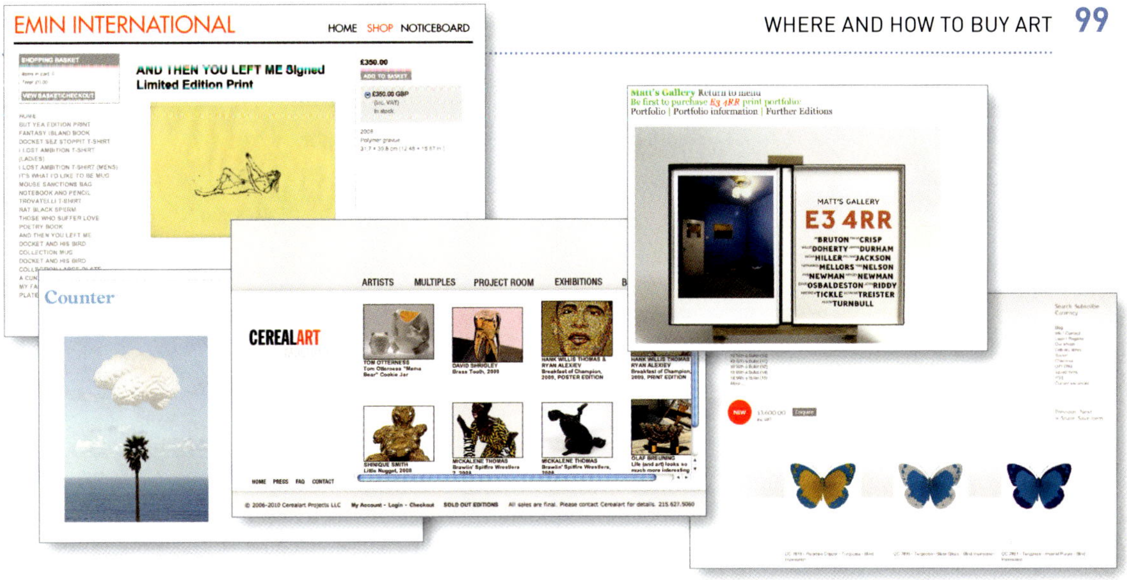

* Without a physical space it can be tricky to get a sense of the gallery or auction house's credibility and permanence.
* There's no official monitoring body for online galleries.
* Online galleries often don't represent artists in quite the same way as a gallery space, gallery space, which nurtures or mentors the artist, and some simply provide an indiscriminate platform for selling works.
* You can't discuss the work of art or the artist in person.

Online buying options are enormously varied. Aside from galleries with a physical space, there are many ways of buying using the internet.

Artists' own websites

Artists themselves often have websites, which is a brilliant way of buying from them directly and building a relationship with them independently.

Platforms for graduate art

There are many online galleries that scour graduate shows and sell work by promising recent graduates and unrepresented artists. Experts such as those at London-based gallery www.Newbloodart.com

sell work by graduates from UK-based art schools, while US-based www.ugallery.com accepts submissions from any artist but only sell work by those they consider the best. Galleries like these will have done the leg-work for you and, although it's a gamble as there's no guarantee that the artists will definitely go on to make a name for themselves, it can be a great way of investing in affordable art and contributing to the upward trajectory of new artists.

The alternative is to buy work via galleries with no selection process, which is more of a gamble. At galleries like www.emergingartists.com any artist can simply submit their work, it will then be posted, and the gallery acts as a portal and go-between between artists and collector.

Art social networking platforms

These are online communities where artists and collectors can interact. At the Saatchi Gallery's web saleroom (www.saatchionline.com) artists' pages display their work for sale, while collectors can upload images of their collections. The site also has a list of limited-edition works available to buy, and enables collectors to buy directly from artists, taking no commission.

Gallery hubs

There are also sites which act less as a gallery, more as a hub that gathers works (mostly prints) by a variety of established names. www.photographerslimitededitions.com brings together work by hugely successful photographers across a variety of disciplines – from art to fashion and portraiture. US site www.20x200.com offers two works of art for sale each week, which are available to buy in three different sized print editions: Two hundred for $20/£12.50/€14.50; 20 prints for $200/£125/€145 and two prints for $2,000/£1,875/€2,200. UK site Culture Label (www.culturelabel.com) gathers together works sold at a variety of UK public art galleries (such as Tate Gallery and the The Baltic Centre for Contemporary Art), commercial galleries, not for profit galleries (Matt's Gallery), print studios (Glasgow Print Studio) and art collectives (Jaguar Shoes collective).

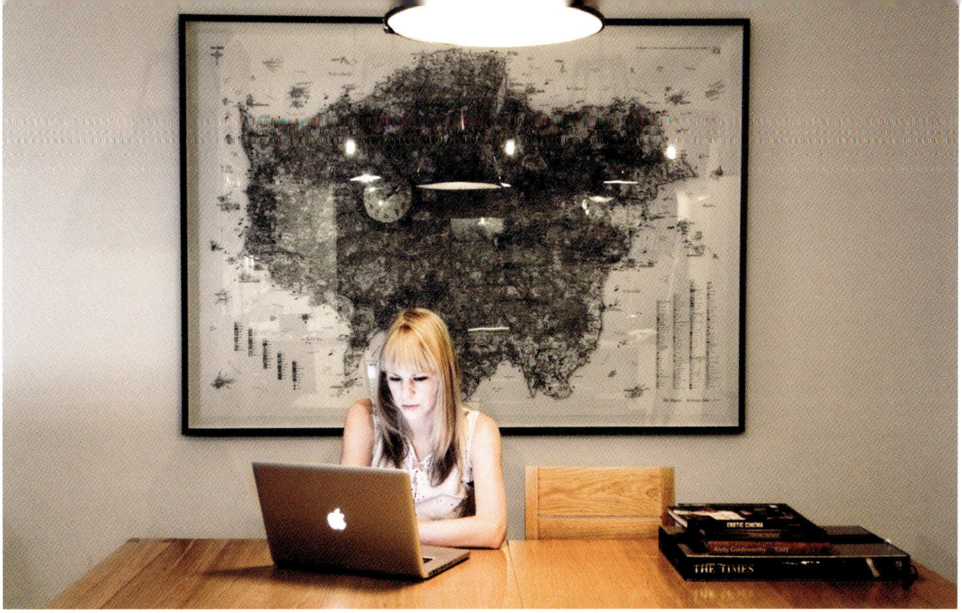

Online art fairs

With an impressive collection of dealers including White Cube, Gagosian, Sadie Coles HQ and New York's Metro Pictures, January 2011 saw the launch of the first online art fair, VIP Art Fair (www.vipartfair.com), which stands for View in Private. It had mixed feedback and who knows if it is the shape of things to come, but it was an innovation in the art world. Works from galleries all over the world can be viewed in relation to the size of a human figure (to get a sense of scale), there are zoom functions for studying specific works, and there is a comprehensive, readily available 360 approach to each work with artist biographies, catalogue essays and artist CVs. Collectors can contact gallerists directly via a multiple of technology platforms such as Skype, telephone and instant messenger. There are even online tours.

Online Auction Houses

In 2011 the former chairman of Philips de Pury, London, Rodman Primack, set up www.Blacklots.com, an online auction house re-selling works by represented artists (gallery representation means authenticity of works presented for re-sale are easier to verify). Chic, sleek and confident, it may herald a new era for online re-sale of contemporary art.

GOOD TO KNOW
BUYING ONLINE

* Establish the credibility of the online platform. Check the biographies of the founders and artists.
* Establish the selection process for the art and artists on sale and the exact way the platform operates. For example, with galleries, do they select artists by scouring degree shows or by accepting submissions online?
* Look for an edited selection of artists. Whether this is small number of artists permanently selling work or a curated online exhibition (as with galleries like www.theportmangallery.co.uk), you want to be sure exhibiting artists have been handpicked with care and discernment, and the selection isn't overwhelming to navigate.
* Check for a phone number. Speak with the gallerist about the artists they sell who you like and try to find out more about them.
* Make sure there is a good returns policy of at least 14 days, although this may vary depending on international sales.
* Establish that their policies (damage, delivery as well as returns) are clear and reliable.
* Ask for certificates of authenticity for works of art when you purchase editions.
* Check feedback from other clients, both on their own website and elsewhere on the web.
* To establish the sense of scale of a work of art you'd like to buy, mark it out on the wall where you'd like to hang it using masking tape – you'll get a more comprehensive sense of its size within a physical setting.

Fundraising

Respected artists whose work is high desirable are often approached to make and donate work for auctions or sales in order to raise money for a cause. These sales can be a brilliant way to discover new artists, especially if there are print collections available to buy which gather together contemporary art by several artists, and prices can be quite accessible. Look out for projects where a host of exciting contemporary artists have become involved. Often work will be commissioned to a brief and sold at a set price (usually an attractive one) and anonymously (the artist being revealed on sale) to raise funds either for a charity or not for profit art organization

The UK's homeless charity Shelter (www.shelter.org.uk) and Cancer support charity Maggie's (www.maggiescentres.org) have both had recent exhibitions with work commissioned by artists to a theme – the former asked artists to create one playing card from a deck of 52; originals of each were available to buy or limited-edition reproductions of a full pack. The latter involved 100 artists creating individual works of art from a sheet of graph paper on the theme 'Joy of Living'. In a similar vein, the AIDS Community Research Initiative of America (ACRIA, www.acria.org/store/store_artwork) have collections of works donated by prominent artists on their website to help the charity to raise funds for research and treatment.

In the UK, the Art Fund (www.artfund.org) raises money to support public collections of art and sells works to raise funds. A recent project was a limited-edition Howard Hodgkin brushstroke for £500/€600/$800.

Fundraisers can be a brilliant way to discover new artists and support a worthy cause.

Art book publishers

Many publishers of books about art often release limited-edition prints to celebrate the publication of their book titles. These can usually be found on their online shop. Prices vary depending on the print run, artist and edition number, but some amazing pieces can be found, so it's worth checking in every so often with publishers who print books about artists who appeal to your tastes and interests.

Magazines

Art magazines often produce artist editions and prints. Parkett (www.parkett.com) collaborate with a selection of artists on every issue of their biannual magazine to produce an edition (usually priced between \$1000/£625/€725 and \$3,000/£1,875/€2,200). Past artists have included Louise Bourgeois, Anish Kapoor and Richard Prince. Wallpaper set up Wallpaper Selects (www.wallpaperselects.com) in association with online editions gallery Eyestorm (www.eyestorm.com), selling limited-edition prints of a selection of the photography which has featured in the magazine.

Alternative and creative ways of buying

Buying art can be as creative a process as making it. You can have an enormous amount of fun approaching an art transaction from a new direction.

At the Art Barter Fair (www.artbarter.co.uk), which originated in London but now also takes place in Berlin and New York, all artwork is displayed without a price and is open to buyers' barters. The only rule is that you can't offer money. Instead, art enthusiasts offer services, treats or one-of-a-kind experiences in exchange for art. The not-for-profit fair MACparis (www.mac2000-art.com) also sanctions bartering for goods rather than money as part of its trading rules. On the online gallery Eyestorm (www.eyestorm.com) art buyers are invited to 'Make us an offer' – i.e. suggest the price you'd like to pay for an artwork.

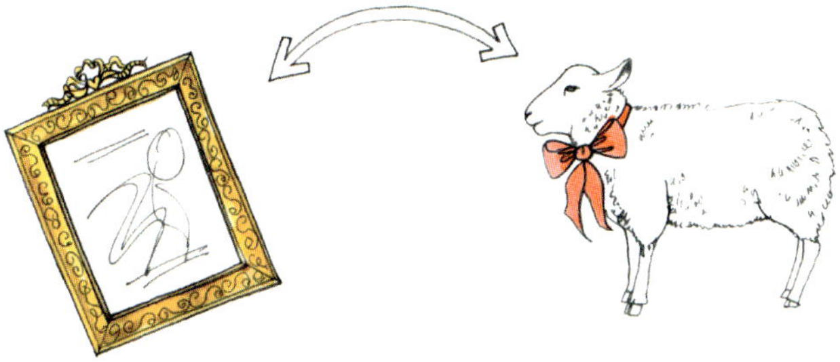

Every November in London, The Royal College of Art stages its Secret Fair (www.rca.ac.uk/secret). Here RCA students together with established artists each create a postcard-sized work of art, which is then sold for £45/€55/$75 (2010 pricing). The identity of the artist behind each postcard is only revealed once the sale has gone through. It's a gamble, but potentially a very lucrative one, and great fun.

At the Art Car Boot Fair (www.artcarbootfair.com) in London, for one summer's weekend, artists including Sir Peter Blake and Bob and Roberta Smith sell artistic wares from the boots of cars, and many participants also create car tax discs available to buy online for £40/€47/$65 (2010 prices).

The grand old establishment The Victoria & Albert Museum holds a summer fete in their courtyard every year. The V&A village fete calls upon artists to create alternative stalls, and invites visitors to pay to play each stall's game, with a chance to win artwork. East London artist Rob Ryan has hosted stalls such as the Play Your Cards Right stand where, for a £1/€1.20/$1.60 fee, winners could walk away with a limited-edition print (worth considerably more).

In purchasing art outside monetary lines, with something that makes the transaction unique to the collector, the story of the winning or trading of a piece adds to personal value for the collector, an active anecdote that cannot be valued in fiscal terms. Embrace these new ways of owning art – they are fun, an adventure, and mean you'll be attached to the piece in a truly special way.

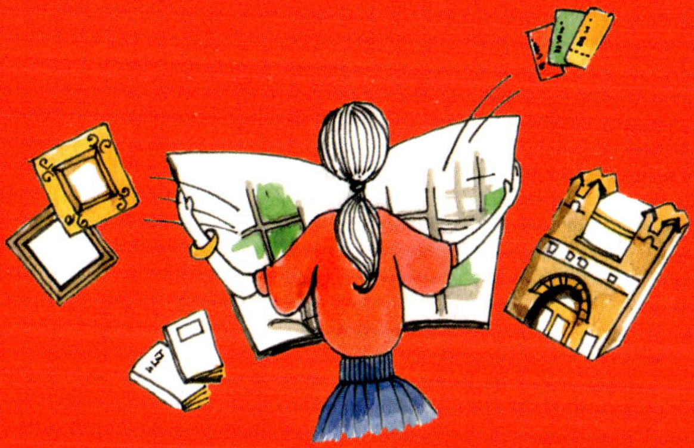

04

Navigating your tastes

Navigating your tastes

BUYING ART YOU LOVE is a great place to start when building an art collection. However, although it's a trustworthy maxim to hold dear, there are a few caveats which are helpful to bear in mind in order to build up a collection that's *more* than the sum of its parts, whatever budget you are on; a collection that has a coherent, individual and lively shape.

Take inspiration from the collections of others

The personal contemporary art collections of influential and celebrated collectors are an incredibly inspiring guide for collectors of every level wishing to develop and shape their collections. Many of these collections are open to the public or allow art societies to conduct group tours (see box below). Think about how collector tastes are explored, pushed, challenged and indulged as you look at the collection as a whole and in curated shows; how appreciation of one artist leads to the discovery of, or introduction to, another of a similar style, or how works by different artists react *against* one another as the collection goes off on a tangent.

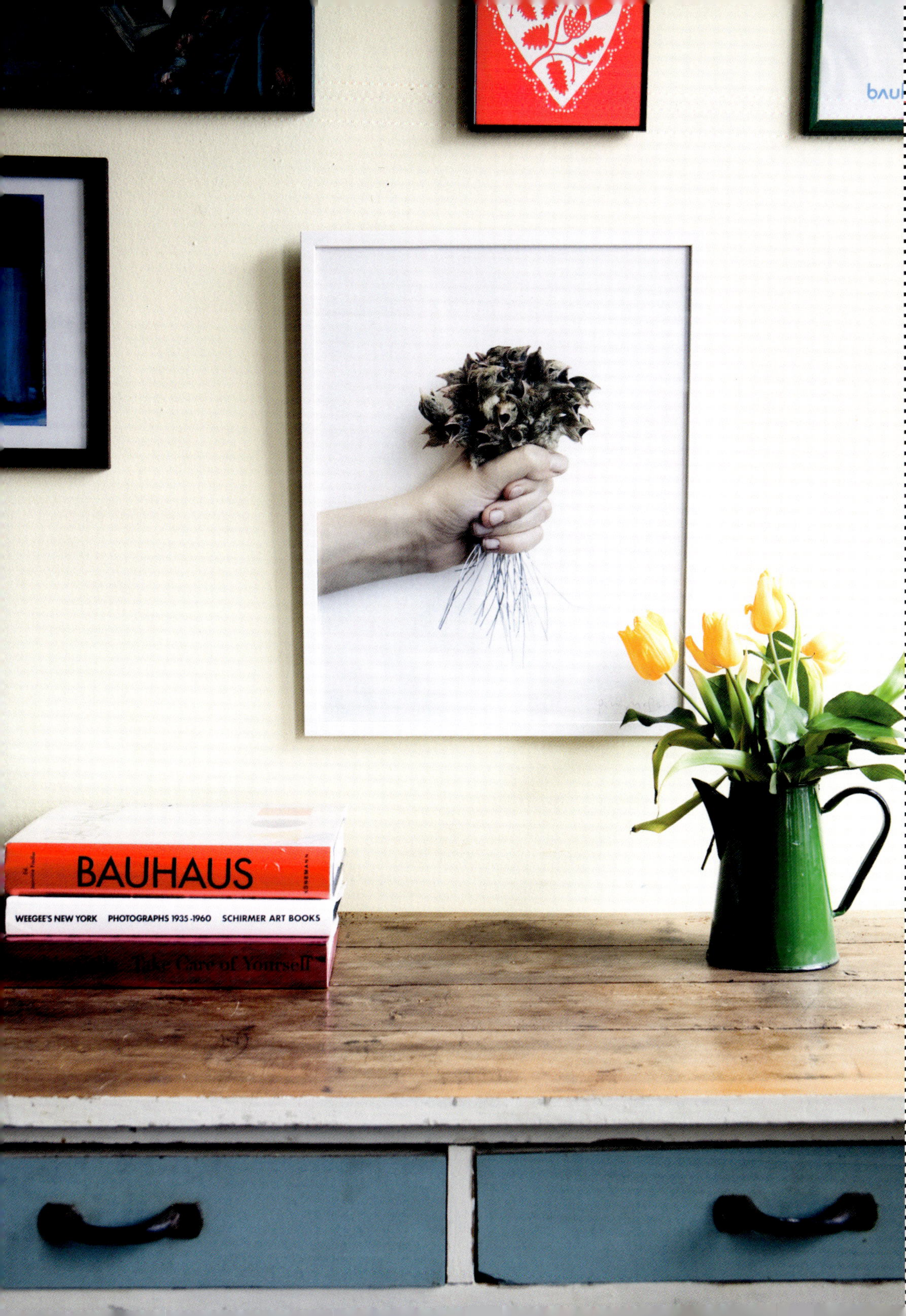
BAUHAUS
WEEGEE'S NEW YORK PHOTOGRAPHS 1935-1960 SCHIRMER ART BOOKS
Take Care of Yourself

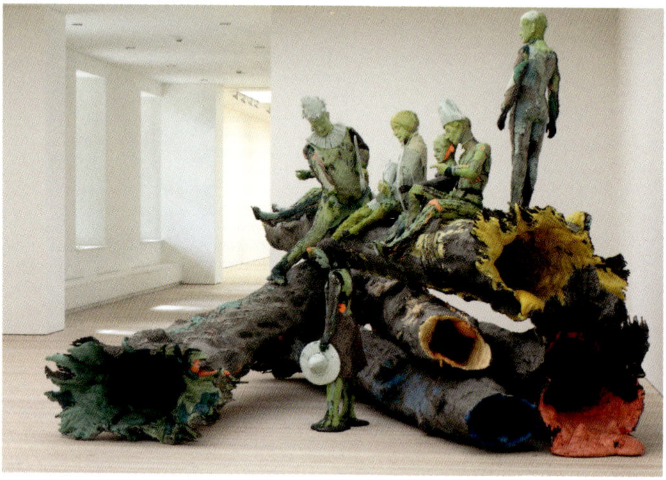

The Saatchi Gallery.

A selection of private collections of contemporary art that are on display to the public

Zabludowicz Collection: the London, Sarvisalo and New York collections of Anita Zabludowicz (www.zabludowiczcollection.com).

Eli and Edythe Broad's Broad Art Foundation in Santa Monica, California (www.broadartfoundation.org).

The David Roberts Collection, London (www.davidrobertsartfoundation.com/collection), which includes over 1600 works by 300 international emerging and well-known artists acquired in the last 10 years.

The Saatchi Gallery (as of 2012 The Museum of Contemporary Art thanks to collector Charles Saatchi's donation of over 200 of his works to the British state).

The Cranford collection: established by Freddy and Muriel Salem in 1999 with the aim of collecting and supporting contemporary art projects.

Cosmetics heir Ronald Lauder's collection of German and Austrian Expressionism shown at the Neue Galery in New York (www.neuegalerie.org).

Buy art you like

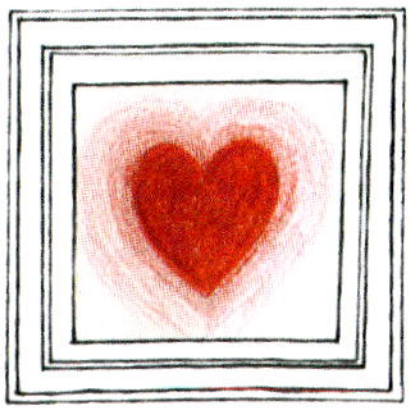

At the end of the day, you are the one who is going to have to live with the art you take home. Don't ever feel pressured, intimidated or overwhelmed into buying something you're not sure about. Buying is as much intuitive as intellectual. You can read all you like about an upcoming artist or latest trend but you may not be drawn to it.

Don't always go for the obvious

It's a risky generalisation to say be wary of words like 'pretty', 'nice' or 'easy on the eye', but as a general rule, such banal praise doesn't really encompass the cut and thrust of cutting edge contemporary art, which in essence seeks to engage viewers in a challenging dialogue rather than a placatory one. Look for pieces which provoke rather than stroke the senses. You are more likely to continue developing your relationship with these sorts of pieces over the years. Sometimes this might be the piece you look at last or the one you initially rejected.

Take time to look at works on your own

Don't feel too guided towards specific pieces by a gallerist. Take their advice and comments on board, then make time to look at works on your own and make up your mind without being unduly influenced.

Explore your own dialogue with each piece

Looking at a work of art should be like having a conversation; a series of reactions and interactions that vary depending on the viewer, their tastes, emotions and sensibilities. The more aware you are of the nuances of each conversation, the more you'll be able to appreciate your relationship with each piece, and see it changing and evolving. Think about how you react to individual pieces, why you like them or not, and ask yourself questions which may make you change your reaction or at least look at the piece from a different angle.

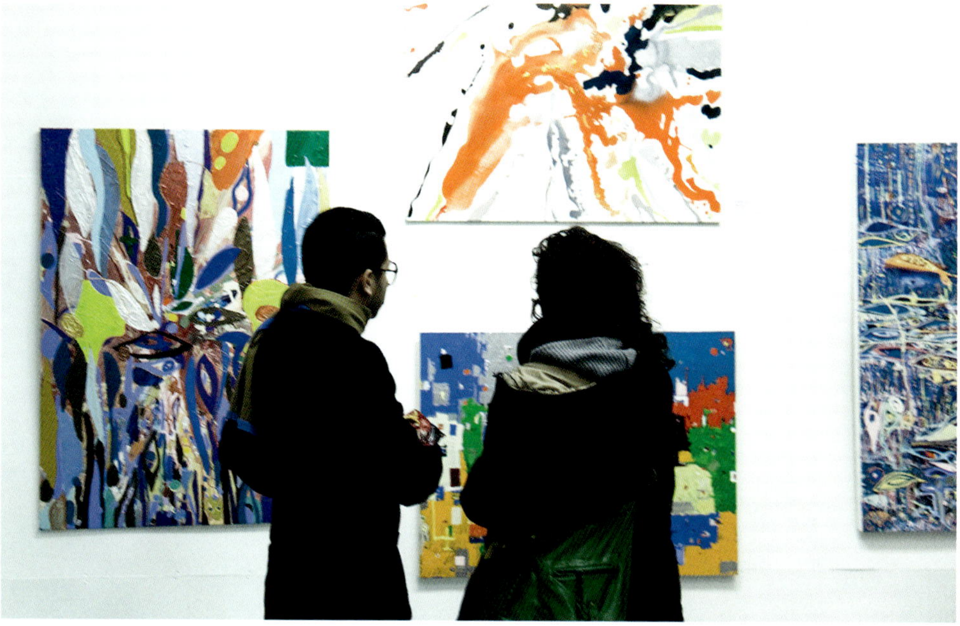

Discover more about artistic narratives

Explore the creative thrust of the art and look at it within an art historical framework. Is it pushing boundaries, challenging the status quo? Is it returning to the principles of an established movement? Is it part of a specific creative movement or marching to the beat of its own drum? Is this movement stylistic, or political? Whether or not this changes your reaction to the work, it will help to give some context to the piece both independent from and integral to your collection.

Think about the artistic medium

Whether you are buying figurative drawings, sculpture, paintings, photography, sketches, collages, mixed media or prints, think about what it is about the work being in this medium that's important to the piece, and how the type of art fits into your collection. Is the medium itself a defining characteristic?

Shape your collection

The world's big name collectors approach developing their collections either vertically or horizontally: The former refers to buying multiple pieces by one artist, in depth, the latter buying across the spectrum with the intention that the collector will own significant works by key contemporary artists. In the upper echelons of the art-collecting world, there's a fine balance between the two. The former can make an artist's career, but if the collector chooses to 'dump' or 'flip' their collection on the secondary market, the art market can become flooded with an artist's work, which can devalue it. Conversely, however, there can be seen to be a derogatory 'I'll have one of everything' approach to more horizontal collecting; a need to have a work by every latest new kid on the block, as a sort of validating cool cache.

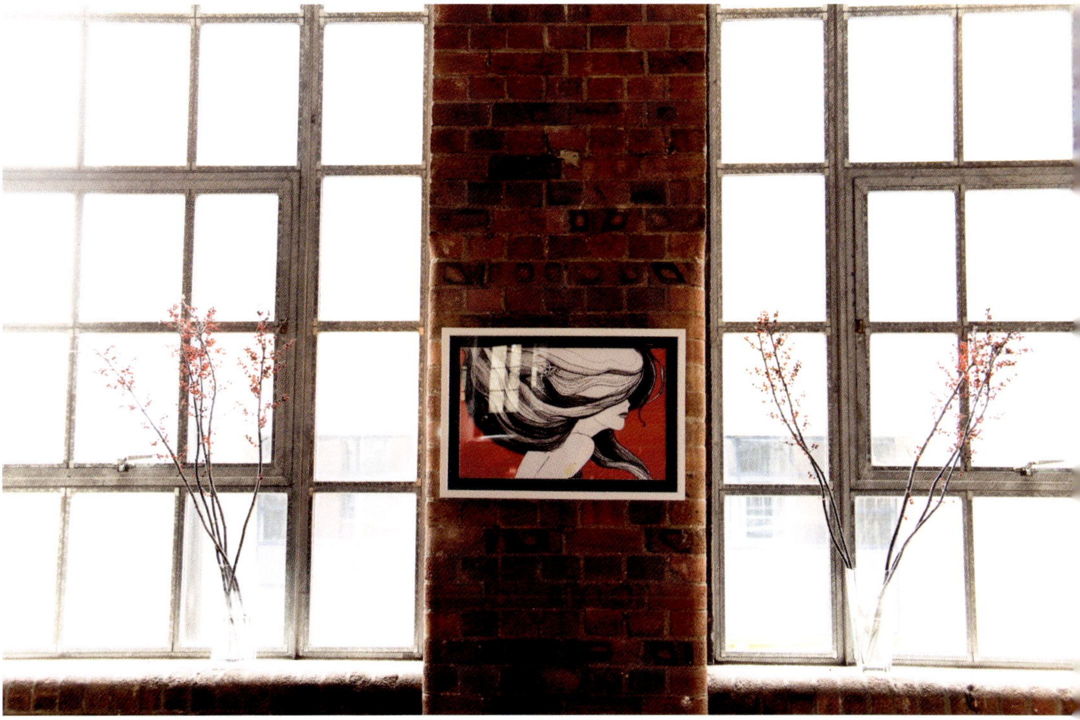

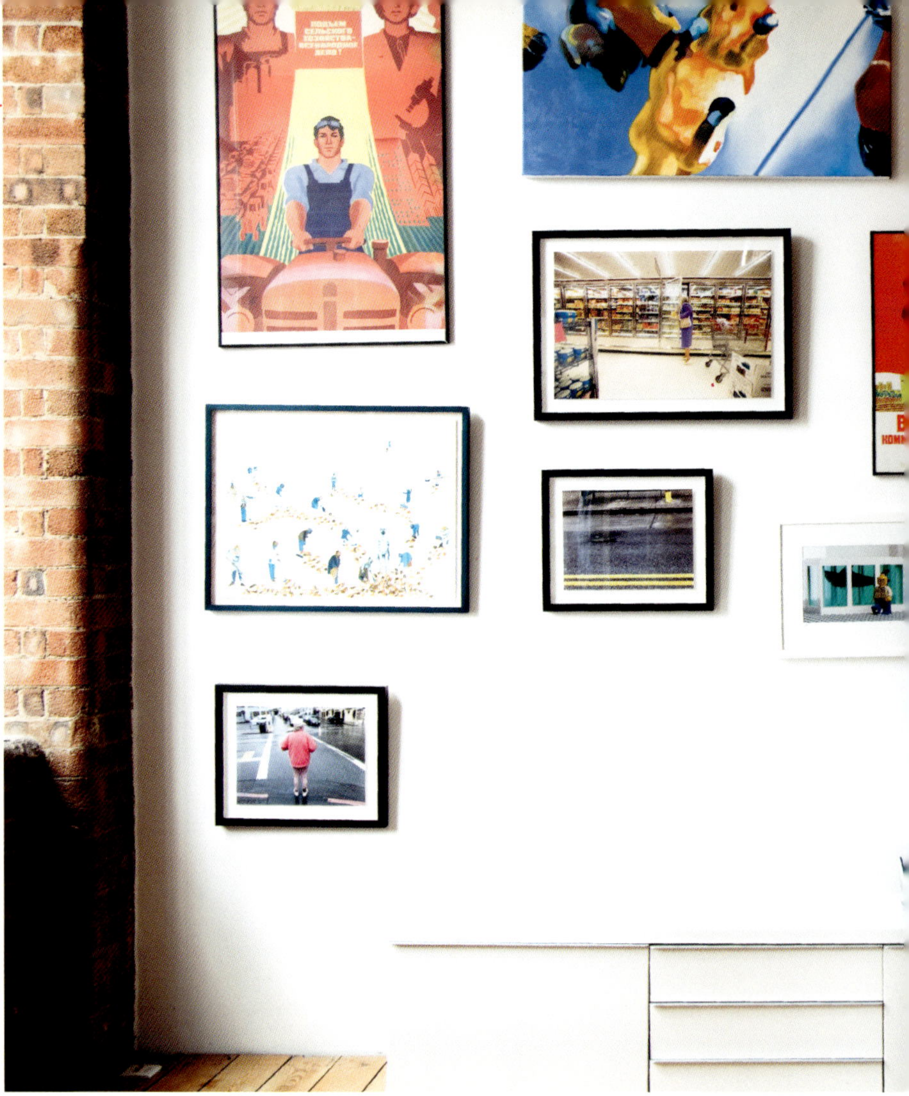

Although vertical or horizontal collecting is a rather alien concept to a more modest collector, the shape of a collection remains a valid consideration. Buying haphazardly or whimsically can have its own appeal, as a collection forms a shape in an organic way, but it can be rewarding to focus your buying.

Initially see how your tastes manifest themselves – it may take a while before you realise you're attracted to works which have a unifying theme. It may only become clear when you look at the collection as a whole. Sometimes works of art *choose you*. You may not be sure quite

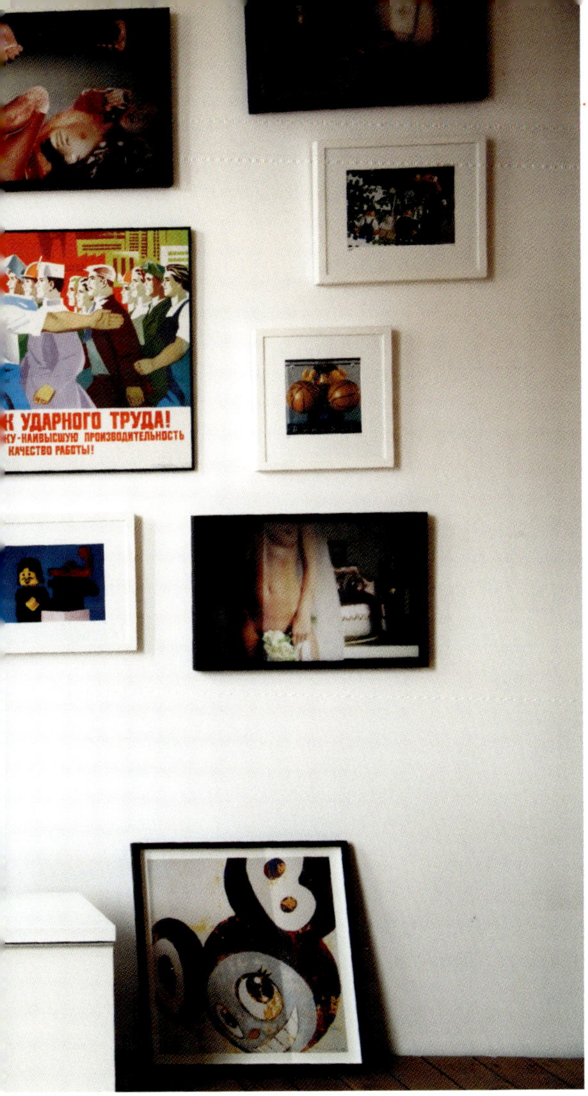

Pushing beyond the boundaries of the comfortable in order to develop your tastes is a vital part of growing as a collector.

why, but you'll be drawn to them. Go with that and see where it takes you, then try to establish what that intangible quality is and try to harness it. It may be collecting original pieces or prints by artists from the same school or group; collecting a certain style – works on paper, miniature sculptures, line drawings, artist studies, paper cuts, book illustrations, posters or letterpress prints; or which have a resonant theme – family, death, sex, nature, the theatre or erotica, for example. There might be pockets of works that naturally align themselves within one collection, as several clusters grow symbiotically.

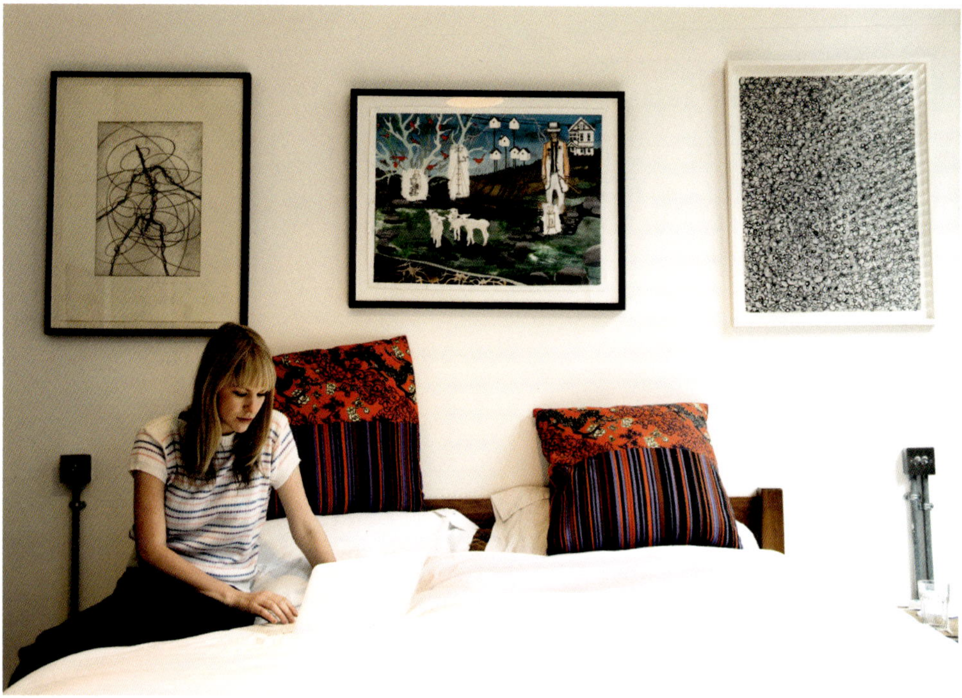

Like collecting anything seriously, from stamps to model cars, adding to a collection can be more rewarding if there's a quest element – a specific aim that can be realised, and satisfaction when that perfect answer, solution, addition, or complimentary piece has been added to the existing pieces. Having a focus to an art collection makes that specific aim more easily identifiable, and pin-pointing the next object of desire and doing everything in your power to attain it is an enormously rewarding process, as well as giving a coherency and structure to your collection.

Challenge and push your tastes

Pushing beyond the boundaries of the comfortable in order to develop your tastes is a vital part of growing as a collector. What can be unexpectedly rewarding is the changing relationship you may have

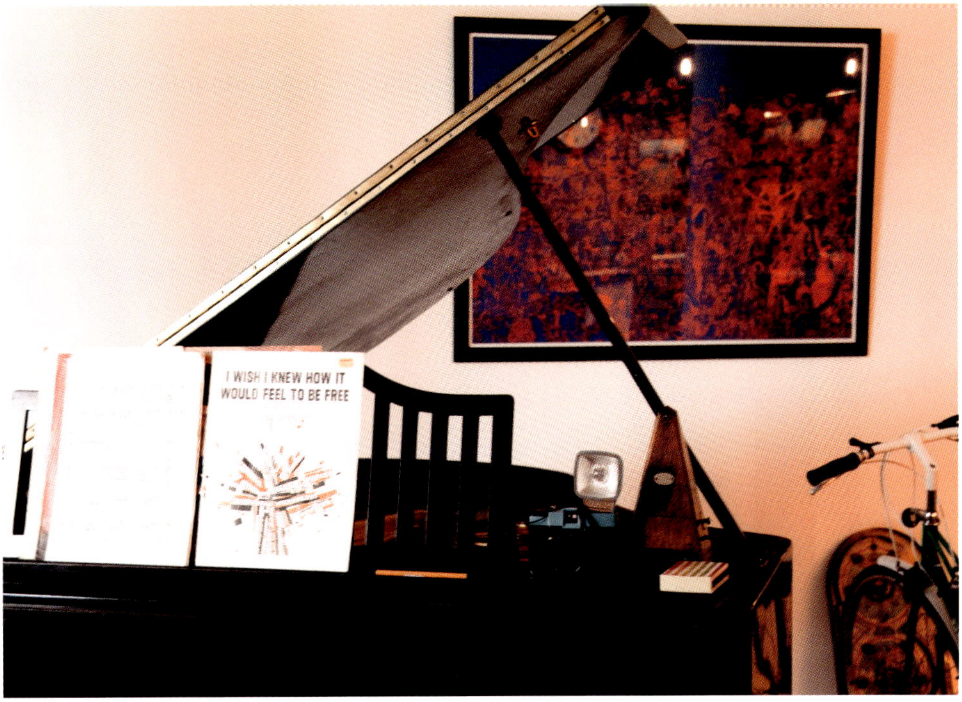

with a work of art. Pieces that once appealed can lose their lustre, while pieces that initially seemed tricky and less easy to live with can grow on you.

There are many practical ways to encourage or even force your hand when it comes to developing your taste in art.

Like collecting anything seriously, from stamps to model cars, adding to a collection can be more rewarding if there's a quest element

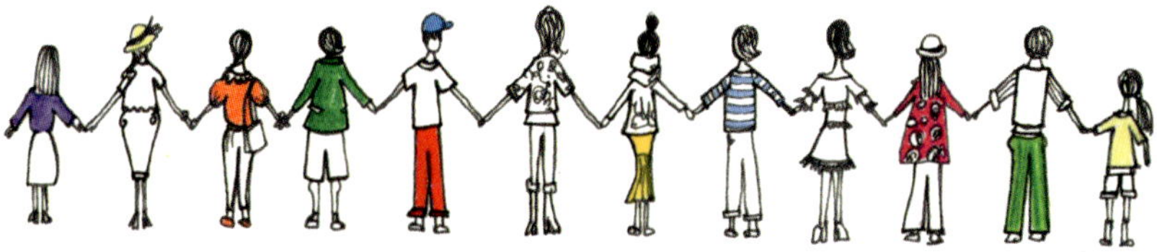

Join a buying collective or syndicate

These involve several friends or households joining forces to buy several works of art, which are then rotated between them. Each household has a work of art hanging in their home for a designated period before swapping. The balance of taste between different members can push each other's choices, and living with the works for a certain period can give more time for your reactions to change, and mature. Members can pay by monthly instalments, or operate a system by investing on a piece-by-piece basis. As a guide, look into the advice given by The Collective (www.the-collective.info), a UK-based advisory service that has helped establish art buying collectives up and down the country.

Take the lead from an arts club membership

Joining in members' club schemes such as The Artist of the Month Club (www.artistofthemonthclub.com) can be an interesting way of discovering new art. For an annual subscription from $3000/£1875/€2200, members are sent a work of art every month for 12 months. Each work is specially commissioned by one of the panel of the AMC curators from an emerging or established artist they consider to be collectable. It's an experimental art subscription, and guaranteed to challenge the boundaries of your taste.

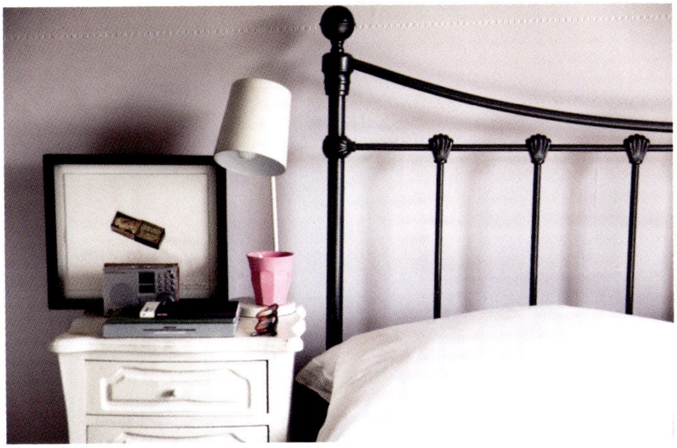

Invest in print portfolios

As mentioned earlier, many art galleries and artist collectives put together print portfolios, which gather limited-edition prints by a selection of artists. This is a fantastic way to buy a collection of pieces from a trusted source and familiarise yourself with new styles, artists, and genres. Since more often than not the portfolio will include works that you wouldn't necessarily have chosen yourself, it's an opportunity to try living with pieces and see how your interest in them and reaction to them changes. It can be revelatory.

Re-hang your collection

No matter how small or large your art collection, re-hang it every so often – say six months or so. It'll inject new life into it and make you look at it with new eyes (plus it can help avoid light damage). See how different pieces look together and how they respond to a new setting – perhaps group the works by theme, colour or size. It might inspire you to develop the collection in a different direction as new dialogues between existing pieces become apparent.

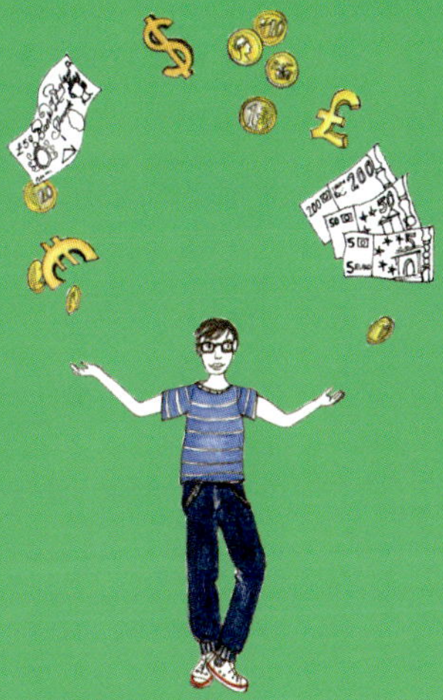

05
What is affordable art?

What is affordable art?

A practical approach to the financial aspects of buying art

AFFORDABLE ART is a tricky term. Firstly, it's pretty arbitrary; for some, 1,000/€1,200/$1,600 may be a negligible amount to invest in a work of art, while for others it's a considerable investment for a luxury. Who's to say what's generally deemed affordable? Surely it's down to the individual judging what's affordable based on an assessment of their own finances. Still, it's worth noting that the various accessible art fairs with an upper price limit set it at around the €5,000/£4,300/$6,900 mark. Secondly, the art world isn't a fan of the term 'affordable art'; it's seen as cheapening and diminishing of the art. 'Attractively' or 'accessibly' priced and 'entry-level' pricing works imply more all round value rather than a crude reductive commerciality. Thirdly, the art market is unregulated – there's no FSA or policing to stop influential collectors buoying prices. Prices are set by the judgement of few – something can sell in a gallery for one price and six months later be sold at auction for half or double that. Everything should be taken with a pinch of salt.

But anyone spending a significant (to them) amount of money on art wants security in the knowledge of several things: that they are paying the right price for a particular work, and that the value of that piece might increase over the years. The first is a matter of navigating

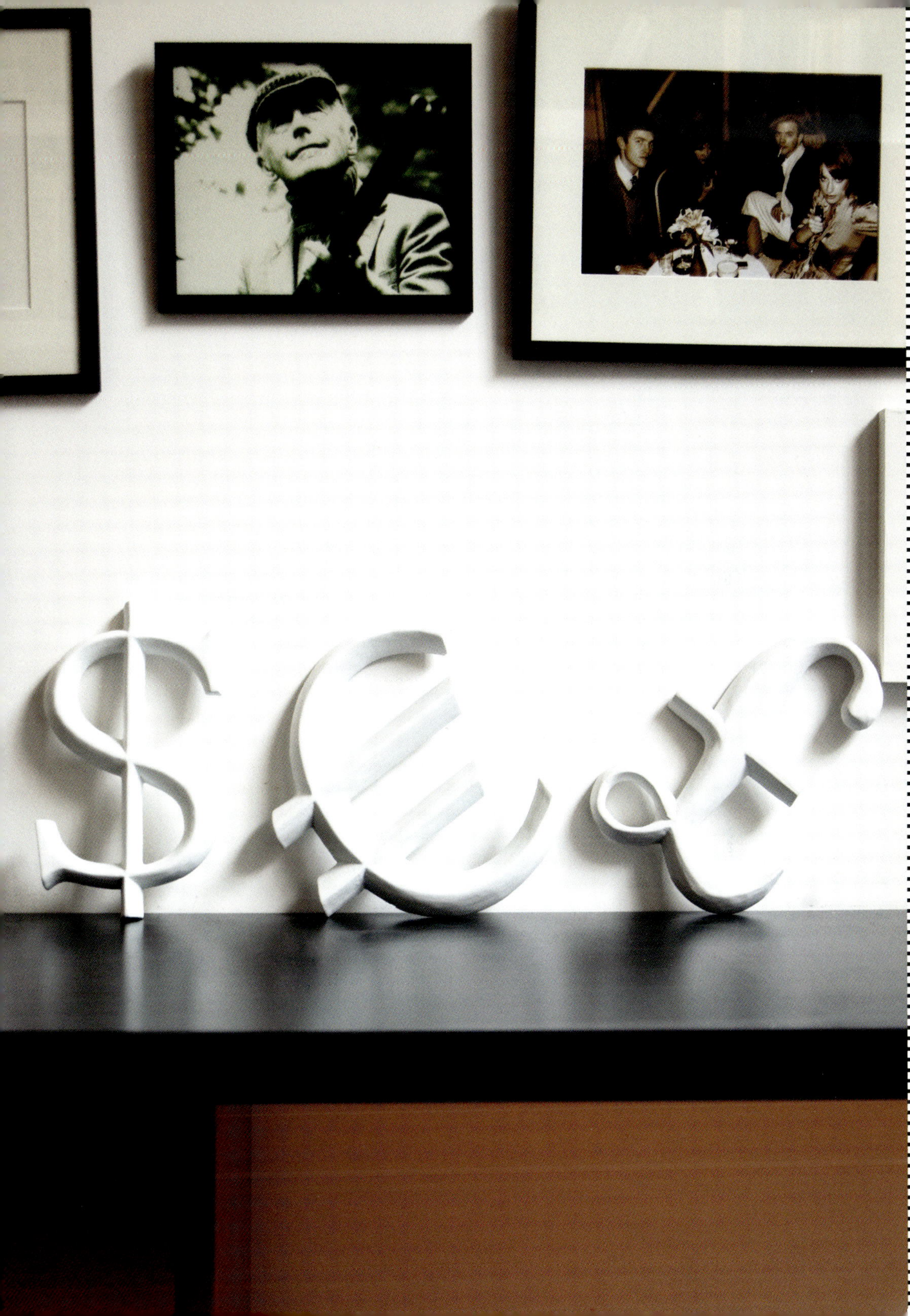

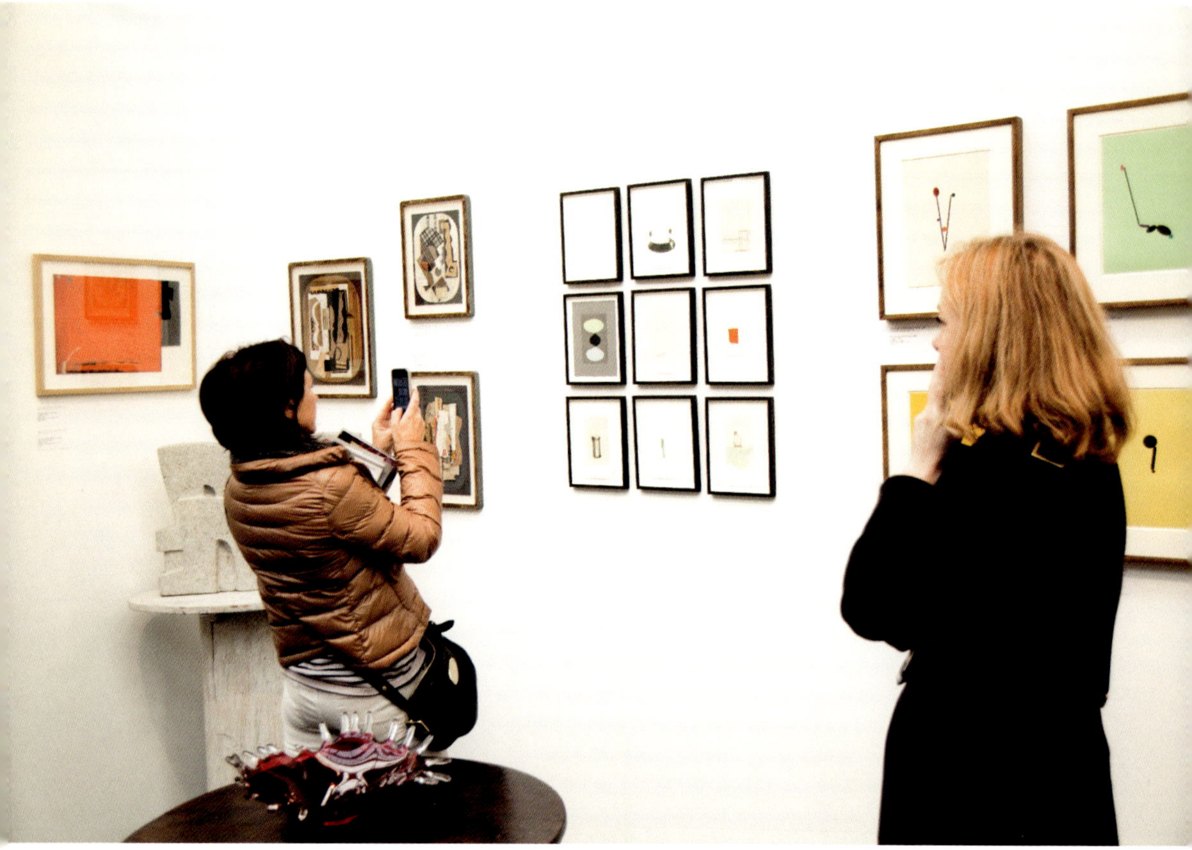

a comfortable path between art market valuation and personal budget, while the second is a careful balance between instinct, research and luck. A rise in price, while it should never be a motivating factor, is in many ways purely a comforting validation that the initial investment was worth it, whether measured in economic or emotional terms. But as a general rule, buying as an investment is a dangerous game. Living with a work of art you don't much like, but which you bought because you thought it would go up in value, is asking for trouble – you're not even investing in your own taste so you've not even really got the courage of your convictions as a defence if it depreciates.

Although there are both art-lover-collectors and art-investment-collectors, buying art to make money is generally frowned upon within the art world. There is no inherent financial value in art that can be measured using a centralised system – there is no one 'price of art' as with say gold or oil, and each artist and each painting is, relatively speaking, valued on its own terms (although prices do obviously affect one another). Art is valued upon essentially subjective criteria: the likes and dislikes, whims and passions, trends and fads of the art world. 'Good art' remains wholly unclassifiable by a checklist of set rules or terms. Skill or technical ability doesn't necessarily take precedence over the ideas or concepts (often ideas in fact trump skill – contemporary artists like viewers to engage with the concept and not just be impressed by technical craftsmanship).

Many contemporary artists working today, from Damien Hirst to Takashi Murakami, employ teams to put together their works of art, but the fact that they didn't manually make the pieces themselves doesn't diminish its value – they conceived the idea so the work is theirs. What makes work by an artist attain a high economic value is the judgement and appreciation of those in the art world. The more levels upon which the art is positively judged, or endorsed, the higher its financial worth.

As a general rule, buying as an investment is a dangerous game.

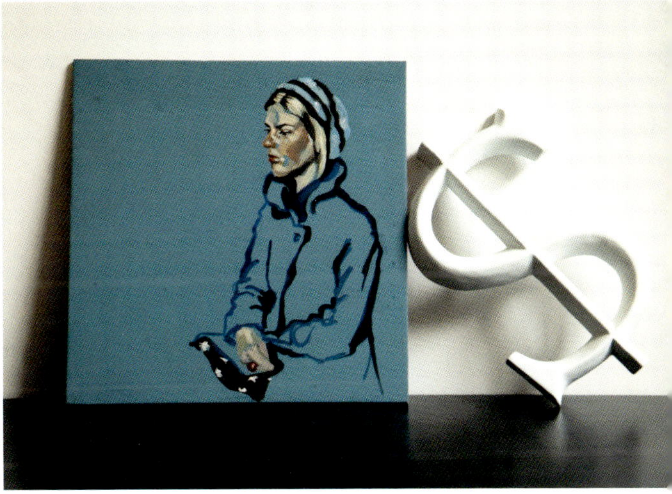

What affects the price of art by a particular artist?

There are various platforms of endorsement that act as a form of quality assessment which directly influence the value of art. The more platforms of quality assurance an artist attains during their career reflects the consolidation of an art world consensus that praises and validates the work, and so (in general) the higher the value of an artist's work.

MFA

A master's degree in art shows an artist's commitment to their practice, and also the higher level at which they have been trained and made to think about their work. A MFA from a more selective art school, with an exceptional teaching faculty comprised of established artists, and high calibre of students who can push each other's work to a more sophisticated or advanced level, can elevate the artistic training process and thus the quality of the graduate's work. A great example is that of the YBAs or Young British Artists – including Damien Hirst, Anya Gallaccio, Sam Taylor-Wood, Sarah Lucas and Mat Collishaw, who, during the late 1980s, were studying at London's Goldsmiths' College under the tutelage of artists including Michael Craig-Martin and Mark Wallinger. MFA shows from highly regarded schools are also more likely to attract the scouting eyes of established commercial galleries at the degree show (if not before).

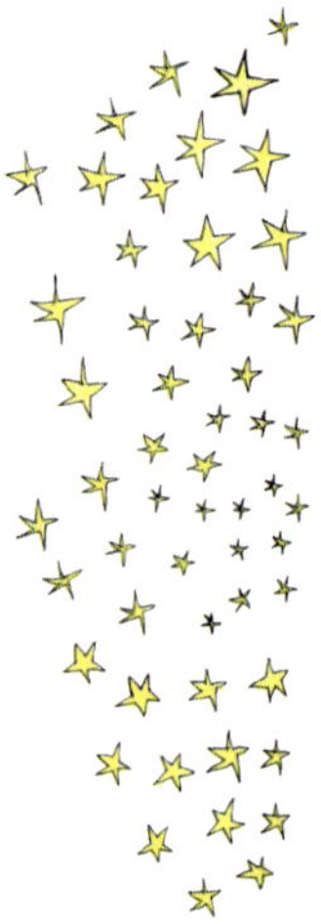

Art world buzz

The buzz or energy around an artist can do nothing but raise awareness, profile and hence prices. This buzz could be around a group of headline-grabbling graduating artists like those just mentioned, or a show that gets people talking – online, by word of mouth, through positive features in magazines and reviews in newspapers. Constant chatter about an artist immediately piques art world interest and sends prices soaring.

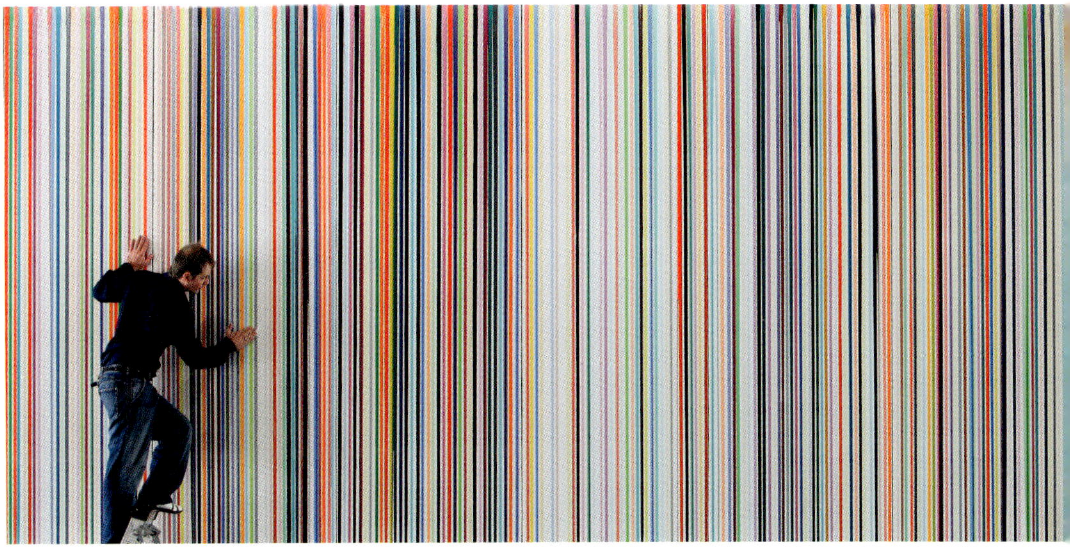

Prizes and awards

Every prize won raises the profile of an artist and also adds to the number of art world eyes who have singled the artist out as being exceptional. It goes without saying that the more prestigious the prize (and the more high profile and highly regarded the judges), the more valued the work of the prize-winner becomes. Nomination in itself is often an accolade.

Being nominated or winning art awards like the Turner Prize (above) is very prestigious.

Gallery representation

In the age of the internet when artists can be contacted directly via personal websites and there are myriad platforms to view art, a gallery is by no means the only channel to an artist. However, commercial gallery representation (especially by a top gallery that already represents established artists of international renown) is highly desirable, nay vital, in order to be seriously successful. Gallery representation is the first major step in art world validation. Every time a gallery with an amazing reputation for discovering emerging talent exhibits a new artist, this signifies that the new artist is *worth* representing, and that they could be destined for the greatness of the artists who have been represented by the gallery before them. Success is by no means guaranteed, but it's more likely. Gallery representation is an endorsement, confirmation that an expert art world eye has faith that the work is good, and that, accordingly, accolades are more likely to follow, prices rise and popularity increase.

Important galleries that throw their full promotional weight behind their artists to increase buzzy reactions, generate news features and internet excitement, in turn raise the artists' profiles and prices. Gallery (and dealer) hierarchies obviously come into play strongly here. The higher both the national and international standing of the gallery, the better it is for the artist. The higher the gallery's profile, the increased buzz around their shows, the more eminent collectors will be introduced to the artists work, and the more popular exposure the artists will get – via gallery shows, presence at art fairs etc.

International shows

Gallery representation usually means gallery shows in one country, unless that gallery has spaces in multiple countries (which is rare). If galleries from countries other than that of the principal gallery invite an artist to exhibit in their space in a group exhibition, put on a solo show for the artist, or want to represent them in that country, then that raises the profile of the artist internationally, exposes them to a broader range of collectors and signifies that there is international endorsement of the artist's work.

Group shows

As well as solo shows at home and abroad, group shows can play a part in raising the profile of an artist, as associations with already well-regarded artists can influence the standing of an artist and the way their work is viewed, and by whom. Being viewed as part of an emerging or exciting movement along with other artists can also generate the sense that they are in tune with the zeitgeist.

Critical acclaim

Positive write-ups (and focussed media attention in general) in the international art news by respected critics can only help an artist's career.

Biennials

Being asked to exhibit work at an international art event such as the Venice Biennale, a showcase for international artists that provides one of the most important overviews for contemporary art, or to be invited to participate in any high-profile international art event is to be at the heart of the interpretation, dissemination, dissection, absorption and discussion of art today.

The Venice Biennale (below) attracts attention from the world's media.

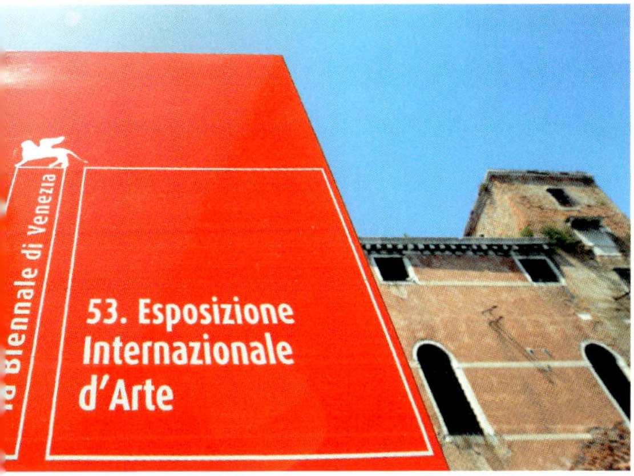

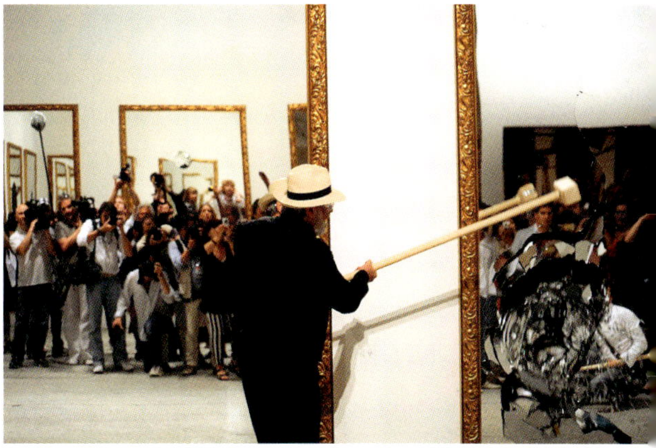

Positive write-ups (and focussed media attention in general) in the international art news by respected critics can only help an artist's career.

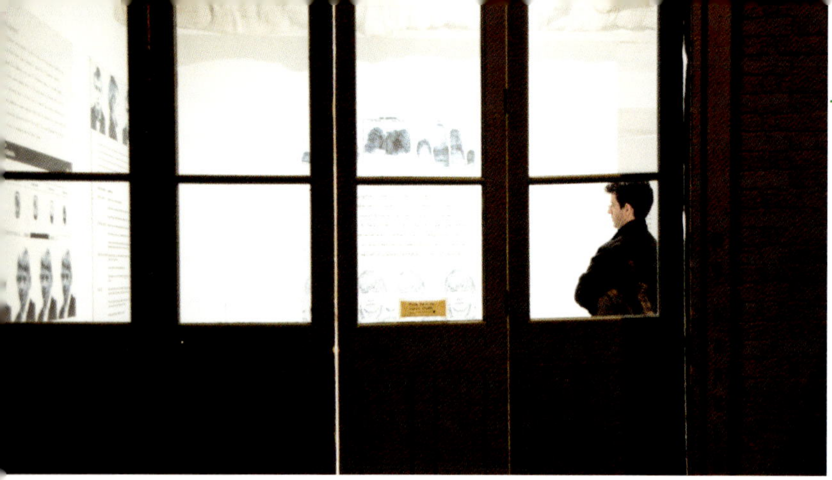

The more popular the artist and the more people want to buy work by that artist, the more prices will be driven up.

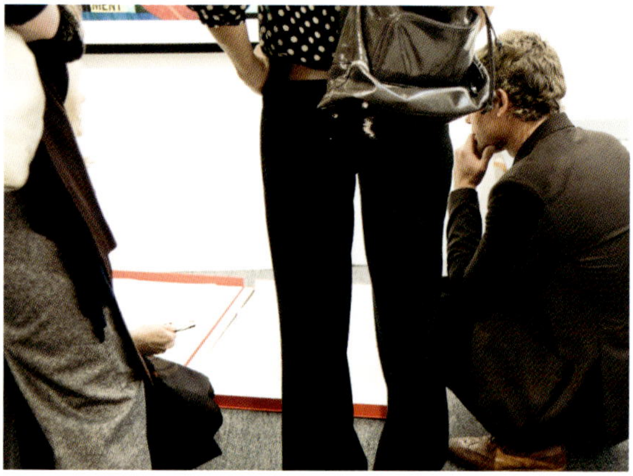

Residencies and teaching posts

When an artist takes up a prestigious lecturing post at a highly rated institution, or they are invited to become an artist in residence, it's a measure of the support that that institution or gallery has for them and is confirming it on a public stage.

Being part of a major collector's art portfolio

When an artist has had work bought by a high-profile private collector, they have been judged, liked and invested in for personal pleasure. That a wealthy, educated art lover with a honed critical eye and a wealth of expert advice has sought to buy an artist's work and thus publicly support an artist is equal to a glowing reference; yet another platform of quality assurance that increases the value of the artist's work as a whole.

Museums

Public displays of art represent a curated collection of high-profile artists who are perceived as important; definitive of an era, a movement, or style that is perceived as having integral significance to contemporary art as a whole. Major commercial galleries have relationships with museums and will work to get their artists' pieces owned by public galleries, and collectors will donate or lend their works to museums as a way of showing their art in a public arena, but also as a tax incentive (exhibiting major works of art to the public can be written off the tax bill). Because a museum will have a panel of art world luminaries who decide which works they will acquire for the gallery's permanent collection, the decision to support an artist publicly is an incredibly prestigious accolade and validation of their work.

Auction

While the primary market remains vital for an artist's career, the secondary market, and the public stage of an auction house sale, arguably provides a forum that confirms the collective appraisal of all of the above forms of support, measured out at each level of the art world – from the teacher to the gallery curator. A high sale price here confirms the highest level that an artist can command for his or her work at that point in time. A quick check on online sites like Artnet.com is a great way to see recent auction sales figures.

Popularity

As with any commodity that's in demand, the more popular the artist and the more people want to buy work by that artist, the more prices will be driven up.

A practical, scaled-down focus to evaluating art

It's always going to be tricky to define whether an artwork is priced at the 'right' amount and whether it will appreciate in value, but on a small, manageable scale, take into consideration these elements:

Representation

See who represents the artist, and then assess the calibre of that gallery by looking at who else the gallery or dealer looks after, or who they have represented in the past. Are the careers of those artists a good sign that the gallery has an eye for discovering, developing and supporting new talent and the clout and promotional strength to support their artists and projects into critical and popular consciousness? The relative success of the gallery and the success of the artists they represent will buoy prices.

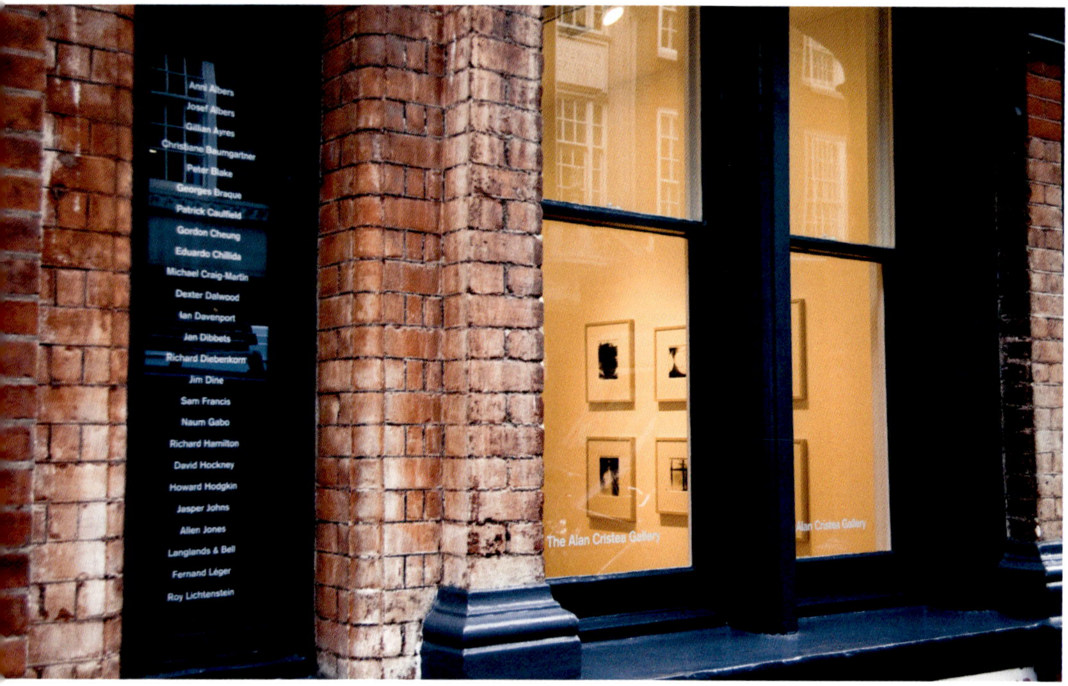

Artist CV

Look at the art school the artist attended and when they graduated; evaluate their commitment to their craft; see where they have had shows, projects they have been involved in, and who they have had group shows with; find out what prizes they have been nominated for and won; and read press coverage or other write-ups. Have they shadowed an established artist or worked as part of an established artist's production team on grand scale projects or worked on an innovative collaboration? Use all this information to build up a picture of the artist's career trajectory and the affect this will have had on their prices.

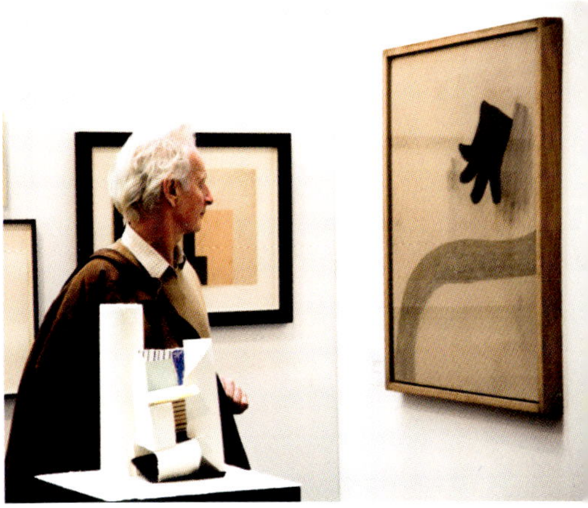

Art world trends

Where does the artist fit in to current art world trends, and might this affect the value of their work?

Specific work value

Things to take into account might be the size of the work; the labour-intensive nature of the piece; the quality or expense of the materials; the visionary direction of the work; whether it's a sketch or a highly developed piece; whether it was a collaboration or made for a specific exhibition or event; and what period in the artist's career the work is from – is it an early work, a current piece or a piece that was made at a significant moment in the artist's life? Ask the gallerist, auction house or seller as much as you can, and look at past catalogues of sales and auction records. For a work of considerable value, if you can, get a second opinion.

Personal impact to value judgements

Each art buyer is in a unique position to judge the value of a work from their particular vantage point. Let's not forget the personal factors that can influence the value of a work of art:

Personal financial landscape

How expensive a picture is to a individual buyer is subjective – evaluated in the context of their own finances.

Personal taste

This remains the linchpin that shapes and drives the development of a personal contemporary art collection. Attachment to a piece, that instinctive attraction to a work that makes it a personal 'must have', means it is much more valuable to that individual collector. Plus art market trends can be more fickle than personal tastes; what's in vogue today may be passé in a few years, so listening to your own taste barometer is an incredibly valuable skill.

Emotional connection

A higher personal value can often be added to art that's bought as a present or to celebrate an occasion, or bought with special winnings, like a bonus or inheritance.

Collector's item

Assess the value of a work of art as part of the personal art collection – if it's a vital piece in a particular puzzle it'll be worth much more to that collector.

Relationship with the artist

Being a patron or friend of an artist (supporting them at a vital stage of their career) will add personal value to the work.

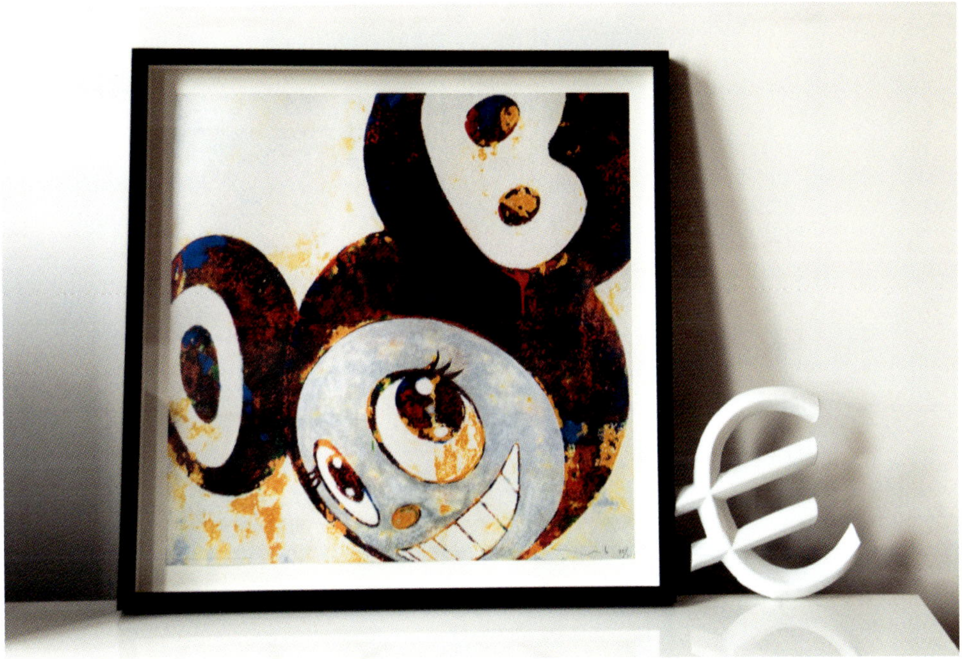

Practical financial approaches

There are a huge number of helpful practical financial considerations to bear in mind when buying affordable contemporary art, and ways of approaching the specifics of the actual economic transaction:

Saving

Setting aside a certain amount of money per month to buy art means there is a clearly defined budget to work with.

Budgeting

You might already know what work you'd like (by a particular artist, say) and are saving in order to be able to buy it, or you'll have a particular amount of money which you are choosing to invest in art. Either way, stick to your budget.

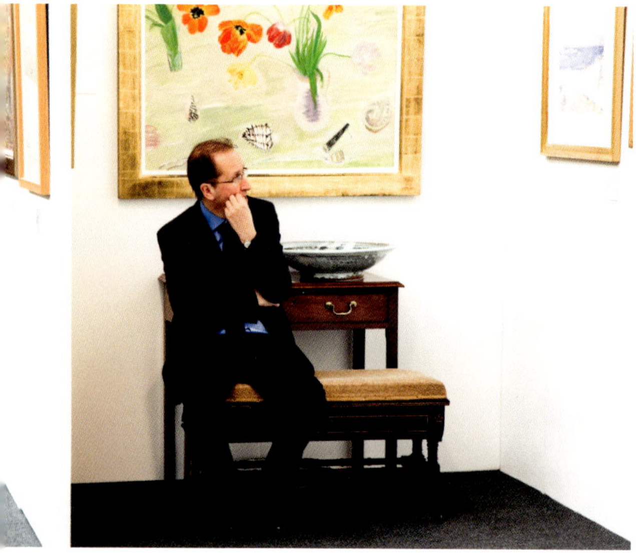

Attachment to a piece, that instinctive attraction to a work that makes it a personal 'must have', means it is much more valuable to that individual collector...

Budgeting for hidden extras

Make sure to consider these before you purchase:
* The cost of framing (which will be influenced by the size of the piece rather than its value.
* The buyer's premium at auction (around 20%; details should be in the auction catalogue) plus VAT.
* Artist's resale price for secondary market sales (see small print in auction house catalogues, or online not-for-profit visual arts rights management organisation DACS www.dacs.org.uk. In Europe this is usually 4% between €1,000/£850/$1,350 and €50,000/£45,000/$67,000 and from then on it follows a sliding scale – meanwhile, in New York, the law does not acknowledge the practice of resale royalties).
* Import tax on works imported from abroad (which differs from country to country but is usually about 5%). However, if you are exporting the work, make sure you deduct sales tax (you'll need proof of export).
* Shipping or the cost of transportation.
* Storage costs – check with galleries and the small print of auction

houses which may charge for holding works before they are shipped to the buyer.

* For works with a value of less than €10,000/£8,500/$13,500 the art can usually be insured under household insurance.

Interest-free loan schemes

Britain, France and the Netherlands are among the countries that have financial systems in place offering interest-free loans to buy contemporary art by living artists, repayable through instalments. In the UK the Own Art (www.ownart.org.uk) system will loan up to £2,000/€2,300/$3,200, which is repayable over 10 months, with the scheme covering any interest accrued. This system relies upon galleries' participation in the scheme, but if you have built up a relationship with a gallery or dealer, payment in instalments is also something you can discuss with them privately.

Buying groups

Forming part of an art collective or co-operative that buys works of art as a group and rotates its pieces is a wonderful way of sharing the cost of art and building a collection together. Participating members, usually between five and ten households or individuals, each put a certain amount into a joint account every month and rotate the pieces in the collection every few months between the households. This is a great way of being able to own art that might be beyond the budget of a single individual. For more information and advice, visit www.the-collective.info.

Innovative financial incentives

Some galleries pioneer new systems of returns on investment in art. CAW (Collective Arts Worldwide, www.cawgallery.net), a gallery that stages pop up art exhibitions across the world, has implemented a global profit share system, a rewards scheme for customers who buy art from them offering the chance to earn dividends from the profits.

Such systems can be imaginatively conceived and reap genuine rewards, but, equally, for every honest dealer there is likely to be someone trying to pull a fast one. Be aware, keep your wits about you, do some research into the gallery, and speak with others who have taken part.

Buying from a gallery

Expect levied prices (up to 50%), especially from a gallery with a bricks-and-mortar space (as oppose to an online space). But gallery representation may help the artist's career trajectory (reflected in the rising price of their work).

Buying directly from the artist

Artists can cut out the gallery percentage but they may set their prices to stay in line with gallery prices to maintain market value and because they may not want to upset their gallery or dealer by brokering knock-down deals behind their backs. Artists without gallery representation may also misjudge the value or their work, assessing its value based on factors the market may not take into account (time it took to make, emotional attachment, etc).

Negotiating prices

The etiquette of negotiating a price reduction is interesting terrain to navigate. Galleries are usually amenable to offering discounts, but this obviously depends on a variety of factors: economic climate, the popularity of the work and the price of the work (only ask for a discount if a 10% reduction would be significant).

As you build a relationship with a gallery, and buy more from them, you'll establish yourself as a client who's worth keeping on side and offering discounts to – which is an incentive to foster particular relationships with galleries. Seasoned collectors, however, will almost never pay the ticket price. Try starting with an opening gambit of 10% below the asking price and negotiate from there. This applies to

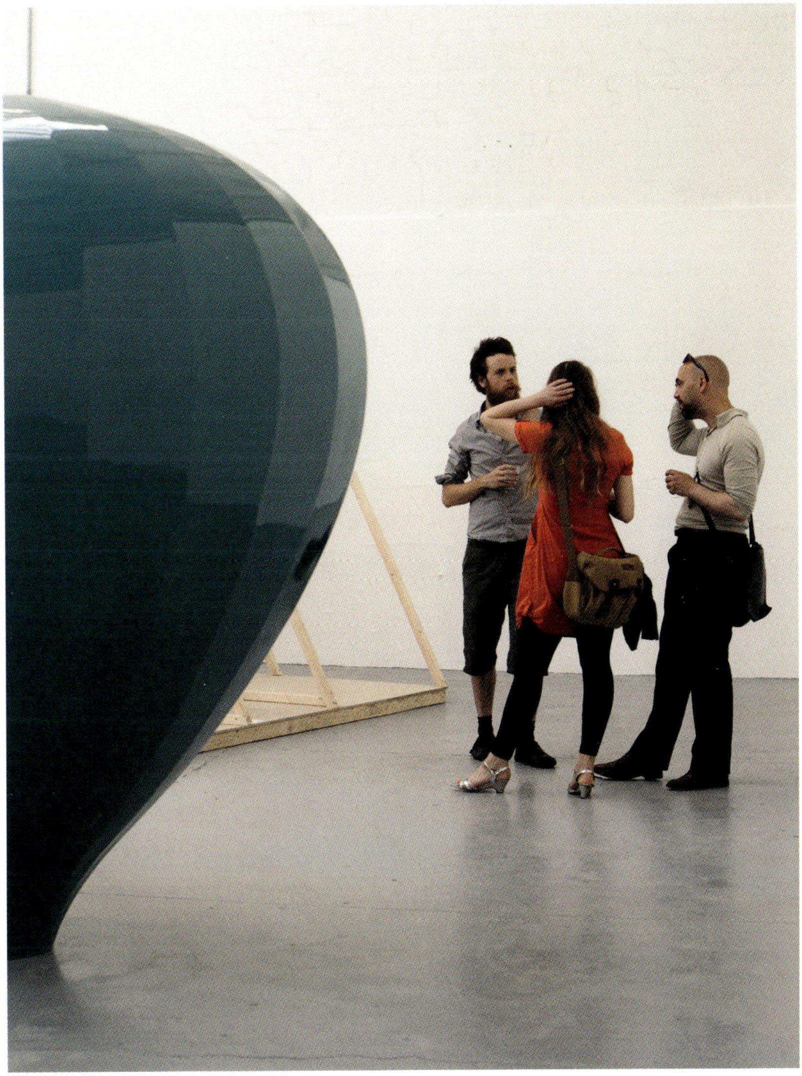

The Royal College of Art's graduate show is a place to discover new artists.

online galleries too – call up and speak to the gallerist and establish yourself as a buyer who's worth nurturing. If you are buying several pieces, that should also give you more leverage when it comes to negotiating a discount.

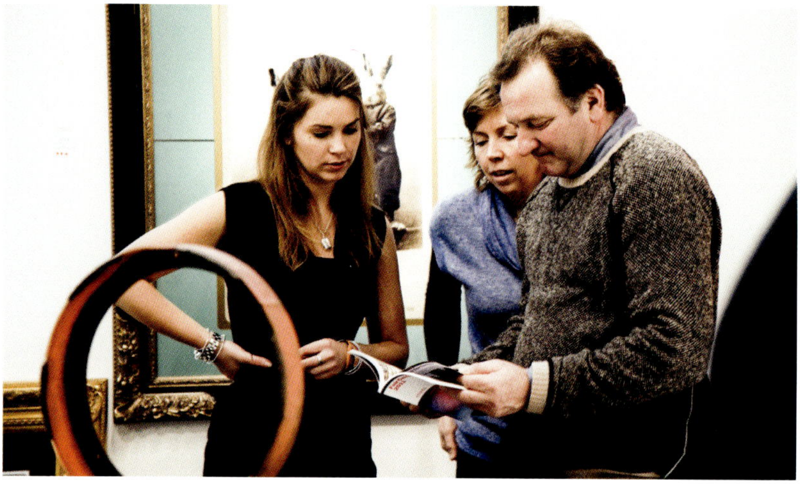

Dos

Be realistic.
Be polite.
Be confident.
Assess the temperament of the gallerist or artist and approach them appropriately.
Explain your budget – discuss the possibility of paying in instalments.
Ask about lower-priced alternatives by the same artist (smaller works, less ambitious projects), if another show is coming up, and if there is more work by the same artist that's not on show.

Don'ts

Don't be intimidated.
Don't feel pressured into buying something at a higher price that you can afford.
Don't *demand* reduced prices or deals on buying one or more pieces.
Don't *expect* reductions.
Don't ostentatiously negotiate. Be discrete.
Don't act in an underhand manner. Be direct and upfront.

Managing price expectations

It's impossible to classify art into price brackets; because of the reasons previously explored – work of one size, scope, vision and technical ability by one artist will be valued differently from that by another – there is no centralised valuation system. But shop around and you should be able to find something to suit your taste, budget and requirements, be that by taking a gamble on an emerging artist or investing in a multiple by an established one, even if that means framing an art/fashion collaborative scarf or limited-edition postcard. Think creatively, be canny, adventurous and bold, and the wider you cast your net when you look, the more you'll have to choose from. Below gives a general idea of what can be found for certain price brackets, with some specific examples available at the time of writing – it's by no means definitive, but it gives some idea of the comparative variety available. Dates in brackets indicate date made; prices in italics and brackets indicate on sale date.

Under £50/€60/$80

Anything from the more experimental and alternative fairs, such as from Free Art Fair, or Art Barter, where art is swapped for goods, services or other art; artist editions of practical items (bags, tea towels, t-shirts); artist and fashion collaborations (entry-level prices); plus work by unrepresented art graduates or students.

£5/€6/$8: Limited-edition greeting cards, pack of 10 (2010) (*2010*) by Turner Prize-winning, Venice Biennale 1990 exhibitor, Anish Kapoor, The Serpentine Gallery, London.
£25/€30/$40: Tracey Emin, *Mouse Sanctions* (2008) (*2011*), a limited-edition cotton tote bag, by the Turner Prize-nominated YBA. Available to buy from www.EminInternational.com.
$28–38/£18–24/€21–28: Artist limited-edition t-shirt designed by internationally celebrated contemporary artists including Jeff Koons and Chuck Close, a collaboration between the Whitney Biennial 2008, and its sponsors, The Gap. Available in 2008 in

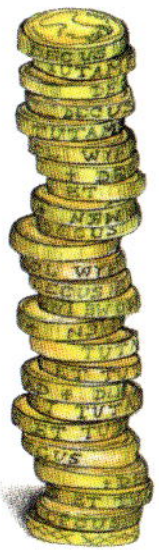

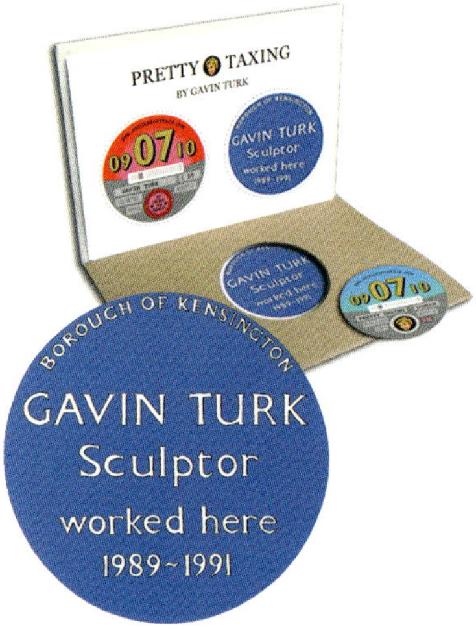

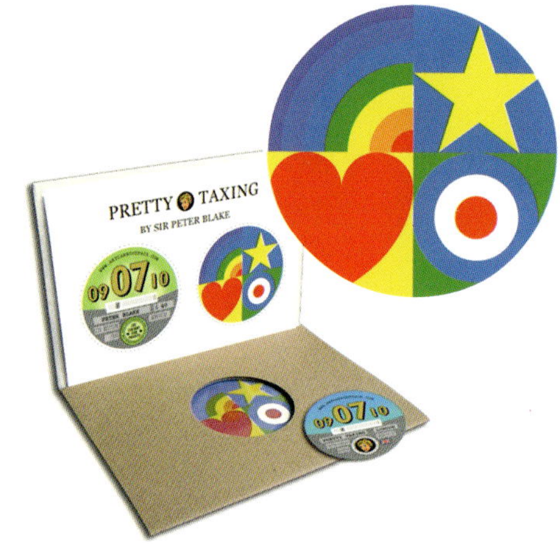

selected Gap stores across the UK, America and Canada, contemporary art museums including the Whitney Museum of American Art, the Museum of Contemporary Art in Los Angeles, and the Paris fashion boutique, Colette.

£30–50/€35–58/$48–80: (*2010–2011*) Tax disc by internationally celebrated artists including Matthew Barney and Peter Blake. Editions of 500, made as part of the Art Car Boot Fair, available from www.artcarbootfair.com.

£45/€55/$75: Original artist postcard from the RCA Secret anonymous postcard show, *2010.* 2,800 postcards contributed by 1,000 established and emerging artists. In 2010 these included Yoko Ono, Olafur Eliasson and John Baldessari.

£50–350/€58–410/$80–560

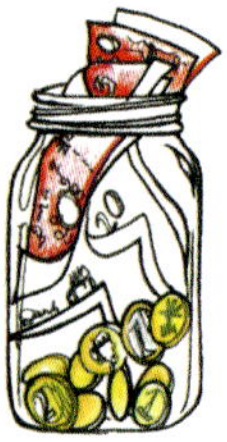

Original drawings by new artists illustrations, work from print studios, limited-editions by established artists made for public galleries and entry-level priced sculpture.

£175/€200/$280: Donald Urquhart, *I'm Living in a Song by the Shangri-Las*, (2010) (*2010*). Digital print on 300 Somerset photo

Satin paper by British drag queen turned draughtsman. Edition of 100 signed and numbered by the artist. Available from The Whitechapel Gallery, London.

£300/€350/$480: Chris Levene, *Grace Jones, Hurricane* (2010), limited vinyl edition includes giclee print, signed by both artist and singer, produced to accompany the album launch. Edition of 500. Sold at The Vinyl Factory, www.thevinylfactory.com.

£350/€410/$560: *Girl in Lake*, unframed sketch in pencil/charcoal by Zoe Hutchinson, an unrepresented graduate (2005) from Central St Martins, www.theportmangallery.com.

£350–750/€410–870/$560–1,200

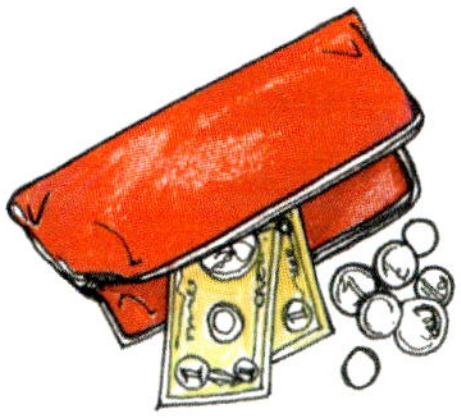

A large limited edition print run by an established artist, a limited-edition from a small print run by an emerging artist, and original works by emerging artists.

£450/€520/$720: Fiona Banner *Book 1/1* (2009), a block print on mirror card by the Turner Prize-shortlisted artist. Original print from an edition of 65 available from www.TheMultipleStore.org.

£575/€670/$920: Michael Taborda, *Untitled* (2009), a wood carving sculptural piece by an emerging artist shortlisted for 2010's ACME studio award. Available from emerging art gallery Murmur Art.

£750/€870/$1,200: Katharina Sieverding, *Die Pliete* (2005), a poster in four parts in a signed box. Edition of 50, KW, Berlin, www.kw-berlin.de.

£750–1,500/€870–1,750/$1,200–2,400

Exclusive limited-edition works by established artists, original paintings or small print runs by emerging artists, and starting prices for exclusive print portfolios.

£950 (£850 for members)/€1,100 (€990)/$1,500 ($1,350): (*2010*) ICA anniversary print portfolio, limited edition of 60,

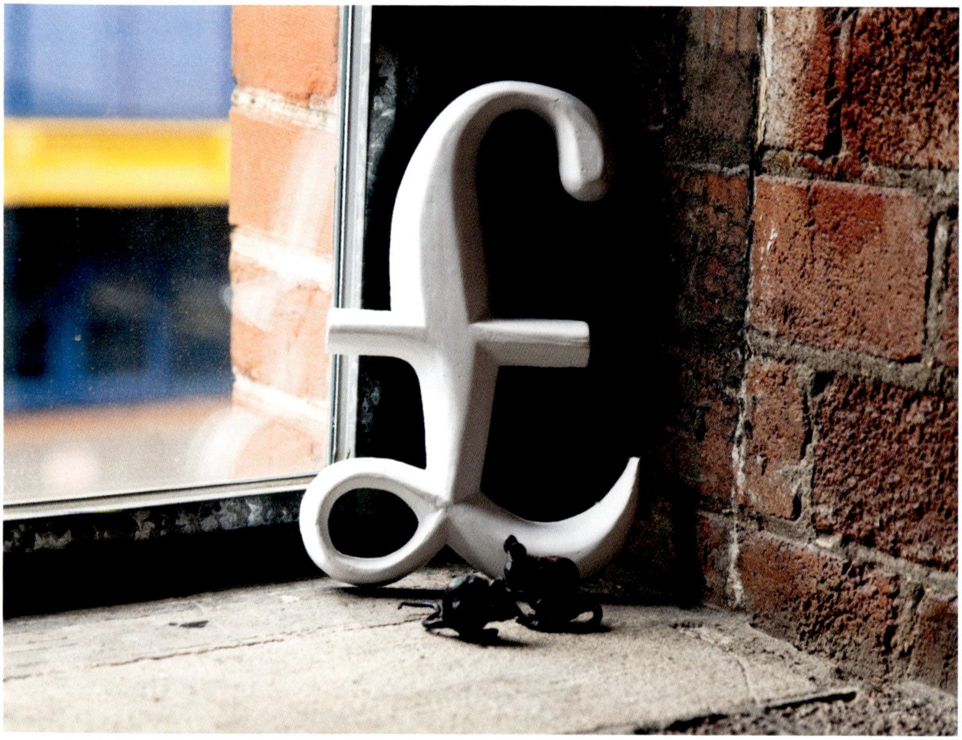

comprised of six prints by internationally acclaimed artists based variously in New York, London, Berlin and Frankfurt, such as Carol Bove, Peter Coffin, Ryan Gander, Judith Hopf, Rosalind Nashashibi and Tomas Saraceno. Prints are presented in a custom-made box.

£950/€1,100/$1,500: Christian Marclay, *Carpe Diem* (2010), a sculpture edition of 40 Sterling silver, steel ball bearings, leather, 25 x 3 x 0.8 cm. Faceless wrist timepiece made in conjunction with Marclay's 2010 video installation at White Cube, 'The Clock'. Available from White Cube Gallery, London (*2010*).

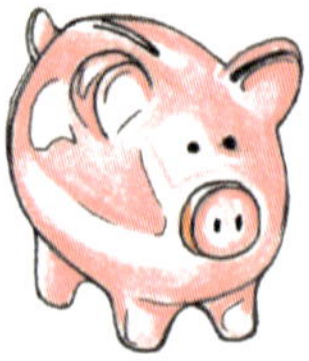

£1,100/€1,300/$1,760: John Baldessari, *Brain/Cloud (with Seascape and Palm Tree)* (2009) (*2010*). Edition of 145 by the multi-international-award-winning Californian contemporary artist, available from www.countereditions.com.

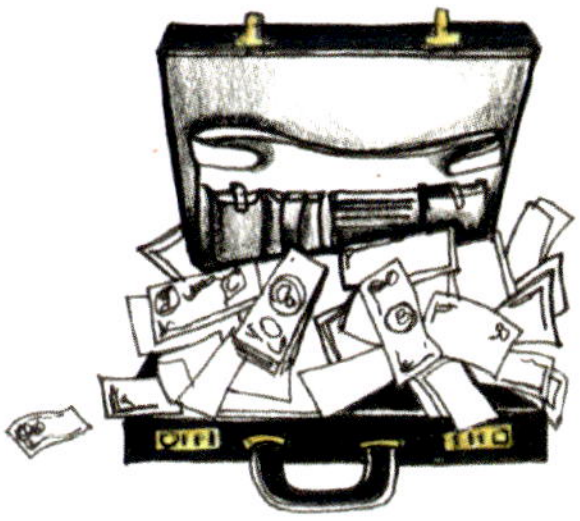

£1,500–3,000/€1,750–3,500/$2,400–4,800

Work by emerging artists who are making a strong international name for themselves, print portfolios, rarer prints by celebrated artists, original works on paper and more substantial sculptural editions.

£1,500/€1,750/$2,400: Alex Prager, *Rita from Week End*, 2009. Edition 2/7. The American photographer's work was shown as part of MoMA's 2010 New Photography exhibition. Successfully sold lot in Philips de Pury photography auction, 2010.
£1,600/€1,900/$2,560: Print portfolio 2010, with four prints by emerging contemporary British artist Edward Kay, acclaimed video artist and Venice Biennale 2003 exhibitor Hilary Lloyd, contemporary American artist Sterling Ruby, and Turner Prize-winning German photographer Wolfgang Tillmans. Available from Studio Voltaire (*2010*), London.
$2,000/£1,250/€1,450: Susan Collis, *No Show* (2010), Silver Screw (hallmarked) with diamond, garnet, smoky quartz, edition of three; a great example of the British sculptor's transformation of the ordinary and mundane into the extraordinary. The Armory Show, New York, (*2010*) www.thearmouryshow.com.
£3,200/€3,700/$5,120: Polly Morgan, *Receiver* (2010), a sculpture by the new gen YBA taxidermist. Bakelite handset, taxidermy quail heads, sculpture edition of 50 available from artist's website (*2011*).
£3,200/€3,700/$5,120: Ed Ruscha, *Angel* (2006). Lithograph on paper by one of the original pop artists. Edition of 50 available from Jealous Gallery, London (*2011*).

Selling art

Selling contemporary art can be tricky since, by definition, the artists are still working, and thus producing new work that's at the forefront of their creativity (there is nothing like death and a finite oeuvre to raise prices). However, that's not to say that money can't be made when you sell a work of art. Whatever your reasons for selling your art, whether you are selling the whole collection or an isolated work, you want to be sure you are getting the best price by selling it in the right space. There are several things to consider:

Appraisal

Begin by researching current sale prices by the artist. This could be online, by speaking to galleries or spaces where the artist has had shows, looking at gallery catalogues, or by looking at the artist's website. Subscriber websites like Artnet.com, Arttactic.com and Artprice.com are a fantastic place to start looking at prices for an artist with an established profile; members can discretely check the sales and auction prices of recent works.

If you suspect that the art might be of significant value, have it evaluated professionally by multiple sources, and go to the original gallery that sold you the work, as well as professional independent art appraisers, so there is no possible conflict of interest; speak to insurance companies who deal with contemporary art and law firms that deal with the art world. These appraisals will not only make sure you get the right price, but they will safeguard against the questions of buyers and officially validate your final price decision.

Location

Finding the right place to sell your piece or collection of art is vital.

Artist: If you know the artist, see if they want to buy their own work back – many artists regret selling all their work (especially as their prices rise after the first sale) or may have a fondness for that particular work.

The artist's gallery: The first port of call when looking to sell a work of contemporary art is to go directly to the gallery where you bought it. The gallery will not only want to protect the price of the artist's work, but they will also have built up connections with collectors who are interested in that particular artist. There are several ways to sell art via the original gallery:

* Direct purchase – the gallery will buy the work from you and sell it on.
* Consignment – the gallery will take the work and sell it for you, taking a commission.
* Part exchange – exchange the work for another one also sold at the gallery, possibly with cost differences factored in.

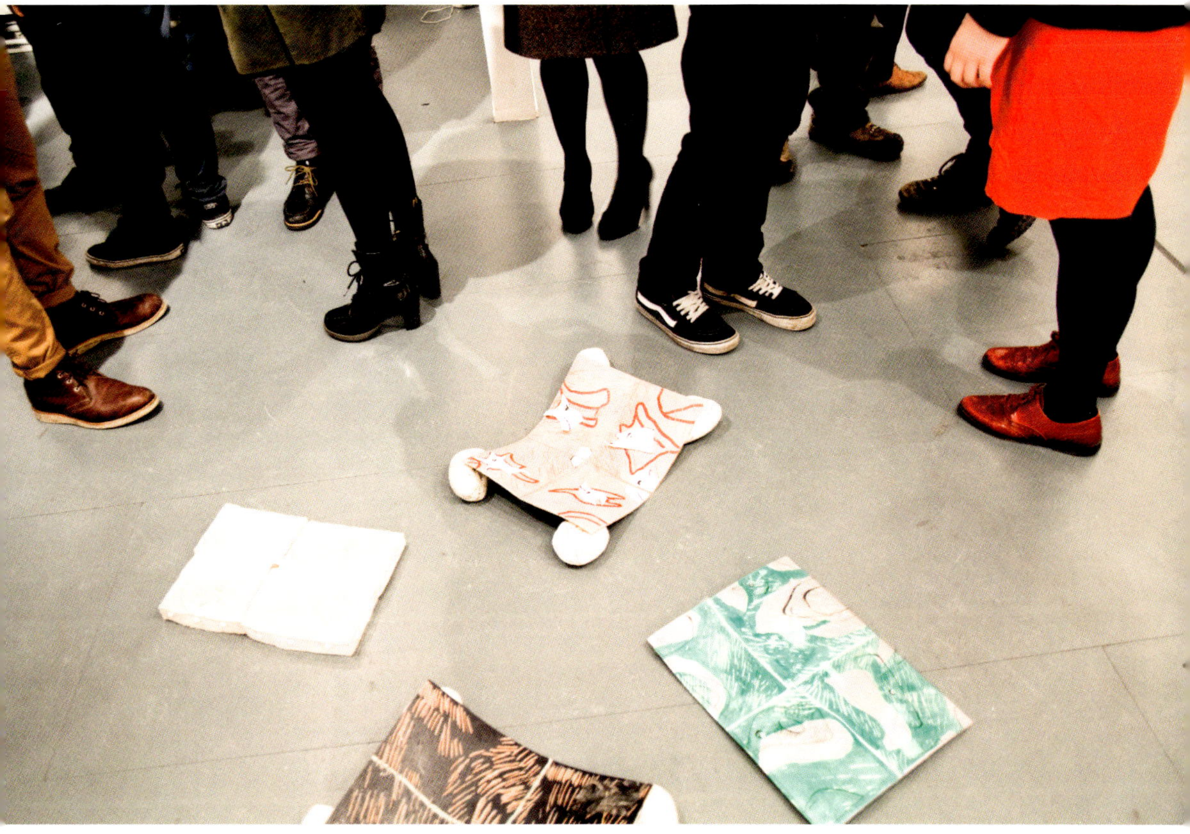

Local exhibition spaces: For less expensive pieces, look at selling in locations such as cafés, restaurants or other popular public spaces.

Online auction sites: These are an easy and effective way of selling art, especially for those with a confident and familiar working knowledge of online auction sites. Be sure to pick the right site for the artwork – a site that sells similar work by artists of comparable success and calibre. This means there will be the optimum targeted traffic already coming to the site. Make sure to label the art correctly in the posting, using key words to maximise SEO – Search Engine Optimisation. List as much information as possible relevant to the piece: style, colour, subject, artist, year, mood of the piece etc. This means it is more likely to rank highly in searches. Test your posting by putting key words into the auction search function and making sure your work comes up. Tweak as necessary. It pays to be straightforward, rather than oblique or convoluted with descriptions.

Bricks-and-mortar auction houses: Going to an auction house and having a work valued can give you confidence in your price and choice of venue, but think about which auction house might be best to approach (in the case of work by an artist with a local significance, it might be better to go to a local auction house, for example. If the work is by an artist with a high or international profile, then one of the larger auction houses might be better). In the main, the interests of auction houses lie with the seller not the buyer, so they will want the highest sale price (they also get over 20% commission on a sale payable by the buyer). However, it's always best to get several opinions to be sure that the estimate is right.

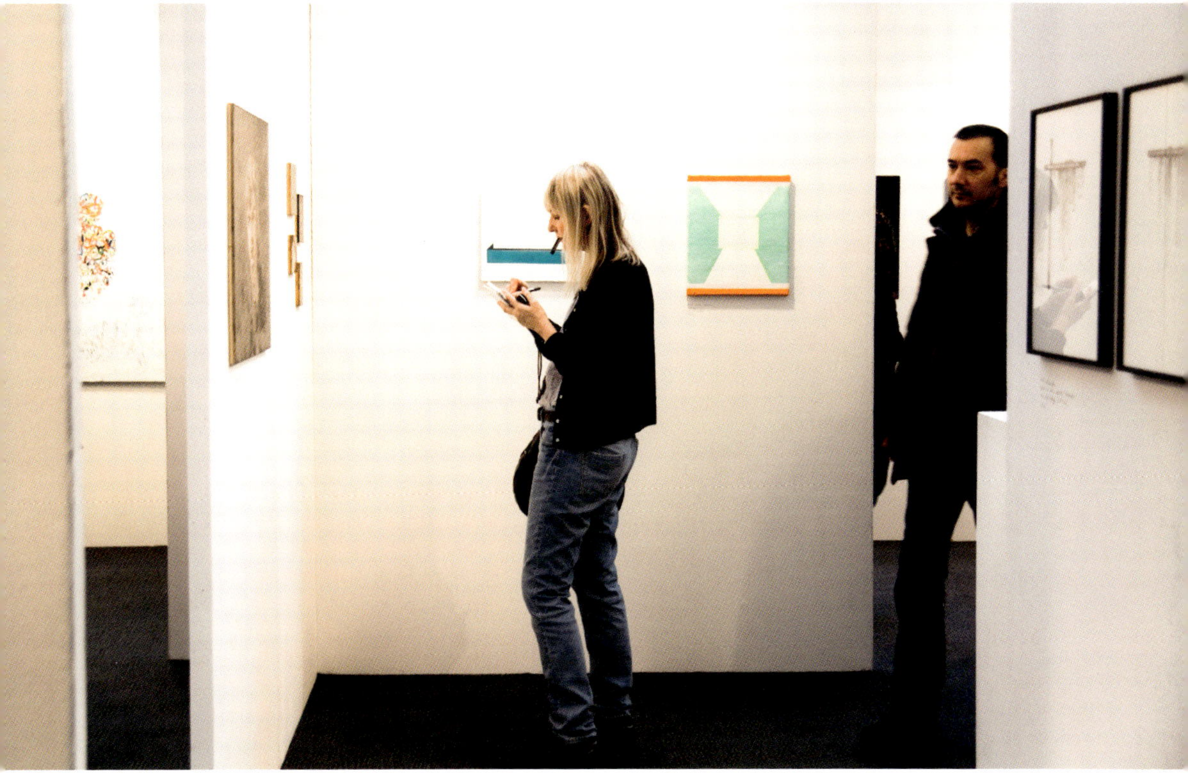

Shop around and you should be able to find something to suit your taste, budget and requirements

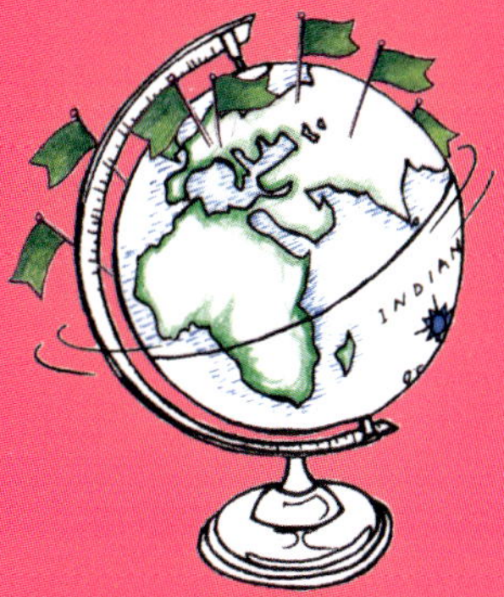

06

Art Fair Diary

Art Fair Diary

THE ART WORLD is tidal, ebbing and flowing around the globe with the current of events – fairs, shows, exhibitions, biennales and auctions. At any one time the focus will usually be on a particular location – where the fairs and major contemporary art auctions are happening; New York in March, Basel in June, October in London, December in Miami...

To follow is a diary of monthly events, highlighting some of the major fairs and biennials plus some of the clusters of satellite events that take place concurrently around the bigger ones (here grouped together). It is by no means suggesting that away from this centre of activity the art world stops, and if you're not at the hub you might as well give up. Rather, it's meant to be a useful guide, giving a sense of what's happening when, so you can engage with those fairs nearest you, or centre a trip around one further afield.

Although most of these fairs are international, the spectrum of galleries (and the artists they show) at each will vary enormously – by shaking up which fairs you go to, you'll inevitably discover new galleries and artists.

A whirl of activity at Art Forum, Berlin.

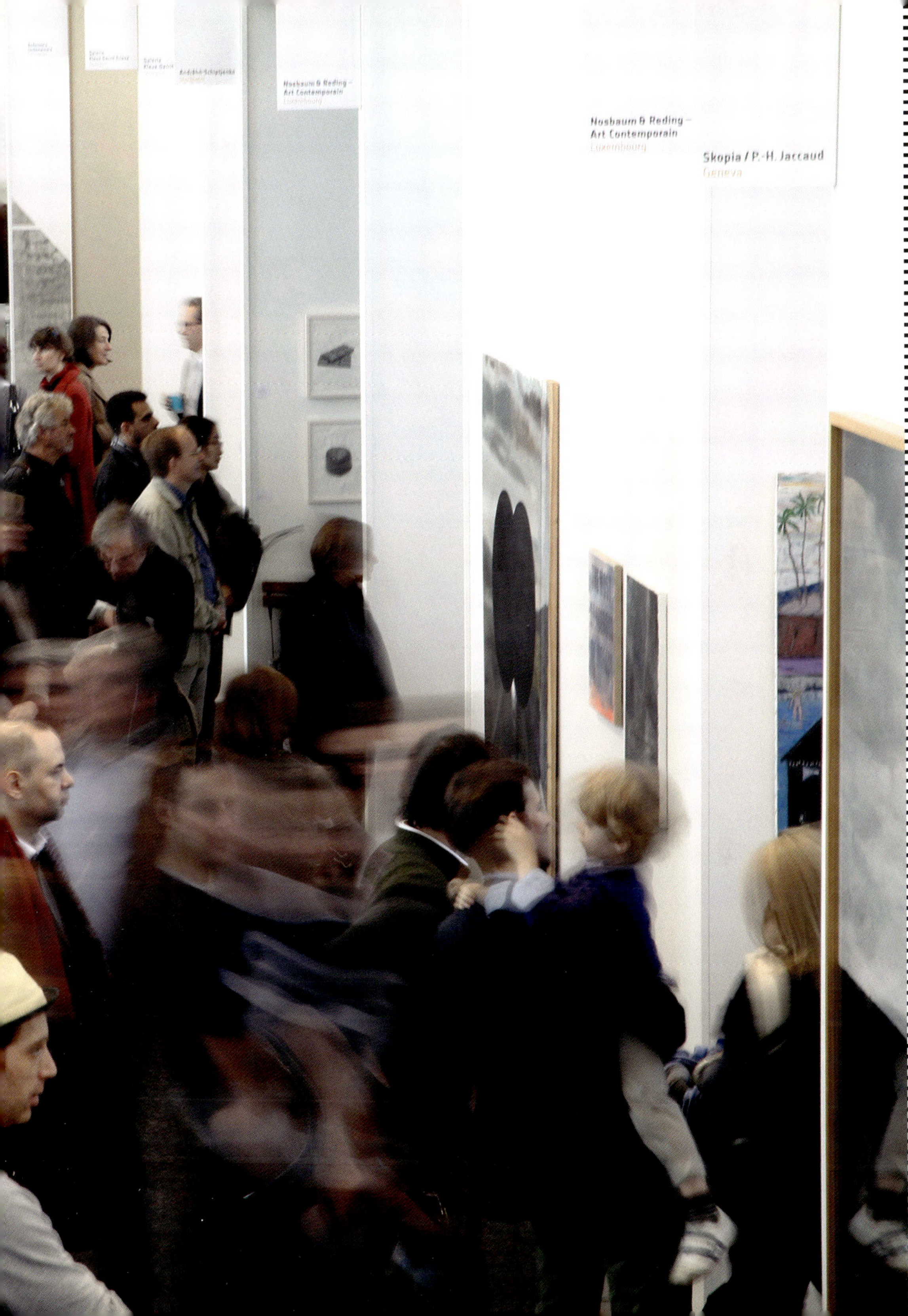
Nosbaum & Reding –
Art Contemporain
Luxembourg
Nosbaum & Reding –
Art Contemporain
Luxembourg
Skopia / P.-H. Jaccaud
Geneva

Good websites to keep an eye on for fair news:

www.artinfo.com, www.saatchi-gallery.co.uk/artfairs, www.artvista.de – these all have listings of international art fairs, while organisations like www.biennialfoundation.org aim to promote structural and organisational dialogue and links between contemporary art biennials. They are a good place to keep an eye on biennials – from Lyon to Liverpool, Istanbul to Gothenburg.

January

London Art Fair, London, UK www.londonartfair.co.uk. Contemporary and modern art with special sections including Photo50 showcasing 50 works selected by a panel of curators, curated group shows with work from international galleries and the innovative project space, gathering alternative galleries and arts organisations.

Arte Fiera (Art First), Bologna, Italy www.artefiera.bolognafiere.it. Look out for satellite events that are part of Arte Fiera OFF; the city's evening vernissage – where museums and galleries around Bologna are open until midnight; and the prize for the best artist under 30.

Accessible Art Fair, Tel Aviv, Israel www.accessibleartfair.com. This is a fair that focuses on a small number of artists who sell directly to buyers. The fair also takes place at other times of year at other locations. There is an upper price limit to works on sale.

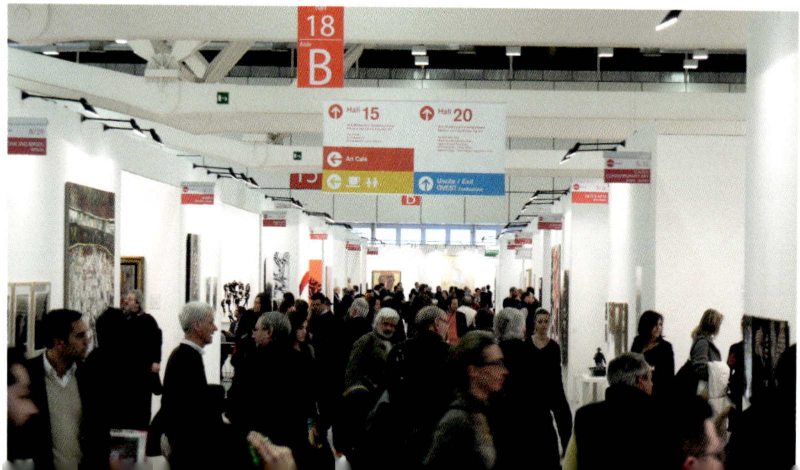

Arte Fiera, Bologna.

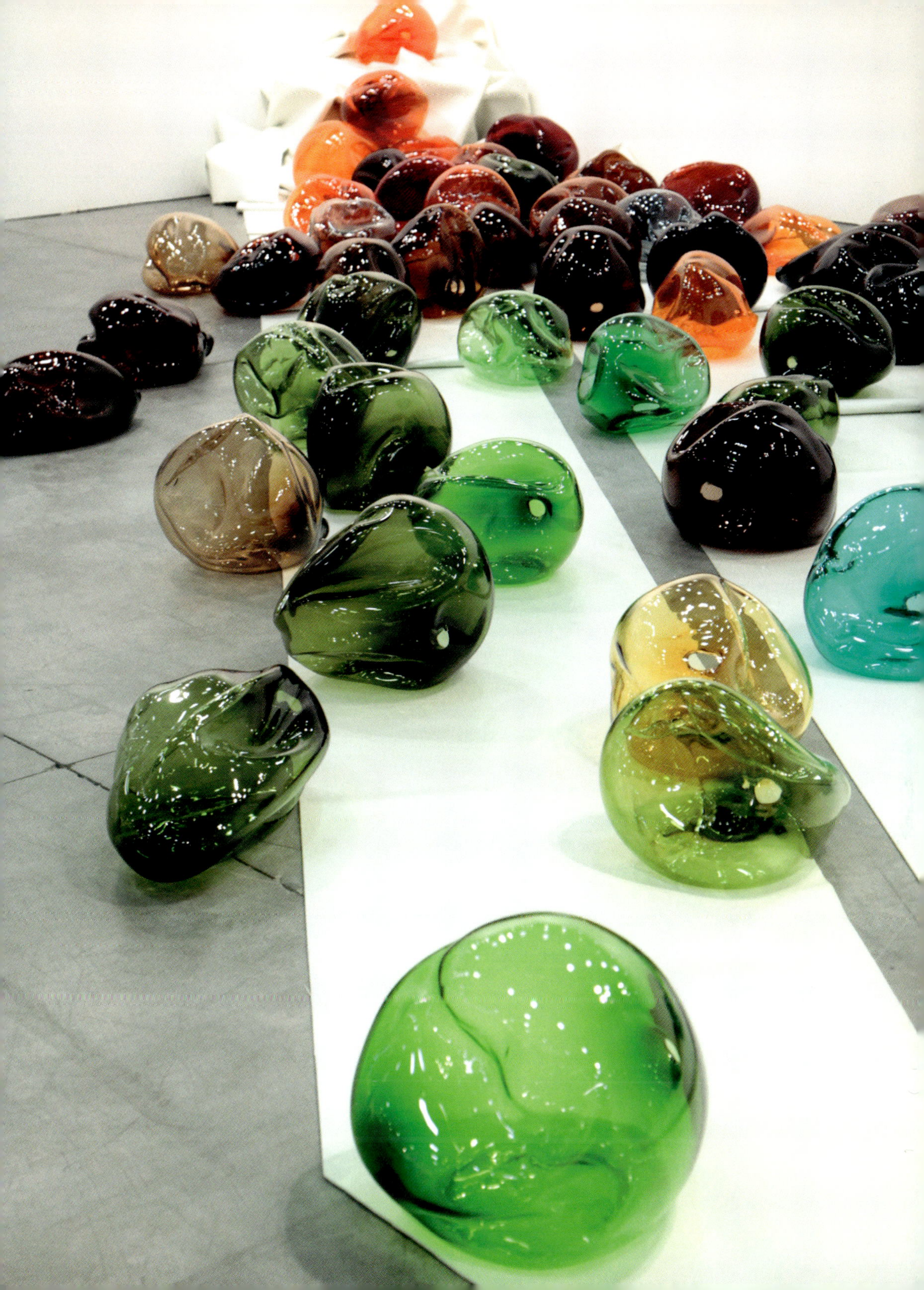

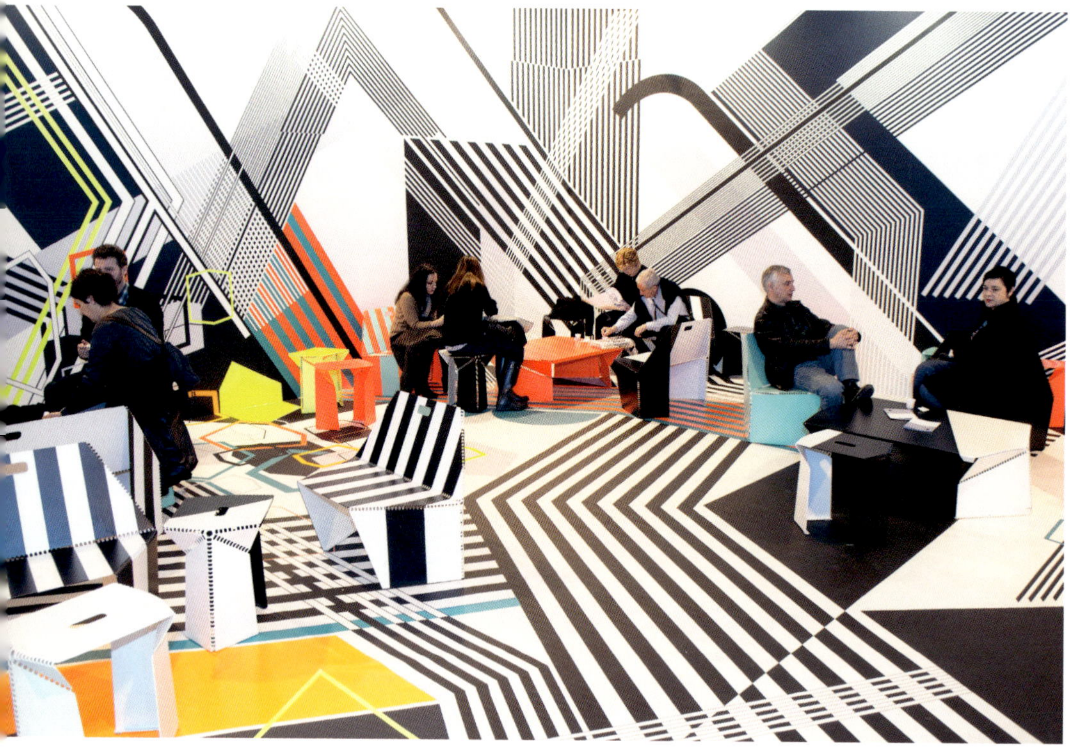

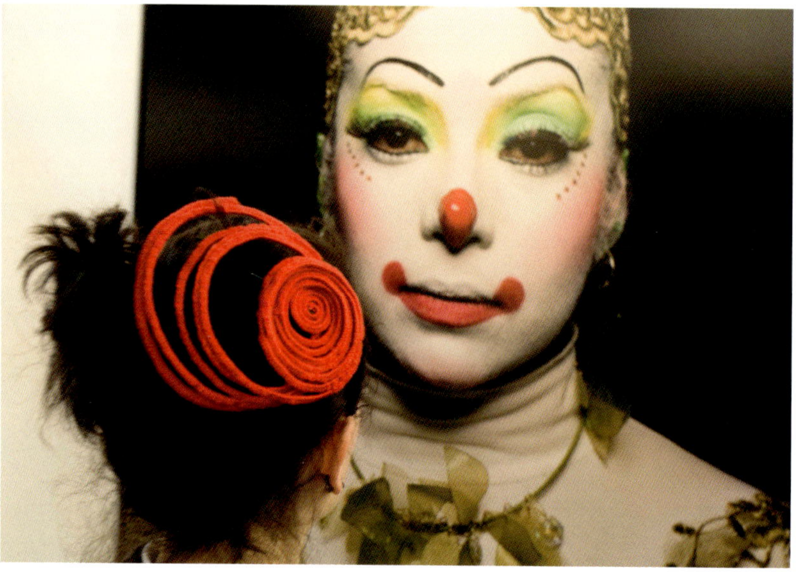

Geometric lines and colour at Arco, Madrid (above and right).

February

Art Innsbruck, Innsbruck, Tyrol, Austria www.art-innsbruck.at. Sitting somewhere between the art markets of Austria, Germany, Switzerland and Italy is this boutique fair, whose philosophy embraces art collectors starting out.

Art Rotterdam, Rotterdam, The Netherlands www.artrotterdam.com. Seventy galleries from 10 countries. The fair Object Rotterdam (www.objectrotterdam.nl), where art meets functionality, runs concurrently.

Arco, Madrid, Spain www.ifema.es/ferias/arco/default.html. Look out for the section with work from a specific country (which changes each year), plus the area for European galleries younger than eight years old.

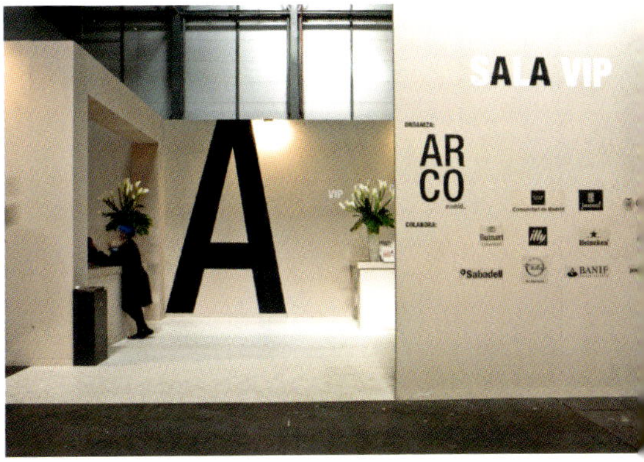

The VIP lounge at Arco, Madrid.

20/21 International Art Fair, London, UK www.20-21intartfair.com. One of the smaller, younger art fairs, with a leaning toward modern and contemporary galleries from Eastern Europe and the Far East: China, India, Japan, Russia, Poland, Serbia and the Ukraine.

Affordable Art Fair, Milan, Italy and Brussels, Belgium www.affordableartfair.com. Encouraging new buyers and creating an un-intimidating atmosphere in which to buy art, this series of affiliated fairs has shows in New York, London, Amsterdam, Bristol, Paris and further afield too – often twice a year in the same location. Works on sale have a capped upper limit.

Accessible Art Fair, Antwerp, The Netherlands www.accessibleartfair.com. This is a fair that focuses on a small number of artists who sell directly to buyers. The fair also takes place at other times of year at other locations. There is an upper price limit to works on sale.'

March

Whitney Biennial, New York, USA www.whitney.org. This rich cross-section of the American contemporary art scene is an important landmark in the emerging contemporary artist scenescape, often making names and setting trends.

The Armory Show, New York, USA www.thearmoryshow.com. This is a major contemporary and modern art fair. It precipitates a broader 'Armory Arts Week' in New York, with public programming including open studios, special museum and gallery discounts, panel talks and discussions, and satellite fairs as below...

The Volta Show NY, New York, USA www.thevoltashow.com. Selected galleries are invited to show the work of one emerging artist only, in a bid to explore the work of individuals under one roof more deeply.

Scope, New York, USA www.scope-art.com. An international fair for emerging art with sister fairs in London, Miami (The Hamptons) and Basel throughout the year.

Pulse, New York, USA www.pulse-art.com. One of a duo of fairs (the other being in Miami in December) which aim to act as a bridge between the central and satellite art fairs taking place concurrently.

The Art Show, New York, USA www.artdealers.org. Run by the AdAA (the art dealers association of America), this show is one with a focussed national outlook, gathering together US galleries that exhibit curated shows.

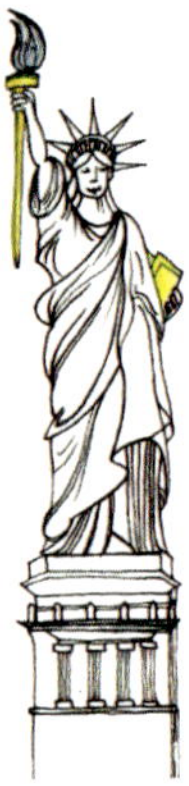

Art Expo, New York, USA www.artexponewyork.com. With no official selection process for galleries (they simply apply), this is a behemoth of an art fair with over 500 galleries. Unpretentious, but occasionally overwhelming.

Verge Art Brooklyn, New York, USA www.vergeartfair.com. The focus is on marginal and newly emerging art, with sister shows in Basel and Miami.

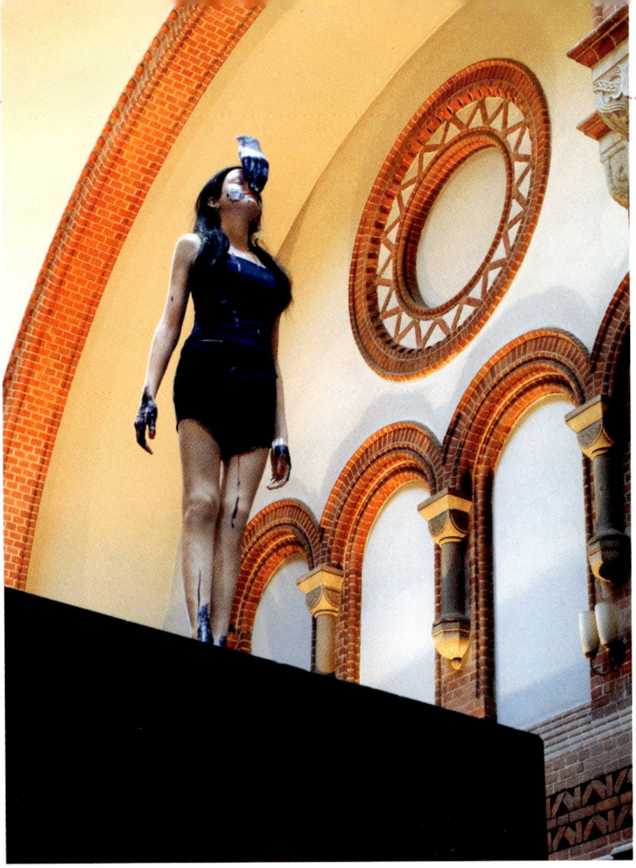

Experimental art at the Berlin Biennale (left). Outdoor sculpture at the Berlin Biennale (overleaf).

Berlin Biennial, Berlin, Germany www.berlinbiennial.de. A relative newcomer with a significant focus on the emerging contemporary art scene – features include changing curators, shifting locations and an active encouragement of the experimental.

Art Dubai, Dubai, UAE www.artdubai.ae. With 75 galleries, a not-for-profit gallery project space and a curated programme of talks as part of a 'Global Art Forum', this relative newcomer has become a hub for collectors, artists, curators and galleries across the Middle East, North Africa and South Asia.

Maastricht, The Netherlands www.tefaf.com. A major event in the art world calendar; whilst there is a predominant focus on art and antiques, there is a section devoted to contemporary art with pieces by internationally renowned artists with high profiles and high prices.

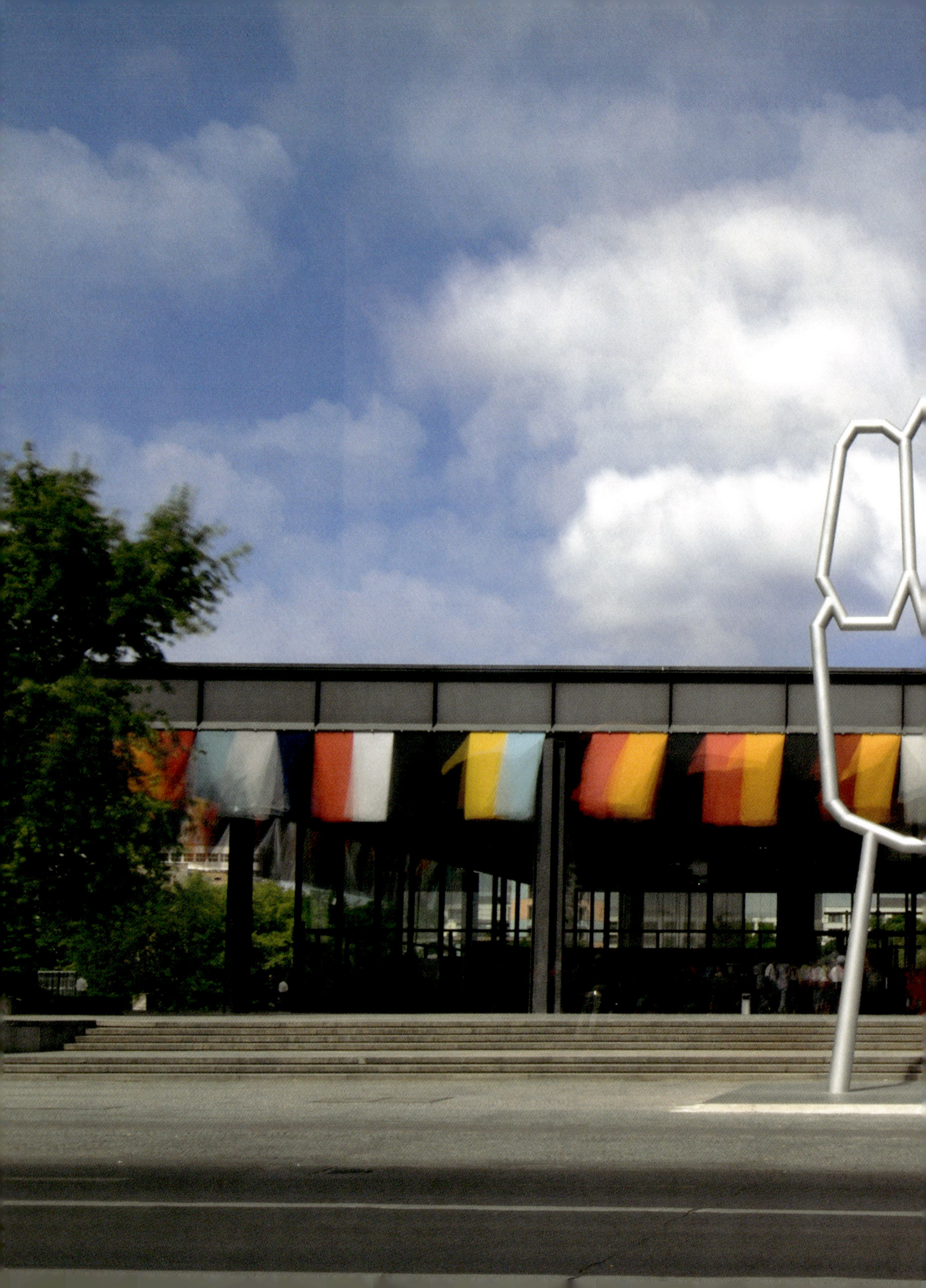

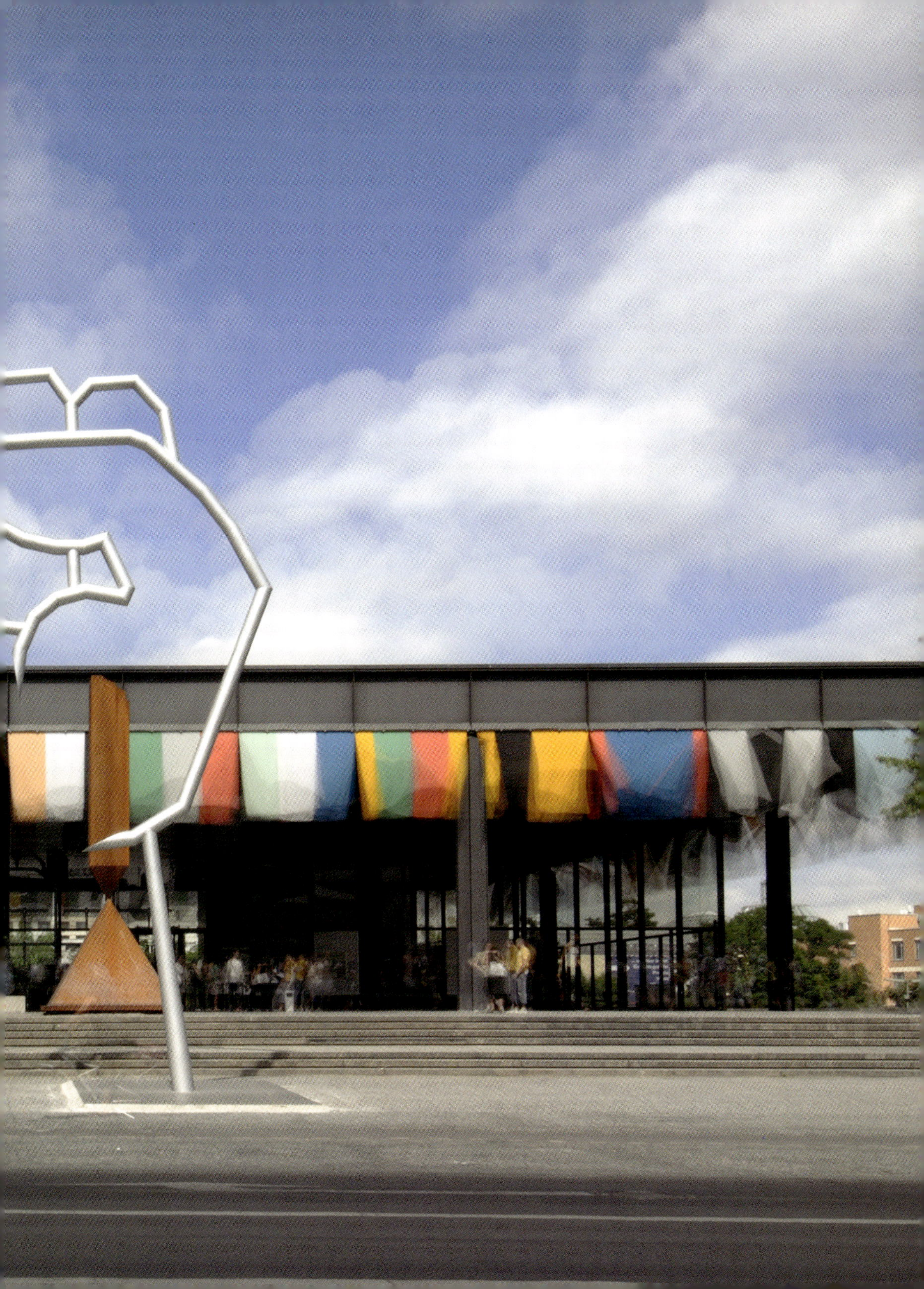

April

Art Cologne, Cologne, Germany www.artcologne.com. New Positions is Art Cologne's sponsored section for emerging artists, while New Contemporaries provides a platform for new galleries.

MiArt, Milan, Italy www.miart.it. Italian galleries (around a hundred or so) gather to sell work by both Italian and international artists, providing a platform for an Italian focus on the international art scene.

Glasgow International Festival, Glasgow, Scotland www.glasgowinternational.org. Local meets international art at this visual arts festival. For two weeks biennially commercial and public galleries have openings, artists throw open their studio doors, plus myriad art events take place across the city.

Art Brussels, Brussels, Belgium www.artbrussels.be. A hundred and seventy international galleries, with a special emphasis on young artists, debates and artist talks, solo shows and a robust out-of-fair program of events running at the same time.

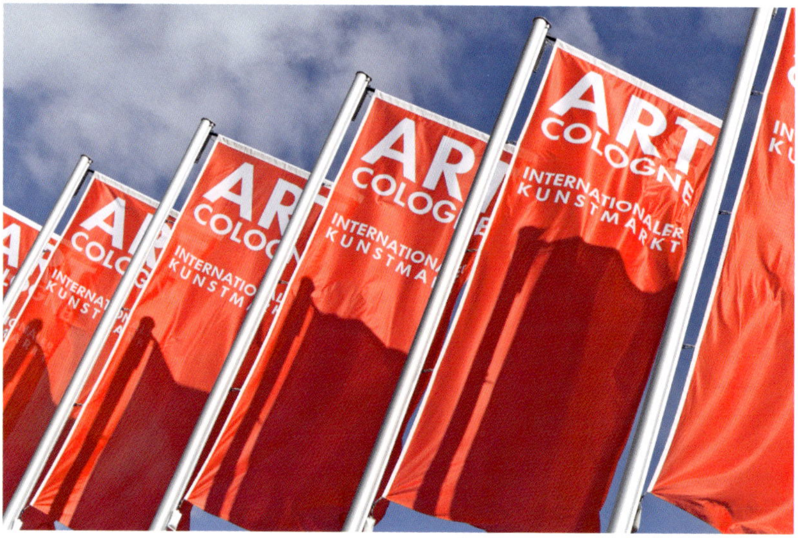

Art Cologne flies the flag.

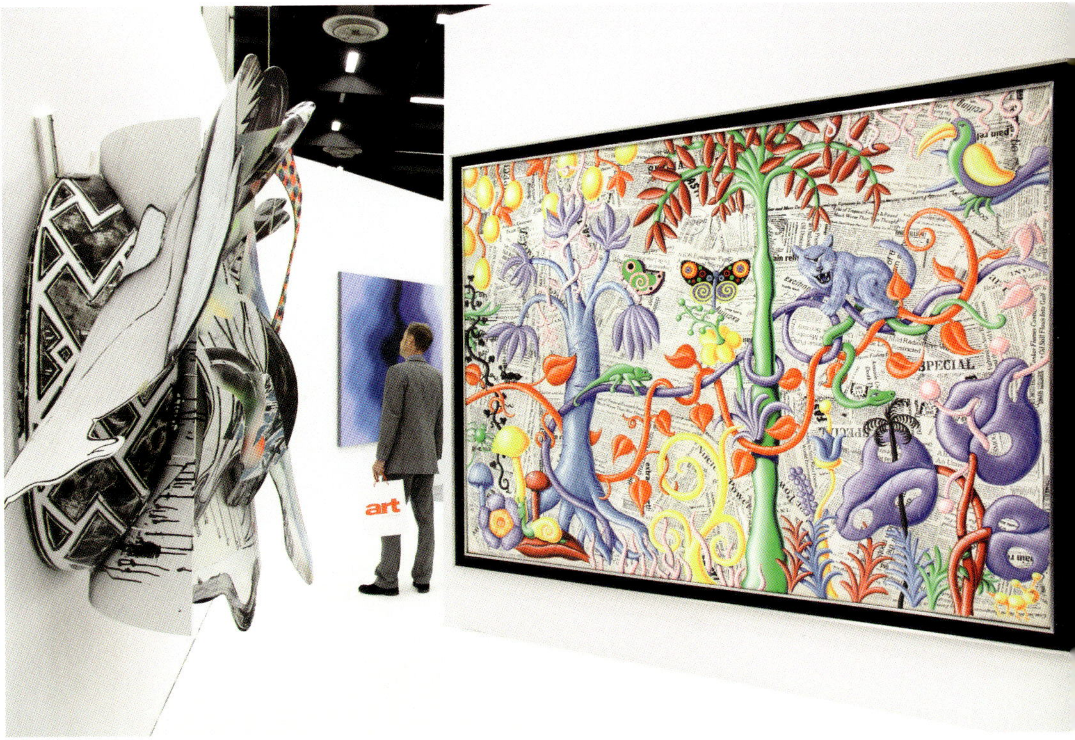

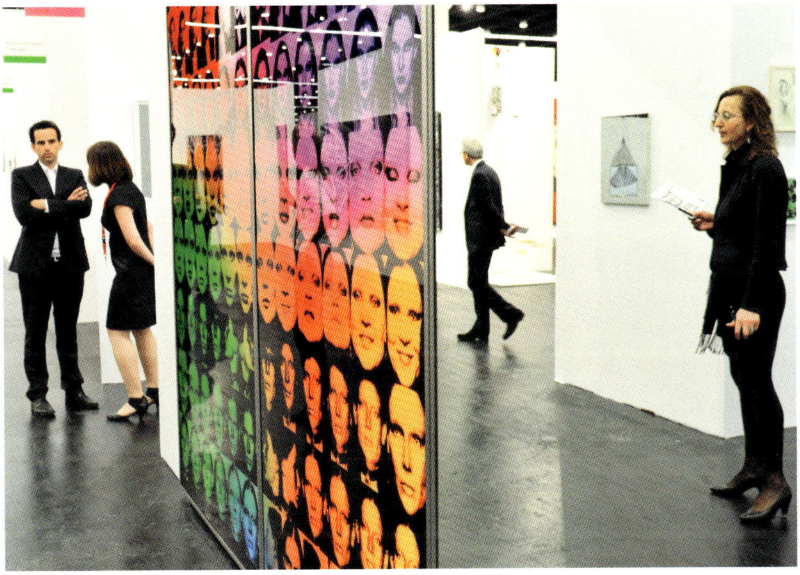

A cornucopia of colour at Art Cologne.

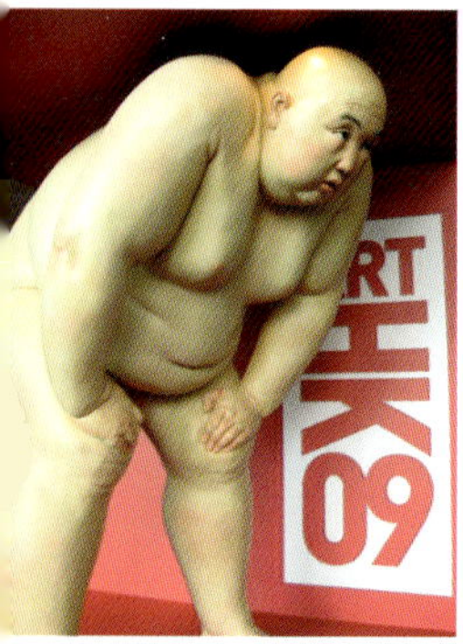

Art HK is an arts hub of the Far East.

May

ART HK, Hong Kong, China www.hongkongartfair.com. The eastern art market has opened up exponentially over the last few years (Hong Kong's auction turnover is third only to London and New York) and in just a few years this art fair has established itself as a major player on the art scene. The section Asia One presents solo exhibitions of Asian artists.

ROMA (The Road to Contemporary Art), Rome, Italy www.romacontemporary.it. Housed in a former slaughterhouse, this is a dramatic stage for work by emerging and established artists.

Vienna Fair, Vienna, Austria www.viennafair.at. This fair focuses specifically on art from Central and Eastern Europe.

Art Amsterdam (formerly KunstRAI), Amsterdam, The Netherlands www.artamsterdam.nl. Over 120 international galleries make this the largest art fair in The Netherlands. Side programming makes art a focus in Amsterdam for the fair's duration.

SWAB, Barcelona, Spain www.swab.es. A boutique fair (40 galleries) held in an old galley arsenal with a focus on emerging talent and young galleries and artists.

Affordable Art Fair, Bristol, UK and New York, USA www.affordableartfair.com (see February entry).

The Brussels Accessible Art Fair (BAAF), Brussels, Belgium www.accessibleartfair.com. This is a fair that focuses on a small number of artists who sell directly to buyers. The fair also takes place in other locationsat various times of year. There is an upper limit on the price of works on sale.

June

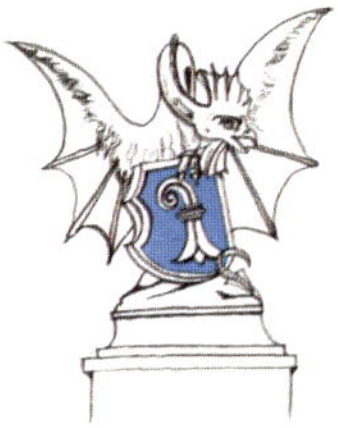

Venice Biennale, Venice, Italy www.labiennale.org. Individual artists from represented countries exhibit in national pavilions. Established in 1895 this is probably the most prestigious of all the art biennials globally; it's certainly the one with the highest profile.

Art Basel, Basel, Switzerland www.art.ch. Over 300 art galleries with 2,500 artists. This is a major event on the art calendar.

Liste, Basel, Switzerland www.liste.ch. This 'young art fair' in Basel shows the work of artists under 40 by galleries less than five years old.

The Volta Show, Basel, Switzerand www.voltashow.com. Emerging and established galleries show art by emerging artists.

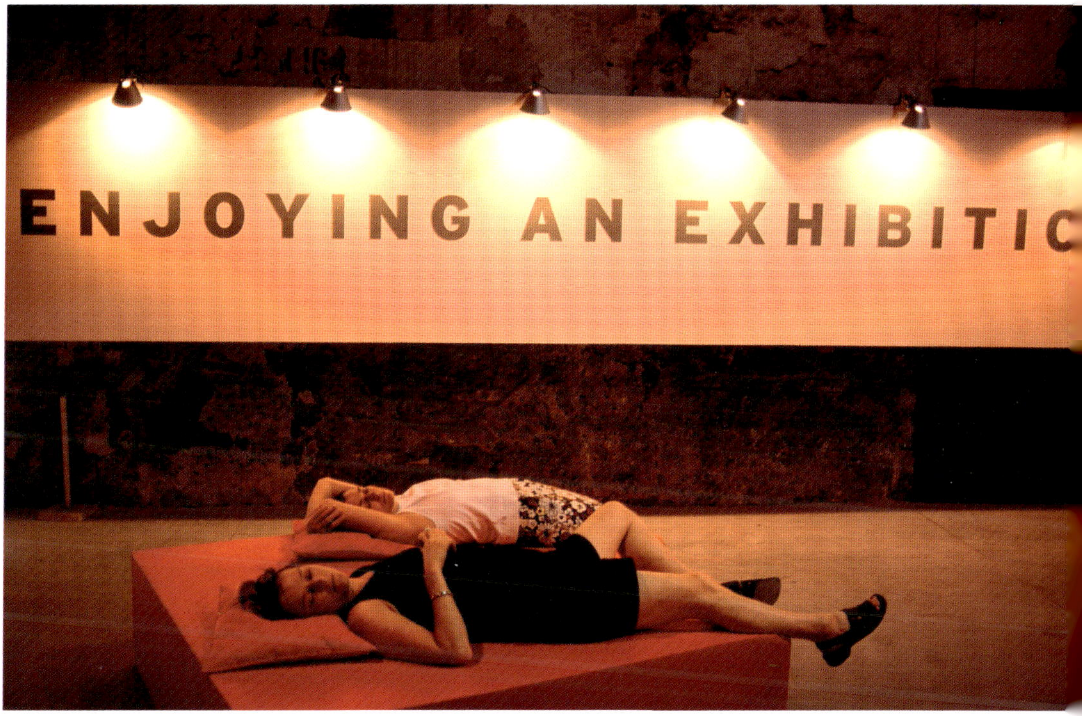

A new way to see art at the Venice Biennale.

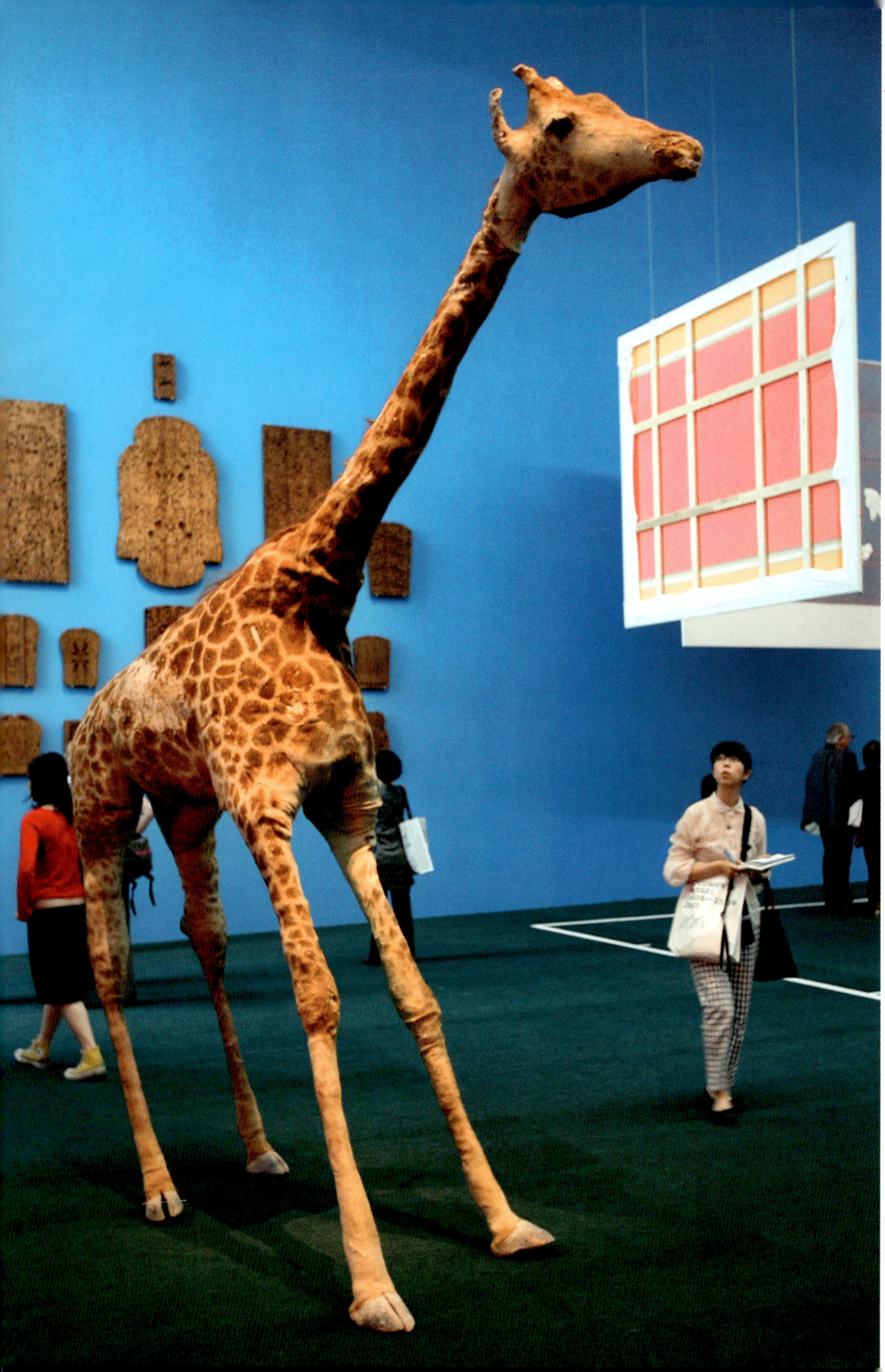

Scope, Basel, Switzerland www.scope-art.com. An international fair for emerging art with fairs in London, New York, The Hamptons and Miami throughout the year.

Verge, Basel, Switzerland www.vergeartfair.com. The focus is on marginal and newly emerging art, with sister shows in Brooklyn (during Armory week) and Art Miami.

Print Basel, Basel, Switzerland www.printbasel.ch. This is a fair for graphic art, with a diverse range of printing techniques.

dOCUMENTA, Kassel, Germany www.documenta.de. This fair runs for 100 days and takes place every five years, with a focus on site-specific art.

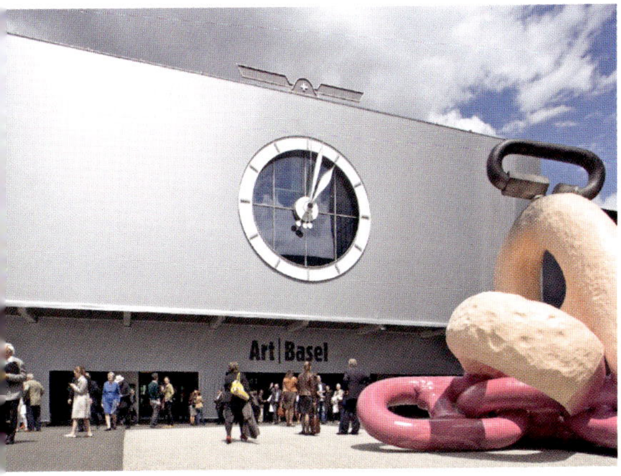

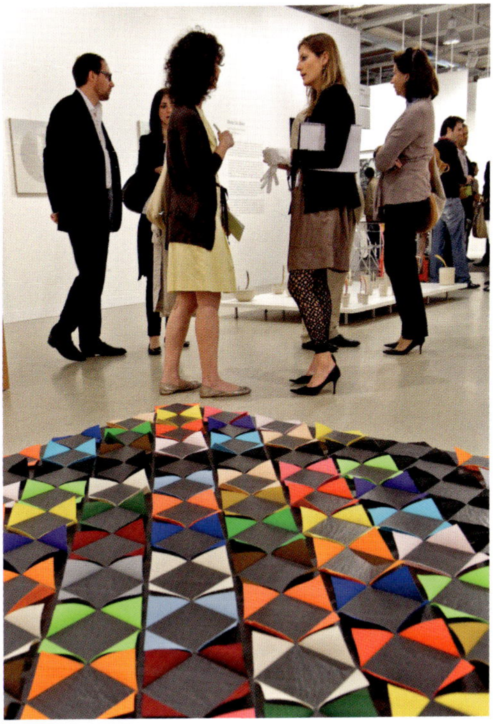

Art Basel always gets people talking (above and right). Outdoor and indoor sculpture at dOCUMENTA, Kassel (opposite and overleaf).

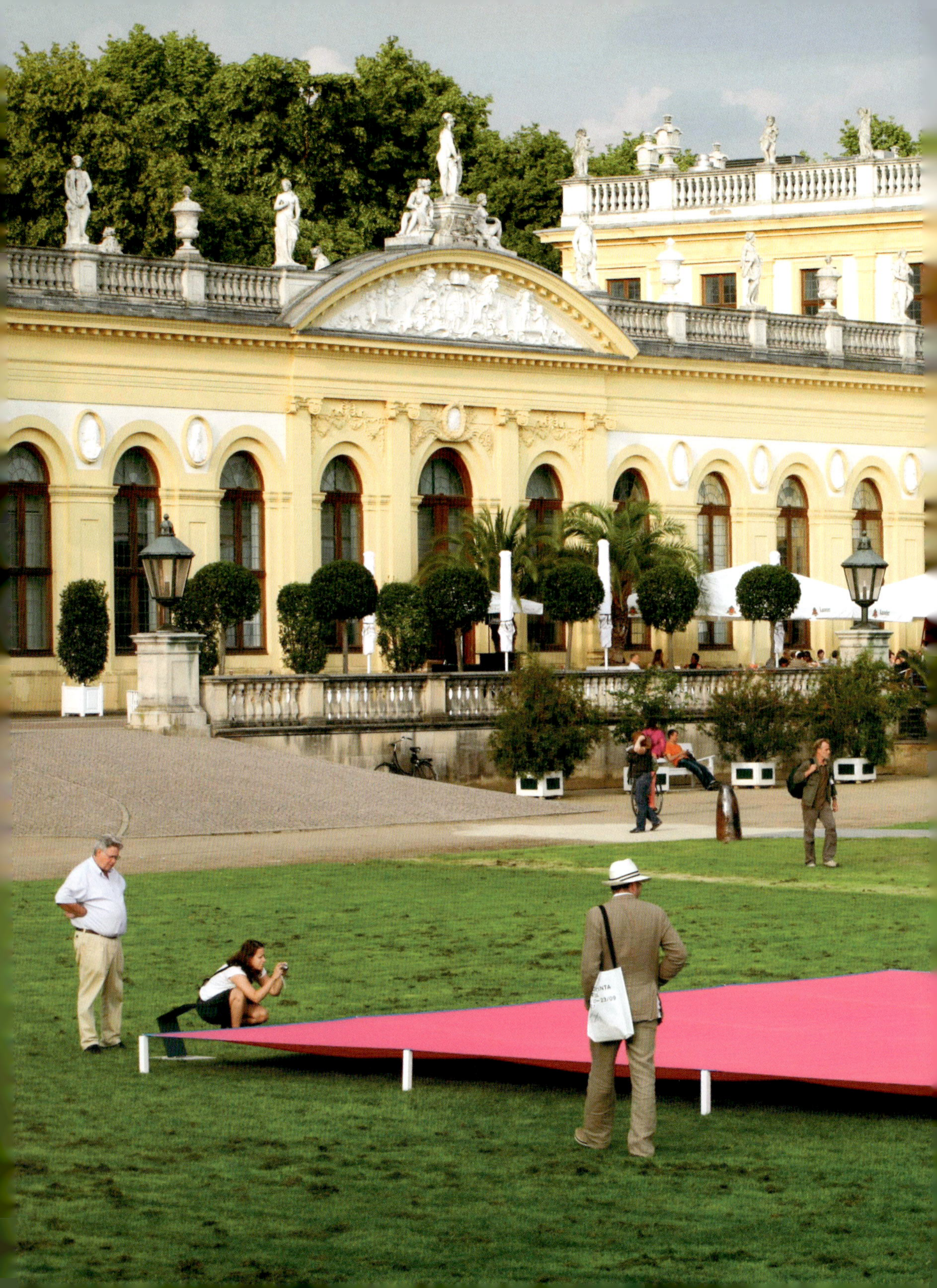

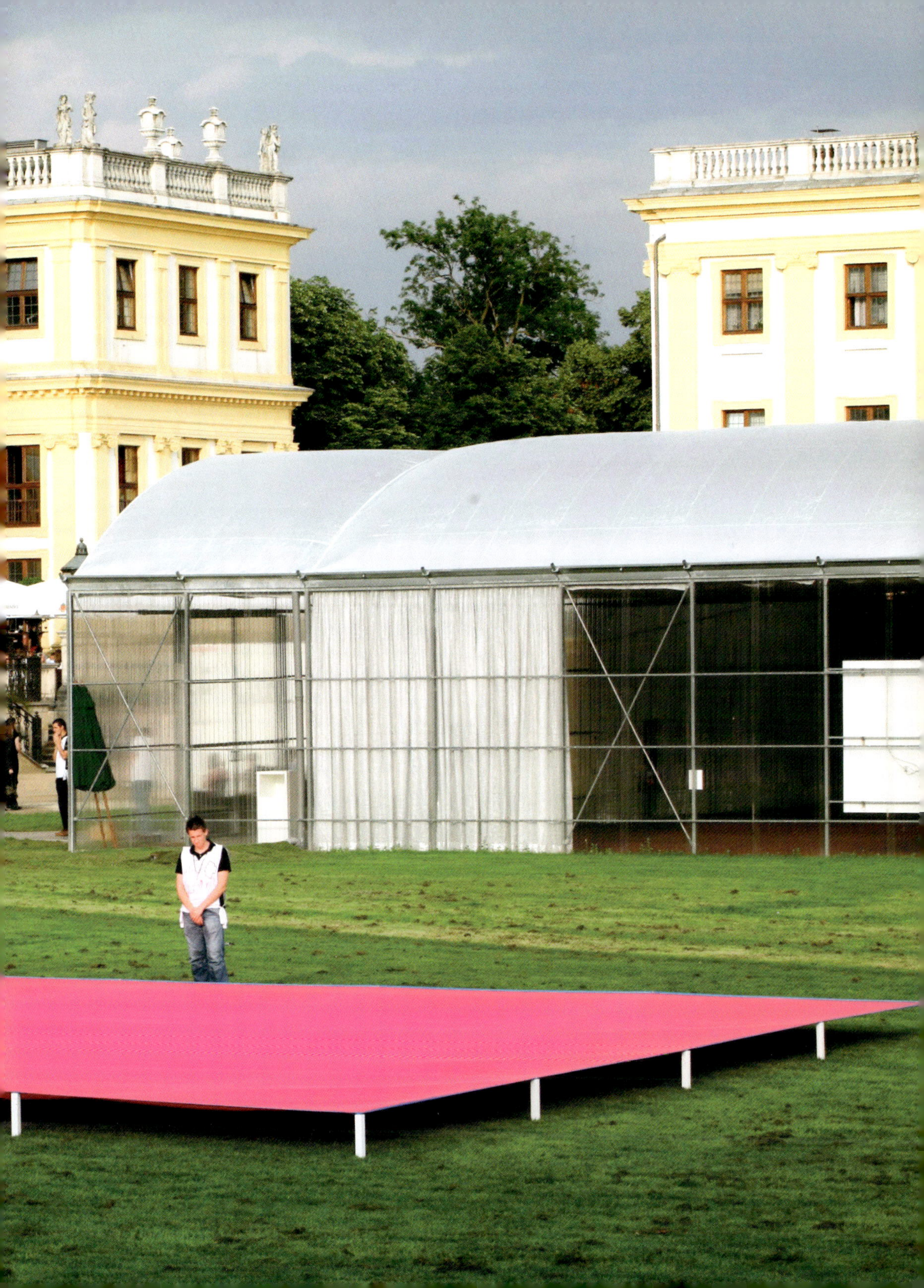

July/August

Arte Santander, Santander, Spain www.artesantander.com. This art fair maximises on the growing art market in Cantabria. In addition to the 50+ galleries exhibiting are a guest country feature and special project rooms.

September

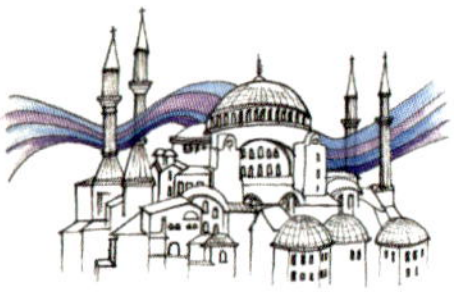

Istanbul Biennial, Istanbul. Turkey www.iksv.org. Established in 1987, a single curator selects individual artists (not representing their nation, simply themselves) to exhibit work within a set conceptual framework.

Lyon Biennial, Lyon, France www.biennaledelyon.com. Established in 1991, an artistic director collaborates with a selection of curators each suggesting artists for inclusion. They then produce work within a conceptual theme.

Docks Art Fair, Lyon, France www.docksartfair.com. This is a boutique art fair that invites 40 galleries to show work by a single emerging artist.

KIAF, Seoul, Korea www.kiaf.org. Priding itself on being a central hub for Asian art (only a couple of hours' flight from most major Asian cities), KIAF celebrated its 10th anniversary in 2011 and, along with ART HK (May), it is an important Far East arts hub.

A bird's eye view at the Istanbul Biennial.

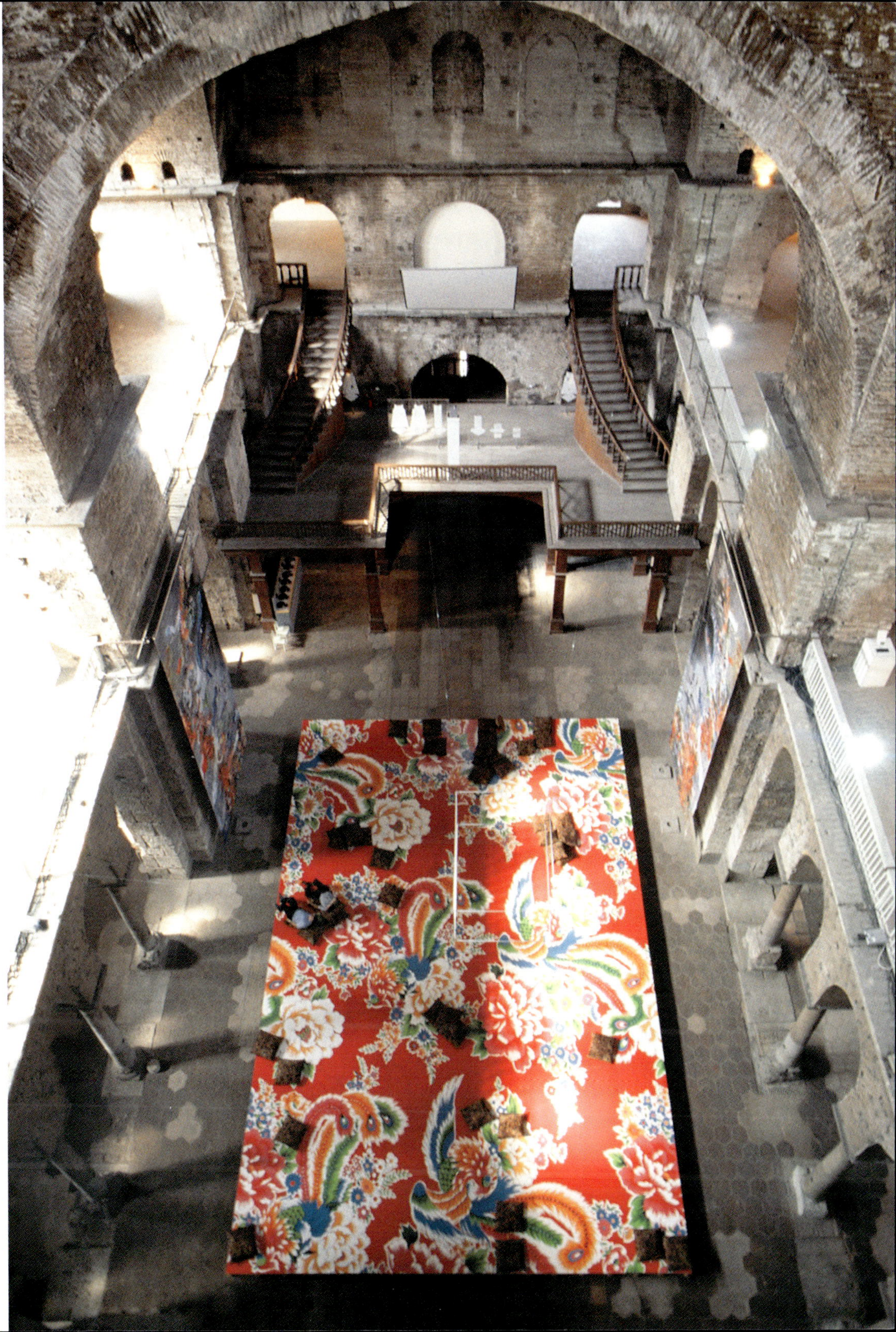

October

Sao Paolo Biennial, Sao Paolo, Brazil www.fbsp.org.br. Founded in 1951, this is the second oldest biennial in the world; it is intended to give international artists a platform to exhibit in Brazil and for the international art community to become familiar with Brazilian artists.

Frieze, London, UK www.friezeartfair.com. Established galleries must have had a programme of at least four exhibitions a year, in order to be eligible to attend, while Frame is a section where emerging galleries can showcase a solo show for one artist.

Sunday, London, UK www.sunday-fair.com. A relative newcomer, this fair originated in Berlin and moved to London during October art week in 2010, giving space to 20 young galleries, with work by 60 international artists.

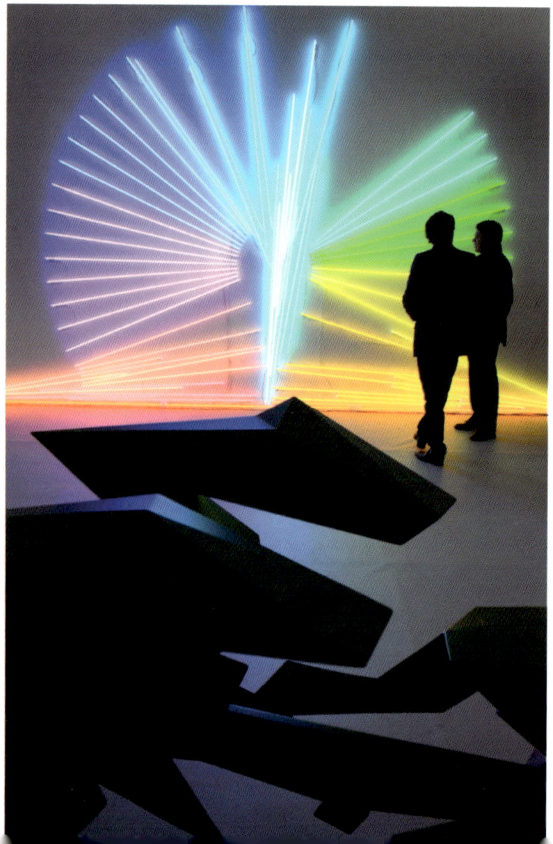

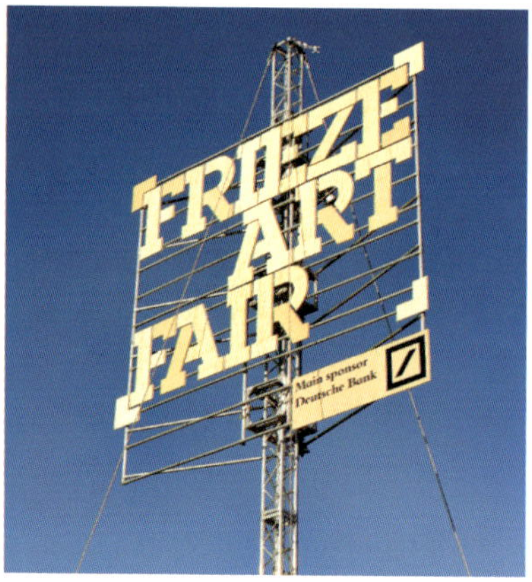

The full spectrum at Frieze, London.

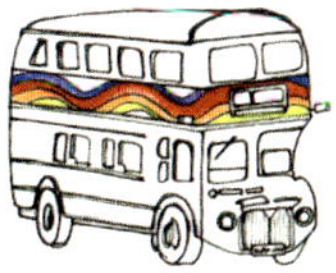

Scope, London, UK www.scope-art.com. This is an international event for emerging art with fairs in Miami, New York, The Hamptons and Basel throughout the year.

Christie's Multiplied Arts, London, UK www.multipliedartfair.com. This is staged for an exclusive 30 (or so) galleries that all sell prints.

FIAC, Paris, France www.fiac.com. Over 200 galleries from over 20 countries, show in three locations, including a grand sculpture park which takes over the Jardin des Tuilleries.

Affordable Art Fair, London, UK and Amsterdam, The Netherlands www.affordableartfair.com (see February entry).

Art International Zurich, Zurich, Switzerland www.art-zurich.com. This is an interdisciplinary contemporary art fair that prides itself on its relaxed atmosphere.

Art.Fair, Cologne, Germany www.art-fair.de. Alongside the 100 galleries exhibiting, look out for Bloom, the area that shines a light on young artists practicing urban art, architecture, video and digital art, design and fashion.

Art Forum, Berlin, Germany www.art-forum-berlin.de. With a hundred and ten galleries from 18 countries with 2,000 artists, there is also a section for galleries younger than six years (selected by the committee) that select two artists to introduce at the fair, and can recommend one other young gallery to exhibit.

Preview Berlin, Berlin, Germany www.previewberlin.de. This is an emerging art fair focussing on the promotion of emerging contemporary artists.

Berliner Liste, Berlin, Germany www.berliner-liste.org. Galleries, artists and projects can all apply for spaces here, with the focus on emerging artists. The different, quirky locations are a highlight every year.

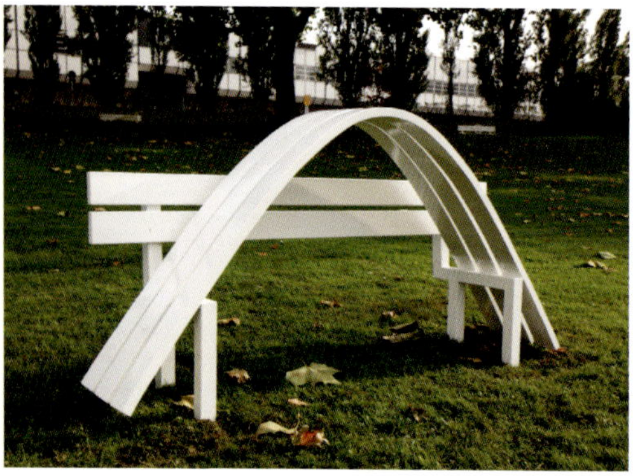

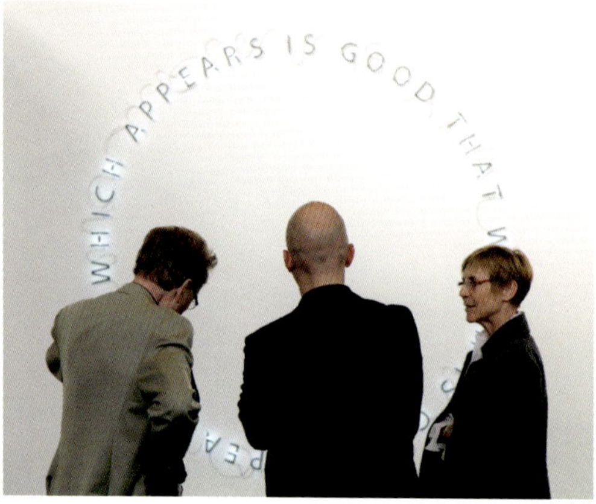

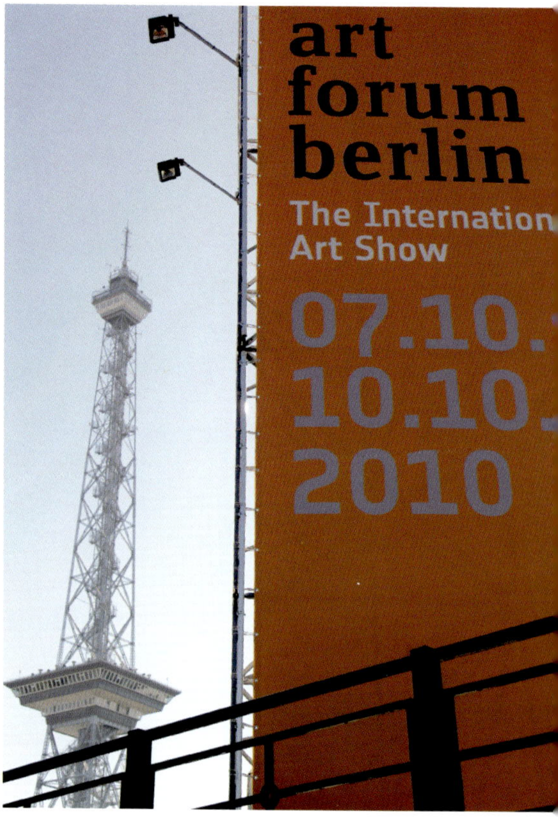

Mind bending art at Art Forum, Berlin.

Art Toronto, Toronto, Canada www.tiafair.com. This is a platform for leading Canadian galleries, plus a broader international cross-section of galleries. The NEXT section is for galleries under eight years old to show work by emerging artists with prices capped at C$7,000.

Athens Biennial, Athens, Greece www.athensbiennial.org. With its penchant for subversive, anarchic and alternative themes that challenge the status quo and notions of art, this is an event that polarises, but always leaves an impression.

November

Paris Photo, Paris, France www.parisphoto.fr. Although this photography fair doesn't (strictly speaking) have a specifically contemporary art focus, its well-established reputation attracts work by leading contemporary photographers. Four emerging artists also have the opportunity to be exhibited as part of the Young Talent Competition, plus the Paris Photo Prize is awarded to an international contemporary photographer.

Artissima, Turin, Italy www.artissima.it. This fair gathers established and emerging art galleries from around the world. One evening is also the occasion of a late-night vernissage (exhibition previews) of contemporary art galleries, unusual spaces and museums.

St-art, Strasbourg, France www.st-art.fr. This event boasts 100 galleries from countries across Europe.

MACparis, Paris, France www.mac2000-art.com. Between 125 and 140 selected artists host a booth of their work. Art bartering is a viable and accepted form of trading in some cases.

The Brussels Accessible Art Fair (BAAF), Brussles, Belgium www.accessibleartfair.com. This fair focuses on a small number of artists, who sell directly to buyers. The fair also takes place in May.

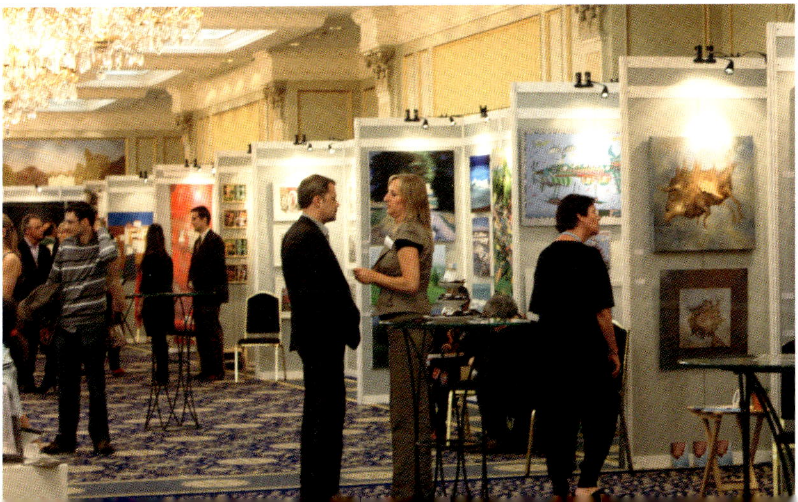

The location of the Brussels Accessible Art Fair is incredibly chic.

December

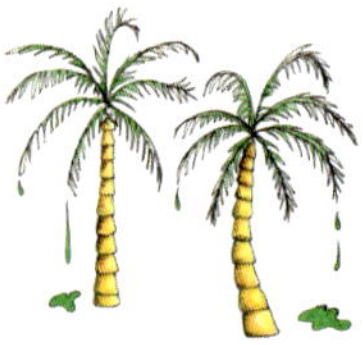

Art Basel Miami Beach, Florida, USA www.art.ch. Over 200 art galleries show the work of over 2,000 artists.

NADA, Miami Beach, Florida, USA www.newartdealers.org. The focus here is on presenting quality art by emerging artists.

Scope, Miami, Florida, USA www.scope-art.com. An international fair for emerging art with fairs in London, New York, The Hamptons and Basel throughout the year.

Pulse, Miami, Florida, USA www.pulse-art.com. One of two international contemporary art fairs (the other being in New York in March) which aim to act as a bridge between the central and satellite art fairs taking place concurrently.

Verge, Miami, USA www.vergeartfair.com. The focus is on marginal and newly emerging art, with sister shows in Brooklyn (during Armory Week) and Basel.

Ink, Miami, USA www.inkartfair.com. A festival dedicated to works on paper by contemporary artists.

Variable date

Manifesta, Europe, roving www.manifesta.org. This nomadic biennial takes a concertedly left-field stance, focussing on minority groups and cultures (amongst other distinguishable elements) and settling itself every two years in locations and venues traditionally not regarded as European cultural hubs (Rotterdam, Luxembourg and Frankfurt have been past locations).

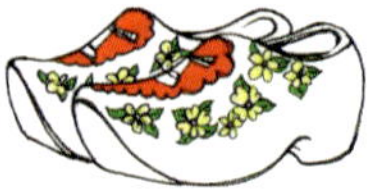

Art Metz, Metz, France www.artmetz.com. A fair that is a contemporary art hub for the Grande Région (Lorraine, Luxembourg, parts of Belgium, Saarland and Rhineland Palatinat).

Satellite Fairs

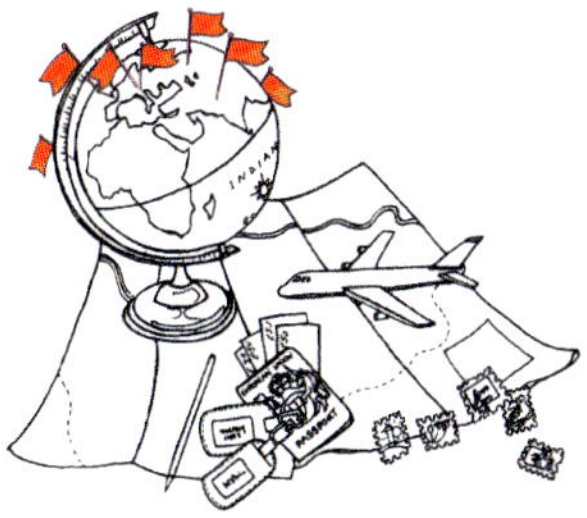

When it comes to the myriad smaller fairs, look out for the left-field ones that gather artists thematically, whether this is by discipline, location or style. Interesting themes for fairs are listed below, together with some examples of each.

Prints and multiples

2010 saw auction house Christie's stage the inaugural Multiplied Arts (www.multipliedartfair.com), which invited galleries selling multiples, limited-edition prints and print portfolios to exhibit, with prices ranging from as little as £10/€12/$16.

Emerging art

Artissima, held in Turin in November (www.artissima.it), Art Forum Berlin's satellite show Preview Berlin in October (www.previewberlin.de), NADA in Miami (www.newartdealers.org), and Volta (voltashow.com), which runs alongside Basel in June, all invite galleries to show work by emerging artists, while Liste (www.liste.ch), also in Basel, invites emerging art galleries (themselves) open for less than five years to exhibit work by artists under 40.

Unrepresented artists

The Art Bazaar Collective (www.theartbazaar.com) in New York invites unrepresented artists to submit their work, which is registered on a first come first served basis.

Artist stands

Volta's sister fair, held in New York in November, MACparis (www.mac2000-art.com) and Brussels's BAAF (www.accessibleartfair.com) are examples of fairs where artists rather than galleries take centre stage, with a single artist (usually selected by a board) having a stand to themselves, showing multiple pieces and selling directly to buyers.

Price

The Affordable Art Fairs (www.affordableartfair.com) are a series of contemporary art fairs that are held in cities across Europe as well as New York, Australia and Singapore. They invite galleries to show work where prices are capped at somewhere between £3,000/€3,500/$4,800 and $10,000/£6,250/€7,250 (depending on location and currency).

Geography

PINTA, held in London in June and New York in November (www.pintaart.com), is one of the fairs that turns its attentions to contemporary art from a particular region, in this case Latin American art, which comes from 50 galleries across Latin America, the United States and Europe. The fair coincides with Christie's and Sotheby's Latin-American art auctions. Vienna Fair has a special interest in showing art from Eastern Europe (www.viennafair.at).

Discipline

ParisPhoto (www.parisphoto.fr) in November gathers together galleries showing work in a particular discipline; in this case photography from over 100 international galleries. Not all of it is contemporary, but it is nevertheless a well represented sector. Craft (Collect, run by the British Crafts council, www.craftscouncil.org.uk/collect), prints (London's Original Print Fair, www.londonprintfair.com), digital and video art (DiVA, www.divafair.com), kinetic art (the Kinetica Art Fair in London, www.kinetica-artfair.com) and urban contemporary art (Graffiti Gone Global in Miami, www.gggexhibit.com or Stroke in Germany, www.stroke-artfair.com) are other examples of discipline-focussed fairs.

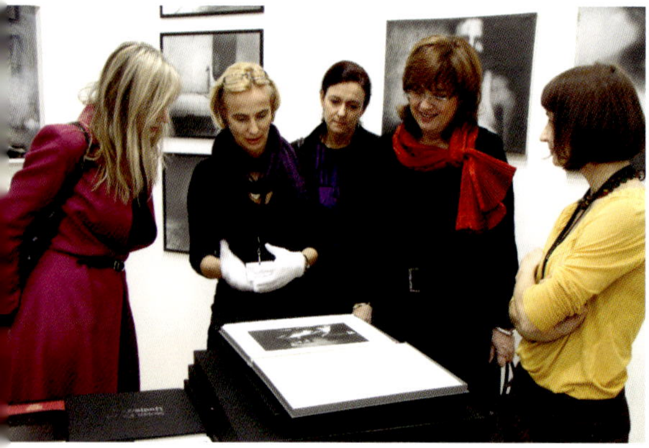

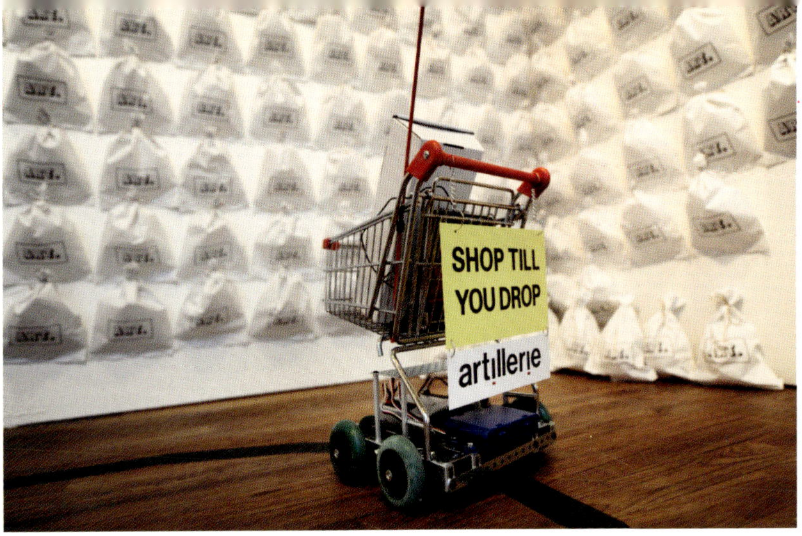

Expect the unexpected at Supermarket Art Fair, Stockholm.

Artist-run spaces

Supermarket Art fair in Stockholm in February (www.supermarketartfair.com) is forging a path in organising art fairs with artist-run galleries, initiatives and collectives as exhibitors, shifting the focus away from sales and commercial enterprise. Others include Nordic art focussed Alt_Cph (www.altcph.dk) on Copenhagen.

Unrepresented artist fairs

These tend to be smaller fairs showing on a local level rather than an international one, but those such as PooL (www.poolartfair.com), held in New York, Miami and Guadeloupe and run by not-for-profit organisation Frere International, and The Artist Project (www.theartistprojectny.com) are notable exceptions, presenting selected unrepresented artists on an international platform.

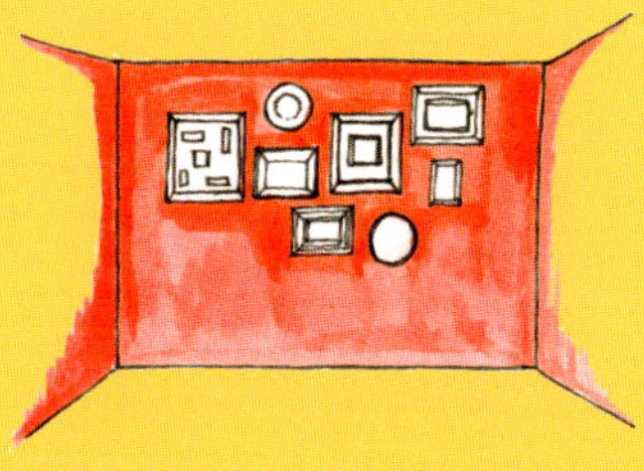

07 Collectors

01

Zoe and Mathieu Laroche

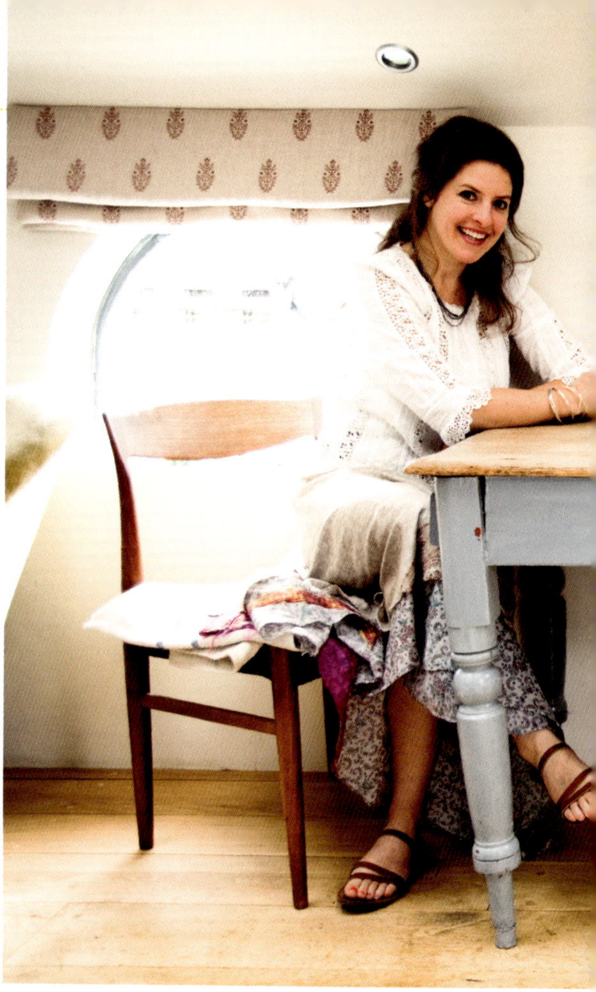

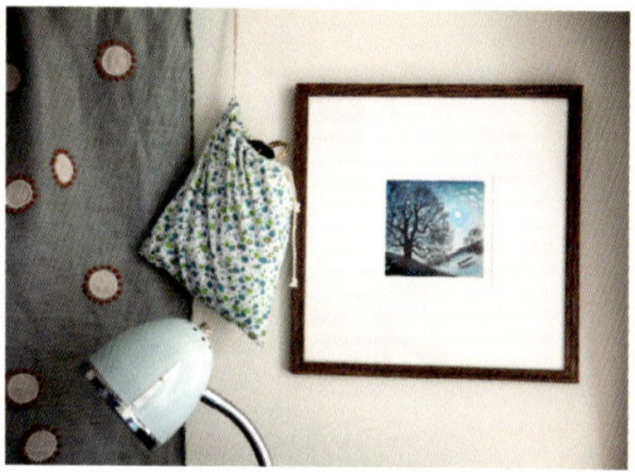

“WE TRY and buy one or two pieces of art a year, together. Each piece is like a little diary of our adventures – rather than putting an exhibition in the diary and remembering it that way, we have a picture there for us to see. We have a joint account that's just for art, we put in when we can and every so often we check it, to see how much we have to spend.

Often we don't go looking for art to buy, it finds us. Sometimes we'll be cycling home and see that a private view is on and stop by to have a look; we've been to art fairs, and have bought from there, but not always, sometimes we just look; and we often buy art from small galleries we find randomly in little towns and villages we visit on trips away from home.

We don't always agree on what to buy, but often a painting will

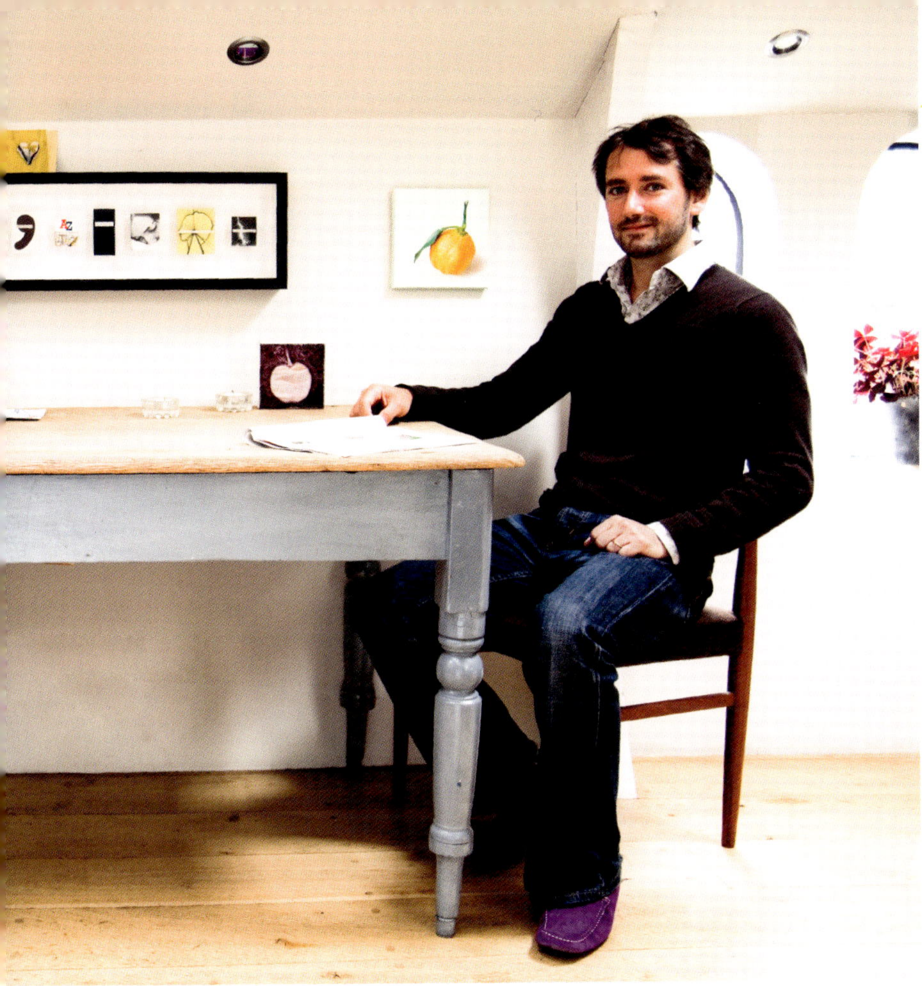

Zoe and Mat as their kitchen table with their cherished Chris Kenny framed miniature books.

'speak' to me [Zoe] and Mat will understand. Mat has a degree in antiques and fine art, so he often spots pieces and appreciates them for their quality and technical skill where as I will fall in love with works on a more spiritual level.

Buying for the first time together was both frightening and exciting. It was of flowers in a jar by Serena Rowe. It captured something of the Dutch masters, something very still, almost haunting. Neither of us had full time jobs, so we bargained the price down from £1700/€1975/$2750 to £1500/€1750/$2400. It was so exciting seeing that orange 'sold' sticker, knowing it was because of us!

Although we mostly buy things together, sometimes we go a bit AWOL. I [Zoe] fell in love with a series of tiny books by the artist Chris

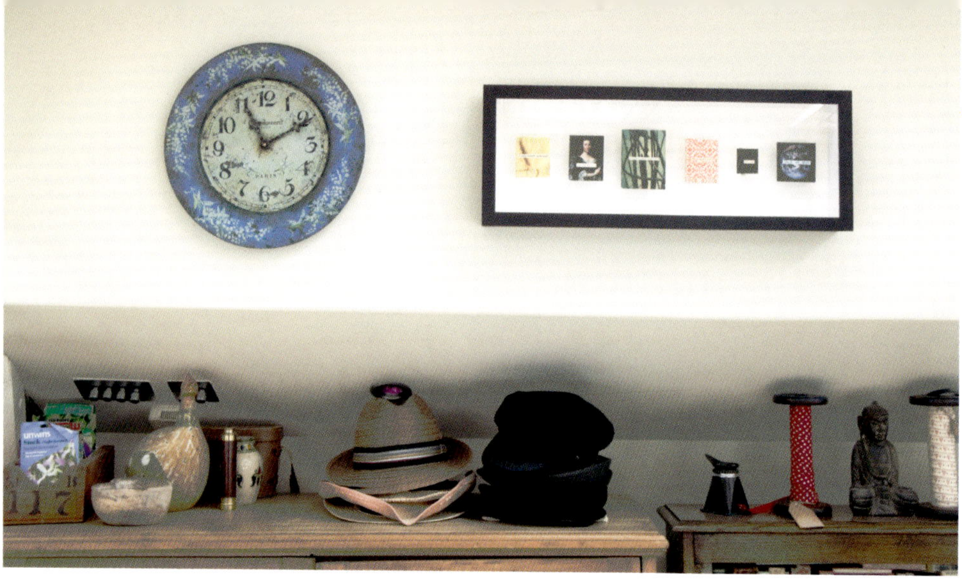

Kenny with designs that reflected the found text titles of the books. As it was the last day of the exhibition I couldn't show Mat, and he didn't understand my description of them at all. But he could see I had to have them. When I eventually brought them home, Mat absolutely loved them. One set is by the table where we eat every evening and I never, ever, get bored of looking at it.

We have a lot of pictures and paintings of lemons, as the boat we live on is called Lemon, and a lot of animals – particularly rabbits as we were both born in the year of the rabbit; sculptures and drawings and two tiles from the Affordable Art Fair. We like buying things we have a connection with.

We always make an effort to meet the artists whose work

Miniature books by Chris Kenny (above); a jar of flowers by Serena Rowe (right) that was Zoe and Mat's first purchase together; and a birthday drawing by Quentin Blake (far right).

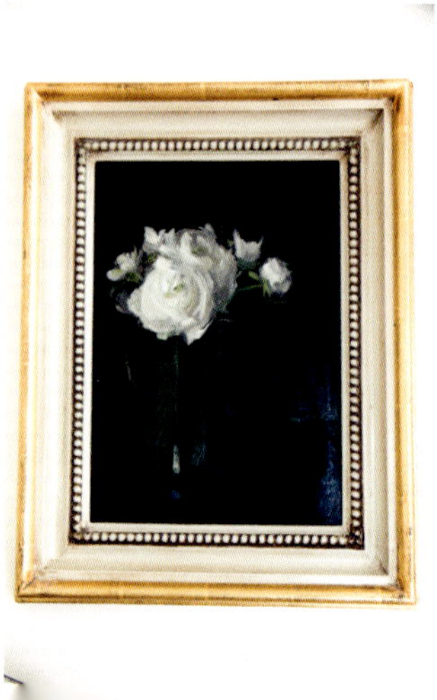

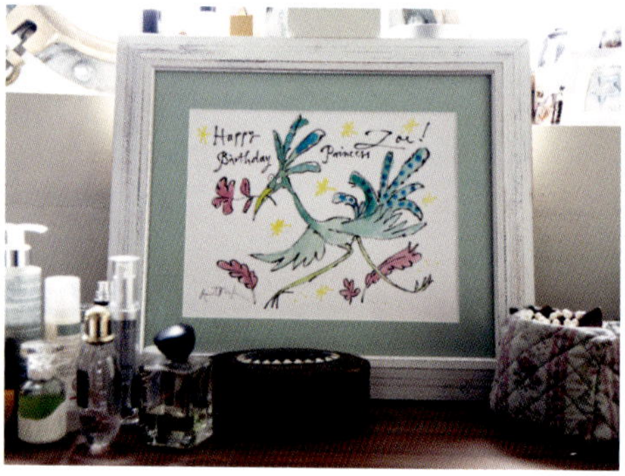

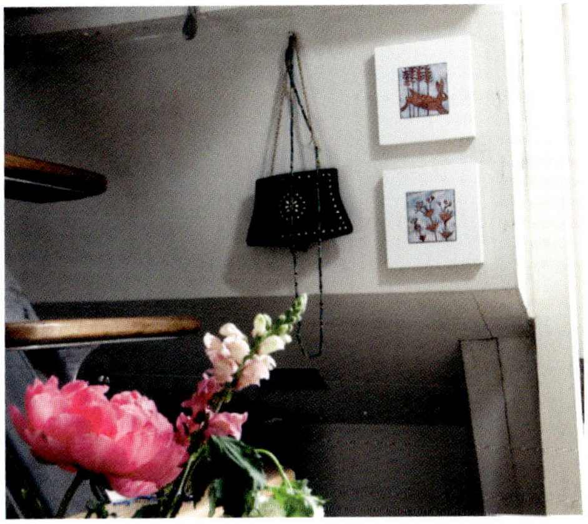

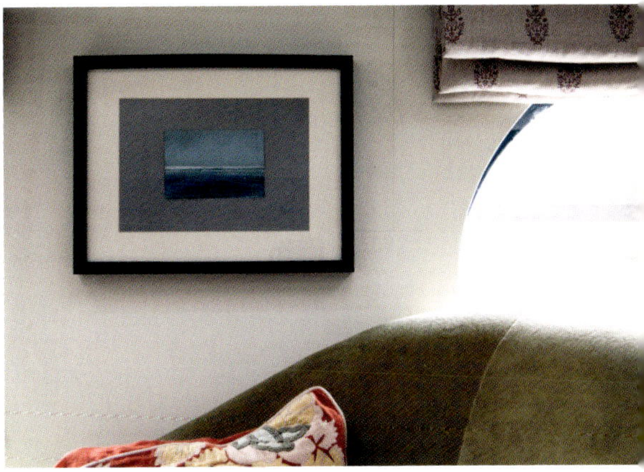

we buy; we like knowing the stories behind each work. The woman who drew the picture we have of a fox running under a moon was very heavily pregnant at the time she drew it; she couldn't sleep one night and saw a fox run under a full moon. We kept in touch, to find out how her baby was, and we are still in contact. We also have pieces by my [Zoe's] yoga teacher, and my sister's art teacher at school. It's wonderful knowing the people whose work you own.

Originality and uniqueness is important to us. We have a few original prints but nearly everything else is a one off. In a world where everyone is wearing and eating so much mass-produced stuff we treasure art that's new and different and that no one else owns, that's not churned out, and has had time taken over it.

Tiles by the door of rabbits (above left) and other purchases by Zoe and Mat.

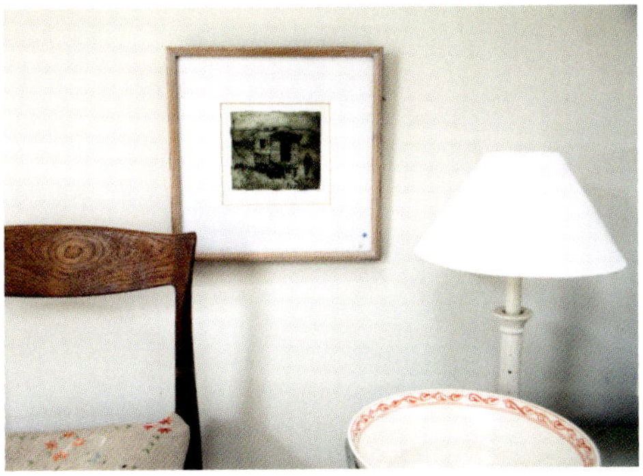

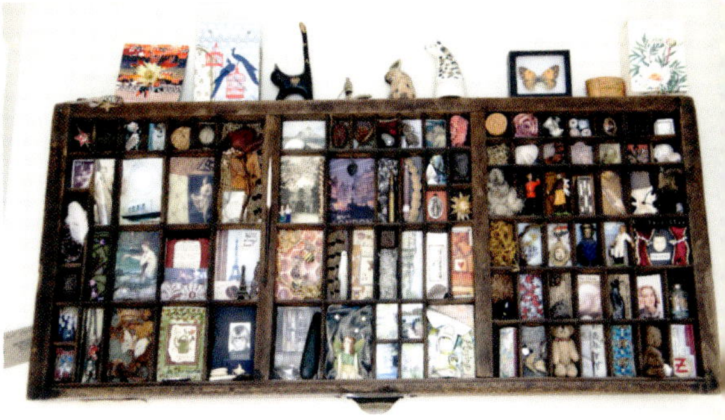

02

Bobby Molavi

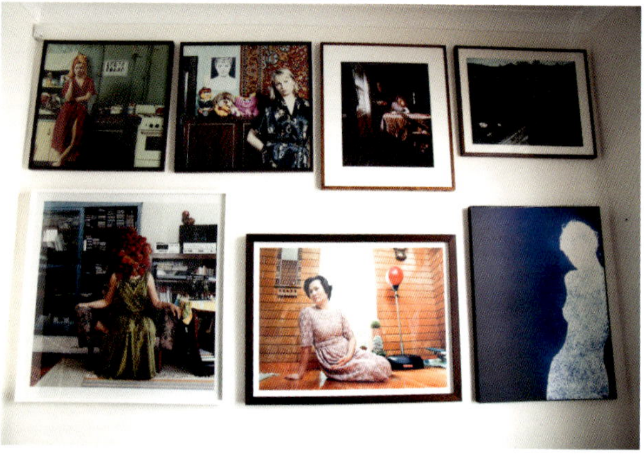

WHEN I first started collecting, I didn't know that much about contemporary art, and I just trusted my eye. I bought my first piece from a small art fair linked to Frieze, called Zoo. It was a big piece by an Italian photographer artist called Luisa Lambri, who shows at the Marc Foxx gallery in LA, and it was about £4,000/€4,600/$6,400. I fell in love with it. The gallery could tell I really loved it, and in the end they let me pay in instalments – the remaining half over a year.

I had a similar reaction to a piece by Idris Khan, a young photographer who I initially saw at his graduate show. He had nothing available there, but I happened to go to Art Basel Miami not long after and I walked straight in and bought one of his Koran pieces immediately. There was no doubt in my mind. And it is still one of my favourite works. Interestingly (as both works were bought on gut instinct) both Luisa Lambri and Idris Khan have gone on to become hugely successful artists.

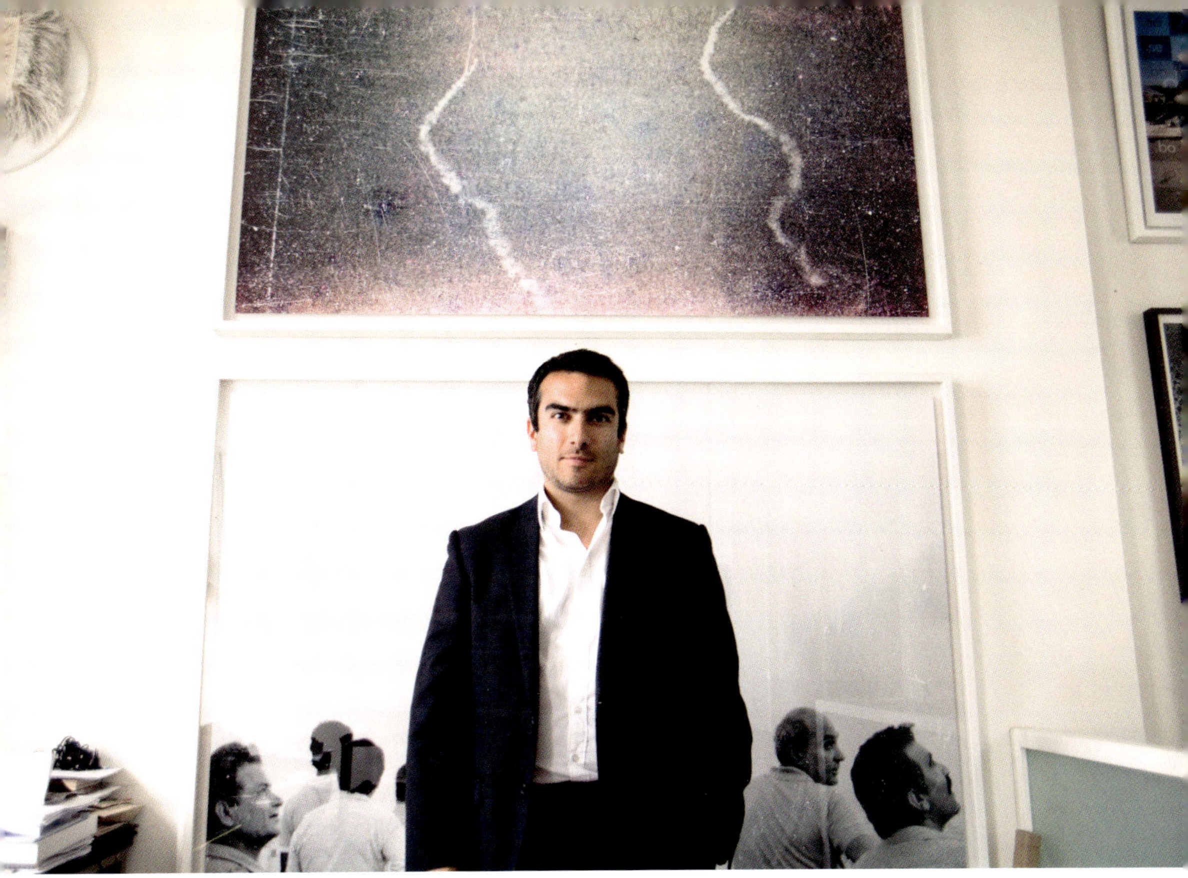

As my collection has grown, my main focus has continued to centre round photography; I have bought paintings, but initially photography was something that felt more accessible and I'm also drawn to it. But I have never bought anything because I thought it fits with my collection, and although themes definitely appear, they tend to emerge looking back rather than looking forward.

Bobby with some of his large-scale photography pieces

I'm now a member of the Future Contemporaries at The Serpentine Gallery – groups like this are great as you can meet like-minded collectors, and members are encouraged to ask questions about art, and are taken round galleries and introduced to artists. Its purpose is to teach rather than to judge or expect anything from the people who have joined.

When I buy art now I am stricter about works meeting my 'requirements'. When I was 25 I would make more superficial decisions, and was affected by what was cool or by what other

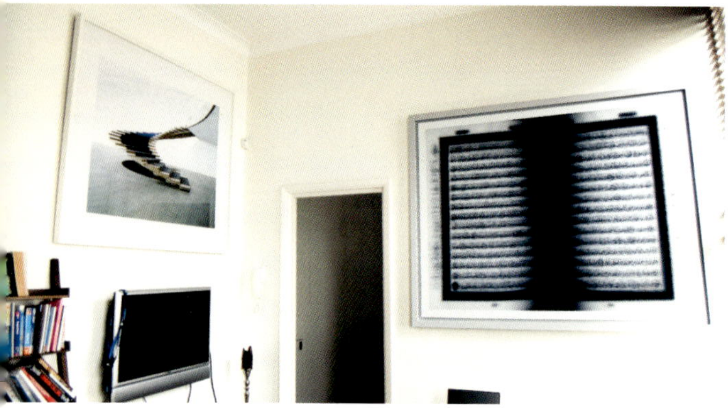

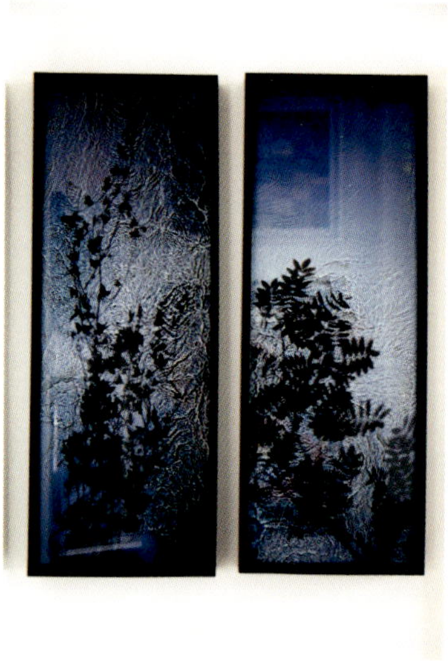

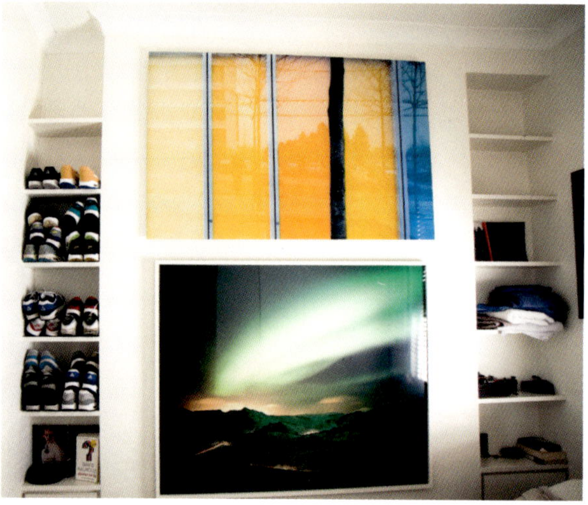

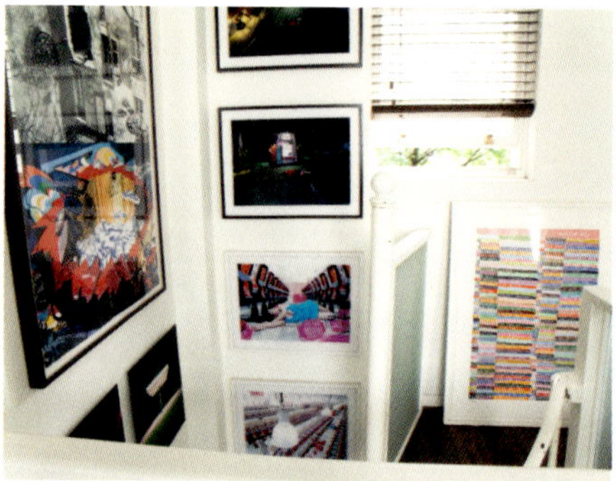

Bobby's treasured Koran piece by Idris Khan (above left).

people said, because I was less sure of what I liked. But now, as well as liking an individual piece, it's important to me that I believe in the artist, and think that their work is developing, and that I like the gallery, and the programme of the gallery. It's also important that I can set an artist in some kind of chronology – that I can see their art historical antecedents, but that I think they are both experimental and building upon an artistic tradition in a new way. My appreciation has to be substantial.

Now I've built up more of an art network, there are people whose opinions I trust, and if they recommend an artist I will make a greater effort to see their work, but I am wary of the herd mentality. In the art

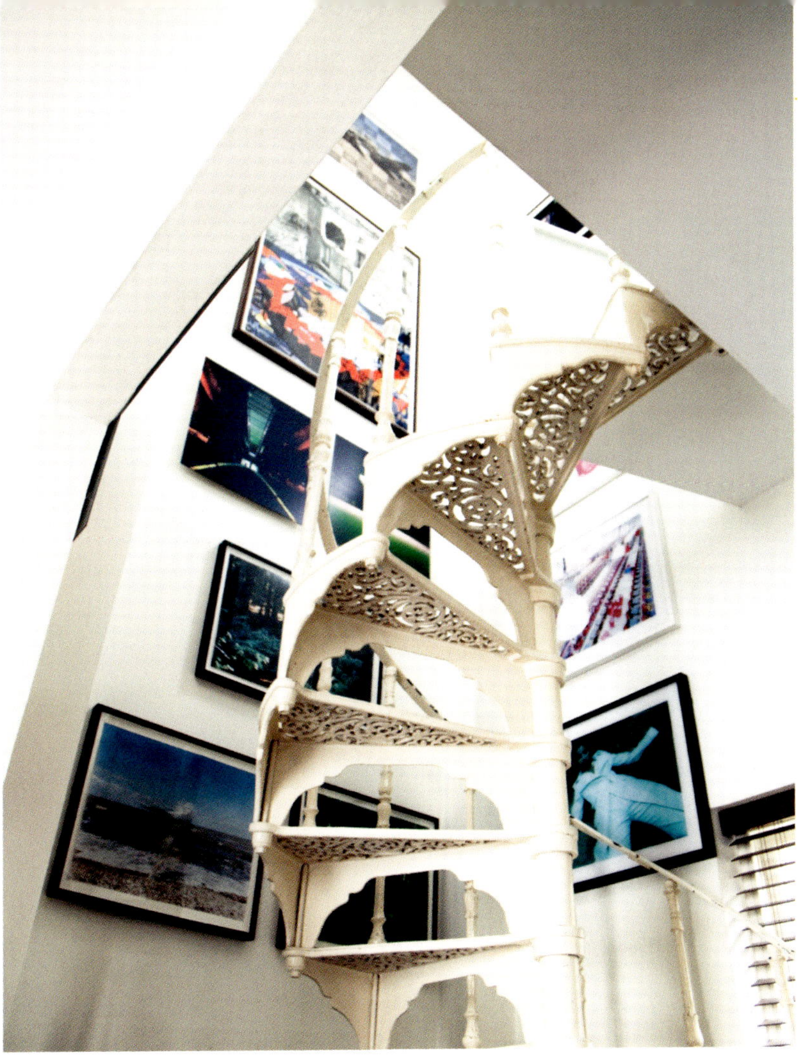

world, things move in trends; the more modest collectors are greatly influenced by the major collectors, but this way of buying is a dangerous way of gambling.

At the end of the day, I buy art that I love and which means something to me, and which I hope I can have a dialogue with for a sustained period. The worst-case scenario of buying this way is being left with a piece of art that you will love for the rest of your life. But buying something because the value might go up or because the artist is seen to be 'hot' means the worst-case scenario is being left with something you don't like, is not worth anything and isn't a great piece of art. ”

Bobby's home is contemporary photography from top to bottom.

03

Jo Varney

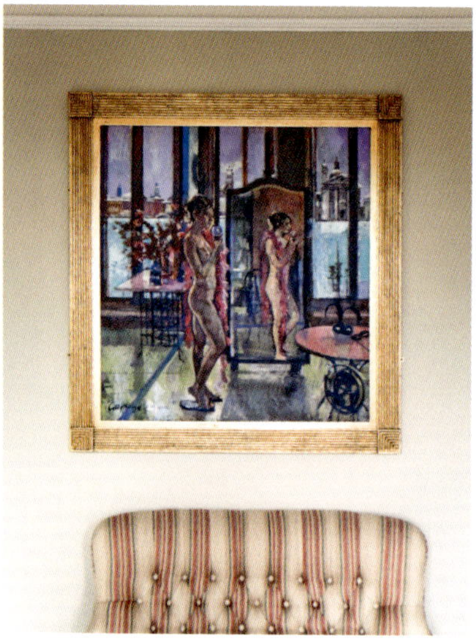

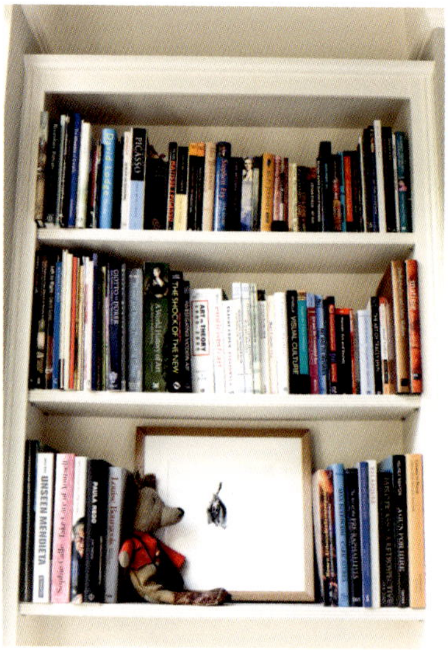

“ I TOTALLY immerse myself in art – I regularly visit all the big public art gallery shows, plus the little clusters of commercial galleries where I live like those on Cork Street, and every time I am in arts hubs like Vienna, Berlin and Basel on business, I make sure I go to an exhibition.

The more art I see, the more I want to understand, so I've done lots of adult education courses to learn about art and the history of art – lunch-time talks, evening lectures, and Saturday morning courses at public art galleries. It snowballed so much that I embarked on doing a History of Art MA in the evenings.

I also read art magazines, like *Tate Etc* and *Frieze*; gallery listings in national newspapers; and I keep up to date with international

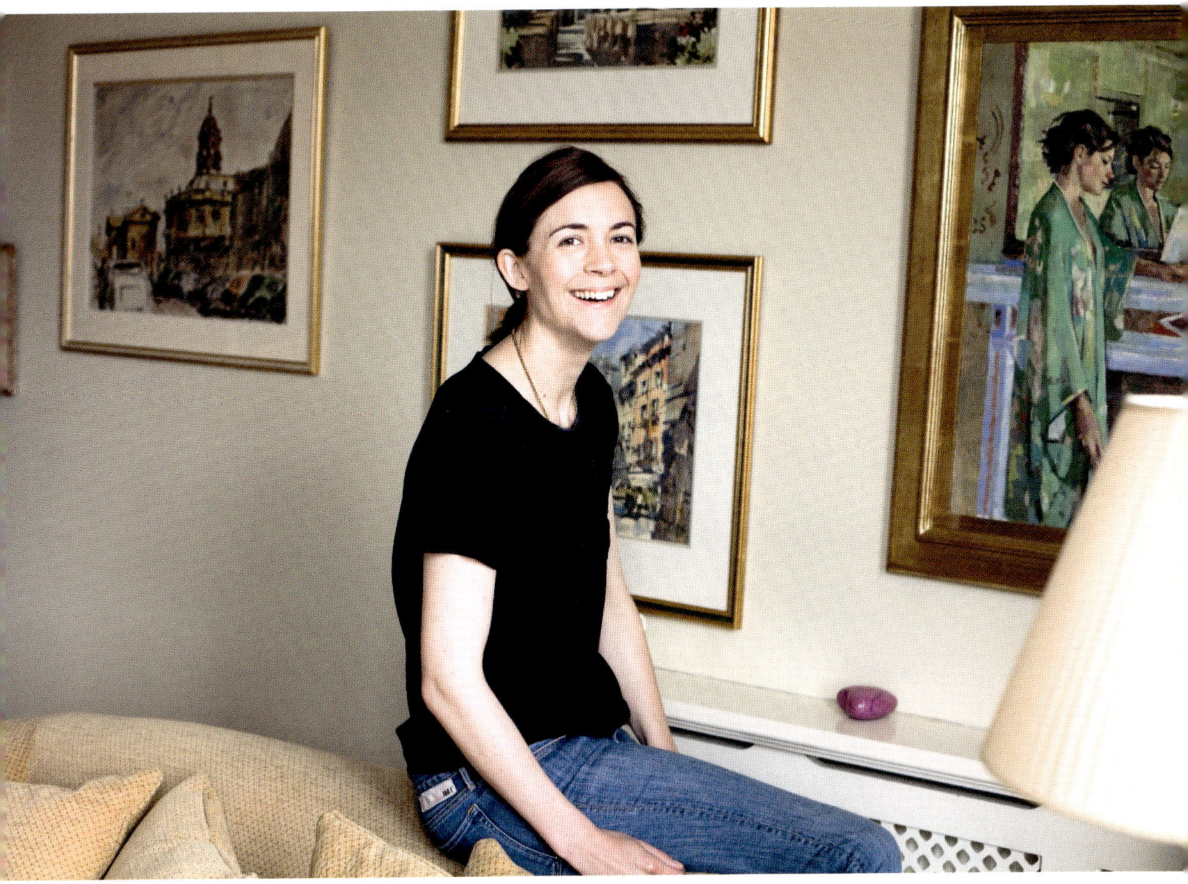

Jo with watercolours and an oil painting by Geoffrey Humphries.

exhibitions via *The Art Newspaper*. I also follow artists, galleries and art publications on Twitter.

With the acquisition of knowledge I've got bolder in my decisions and my tastes have changed. I had never thought about collecting photographs before, but having done a photography course, I bought my first photograph two summers ago. I also never used to quite understand about prints and printing techniques, but again I've come to appreciate them through learning – now I think prints are wonderful, a more affordable way of buying art. Buying an Avigdor Arika print was a big revelation. Someone once told me that Lucian Freud only buys even print numbers, and it's a quirk I like, and have adopted.

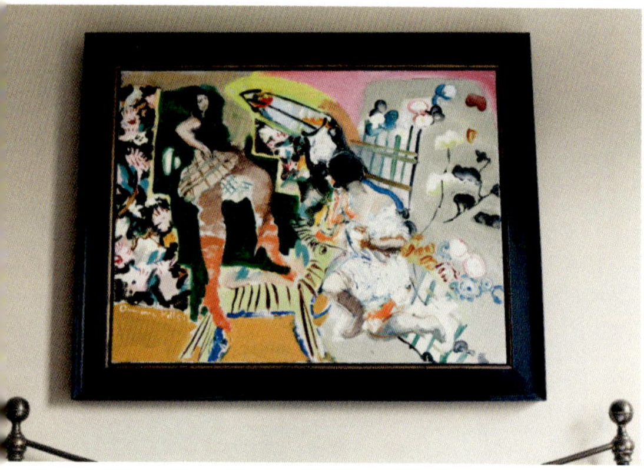

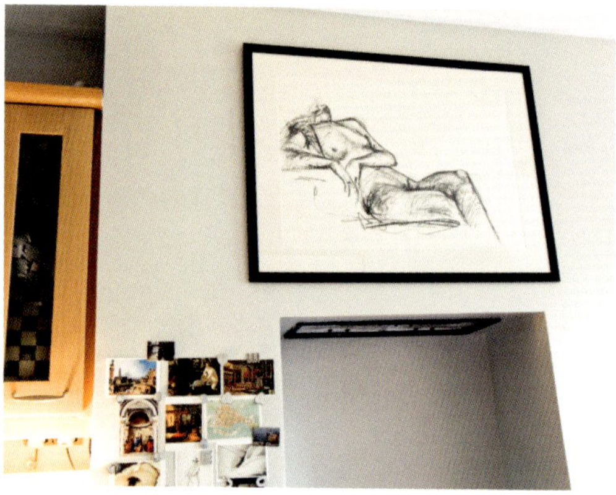

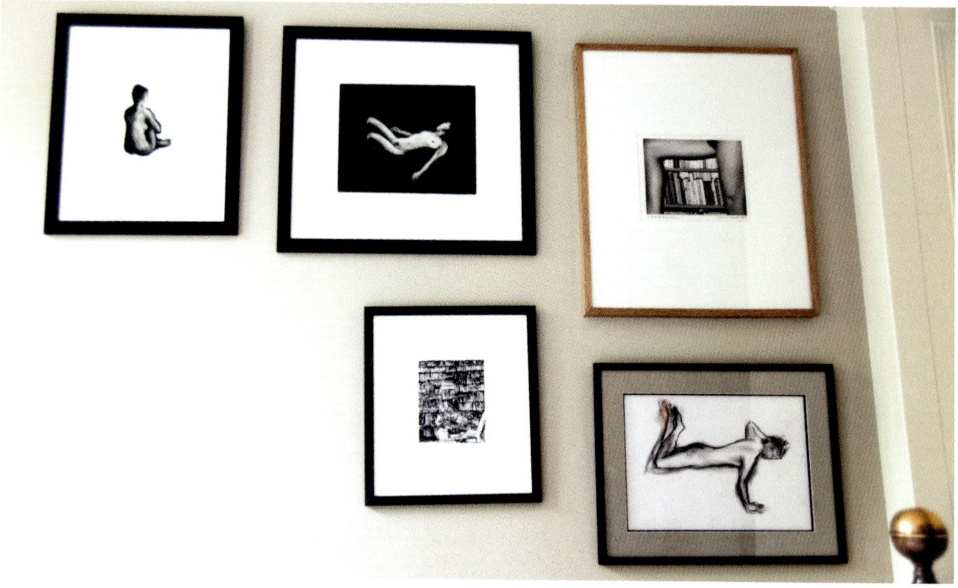

Jo's collection of nudes in her bedroom (above).

My collection is fairly diverse, but if there is a thread of continuity I'd say it was art that relates to the female and the sexual. I am really interested in questions about the female body, and the portrayal of the female body (mostly by men) and how women have been portrayed as objects – something to be looked at. At the moment I am particularly interested in how women present women, so I have started buying art by more women artists.

I like buying directly from artists. I've bought pencil drawings of London from a school friend who has done incredibly well, grand scale oils from the artist Geoffrey Humphries in Venice, and some beautiful watercolours from an artist in Devon. It doesn't take much hard work to buy directly from artists whose work you have seen in a gallery. This way you get greater exposure to their work, can speak to them about their ideas, get to see their studio and can often negotiate a better price – especially if you buy two pieces at the same time. Bulk buying gives you more leverage and I like hanging two works together as a complementary pair. I also often ask if they do student discounts. I've asked a few times now so I don't feel quite so rude – I think you just need to have a lightness of touch.

I try to re-hang my art about once a year. In moving it I see it in a new light – and often it sets up an interesting dialogue between the works. For example I have a pretty cluster of watercolours, and they look really good together because they correspond, and in my bedroom is a selection of female nudes.
Re-hanging also means I can create new spaces on the wall.

For me collecting art is enmeshed together with learning about art. The more I learn and read the more what I like changes. It is a real journey of self-discovery. ”

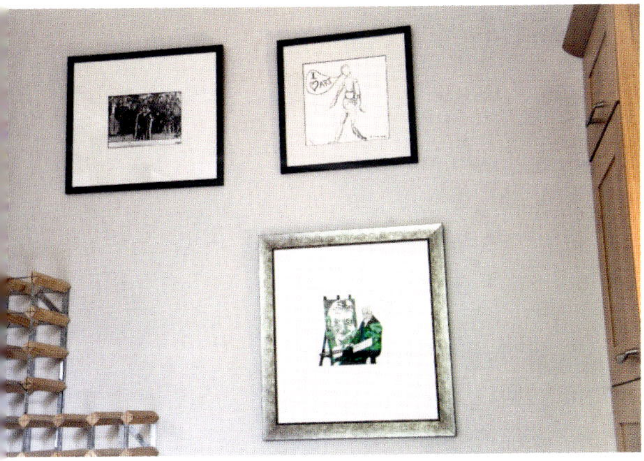

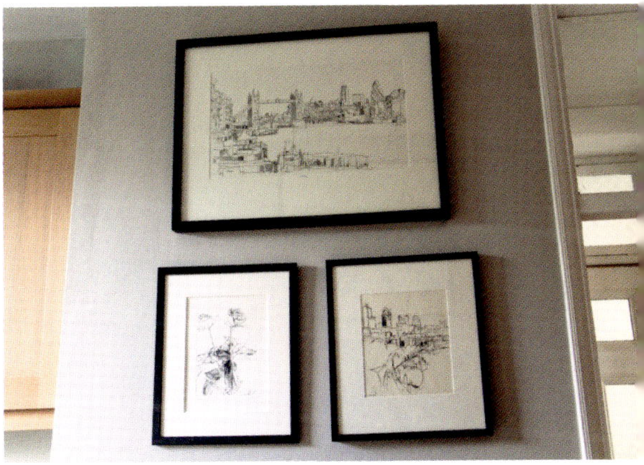

04

Mark Christophers

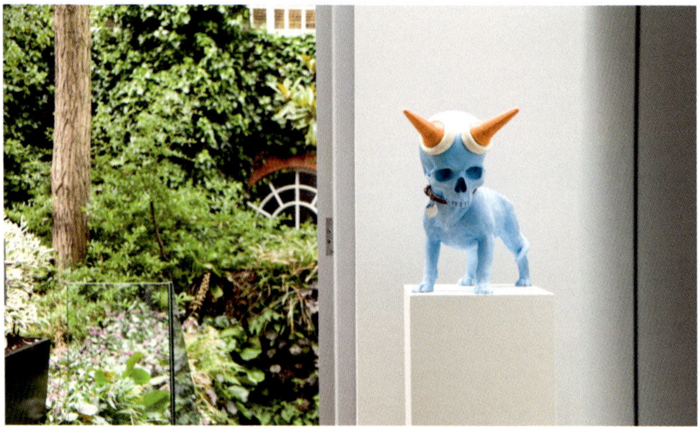

URBAN ART has always appealed to me; it wasn't necessarily a conscious decision to buy it, but I guess my eye has just gone that way. Maybe it is because I have a bit of a rebellious streak, and I am always looking for something different, for challenges to the way things are usually done. I like art that makes a statement – people often either love it or hate it, but I'm not buying it for them, I'm buying it for me.

When I buy a work of art I'll have an idea of the specific space I want to hang it, or where it is going to go in relation to my furniture – for me art sets the tone and feel of a room. I love furniture and I source original 1970s and 80s lighting, and all the art I buy is pretty strong, so it all needs to work together; each piece needs to hold their own but not overwhelm a room.

I'm not a big fan of the whole art *scene* – I just know what I like; I'm not into the 'technical' side of things. Most of the art I have is self-found, by stumbling across things. About 8 years ago I was strolling

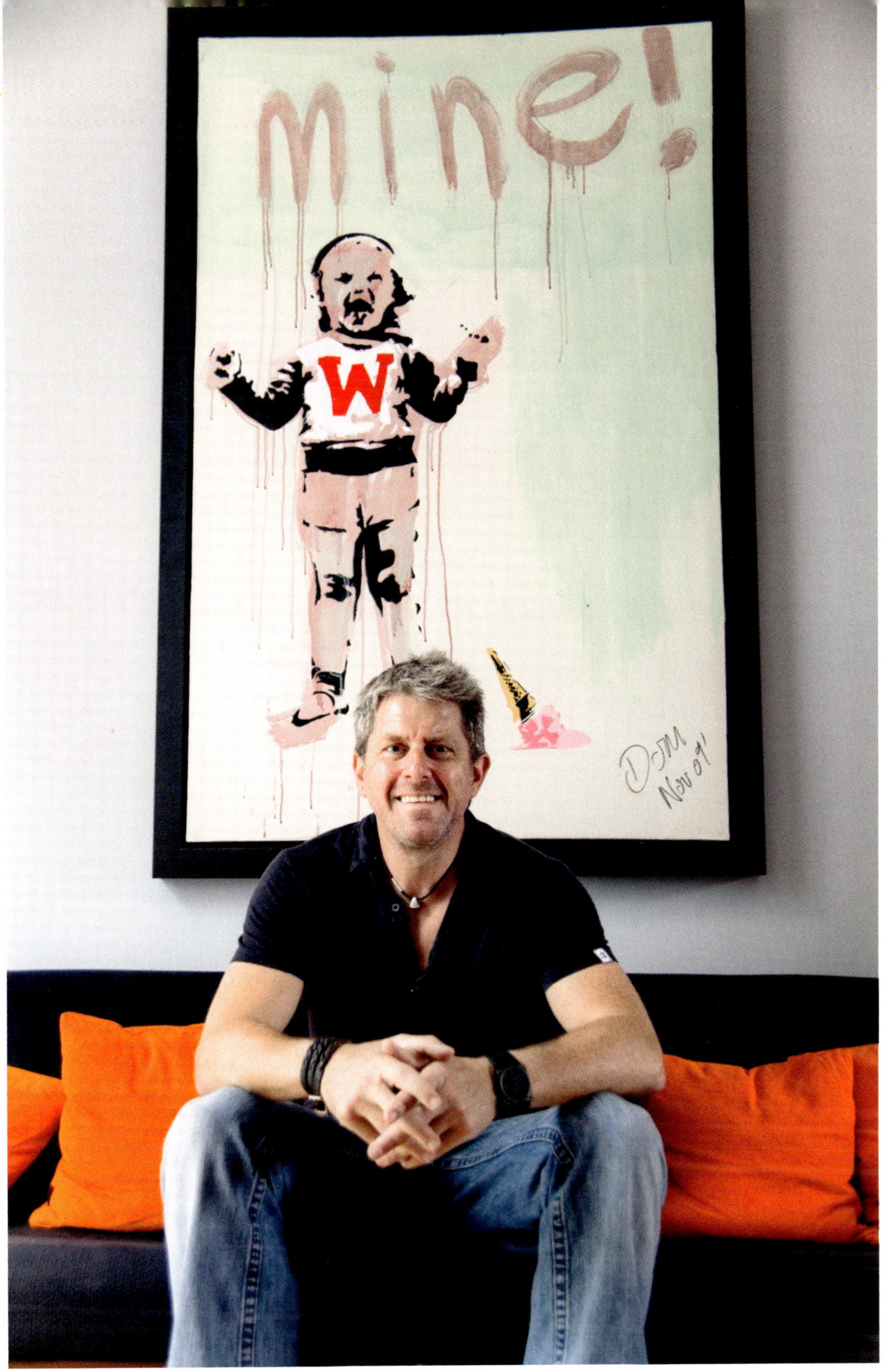
mine!
W
Dom
Nov 09'

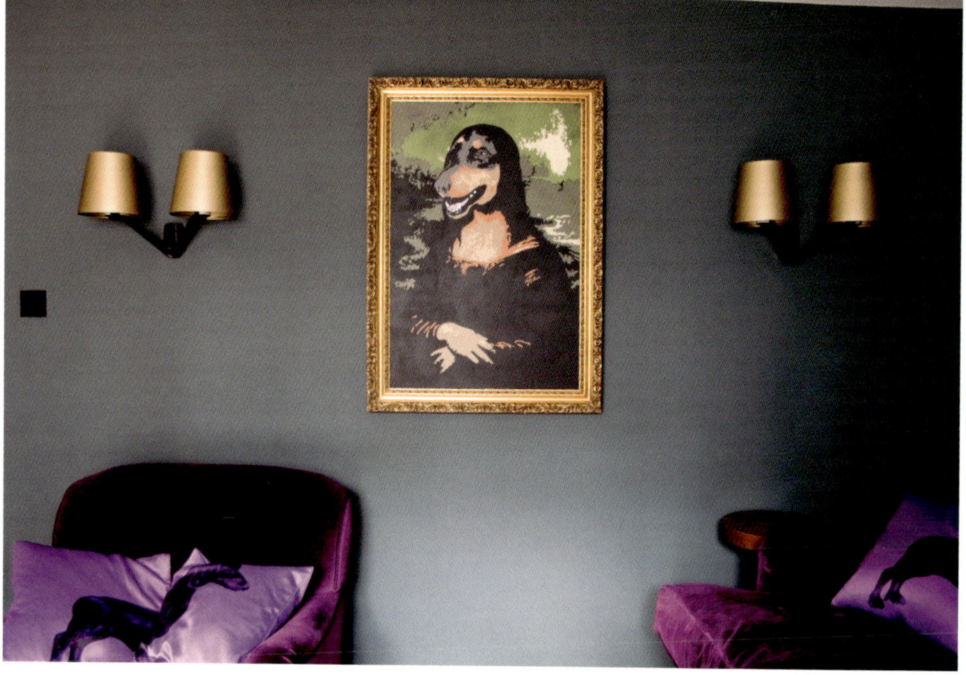

Mark's strong, striking décor compliments his art collection.

along Bayswater Road on a Sunday and there was an artist showing his work by the railings; I really liked his style, got chatting (he was called Lucien Simon) and ended up commissioning him to do a colourful 7ft x 8ft (2.1 m x 2.4 m) piece for me specifically for a space in the loft-style flat I had just bought. The funny thing was that as he was finishing it, he said that *The Times* wanted to do a feature on him, and they wanted to feature the painting I had commissioned as a kind of showpiece. But I would never buy anything *because* the artist was seen to be 'up and coming'.

I bought another work, an original by Dom Pattinson, after I saw it in Selfridges' furniture department. I just kept walking by and thinking how much I liked it. I then got to know Interior Angle who represent him, went to one of his shows and picked up another piece. I've also bought a few pieces recently from Graphic, a gallery that specialises in urban street artists working in different mediums: spray and paint artists, or guys who work on cardboard, metal or stone. It's great to have a base where I can chat about interesting artists, and what's going on.

A lot of the works I own have a dark humour, a quality that is possibly a little disturbing, but they also are clever, funny or have an *interesting* twist – I wonder what's going on with them, and it

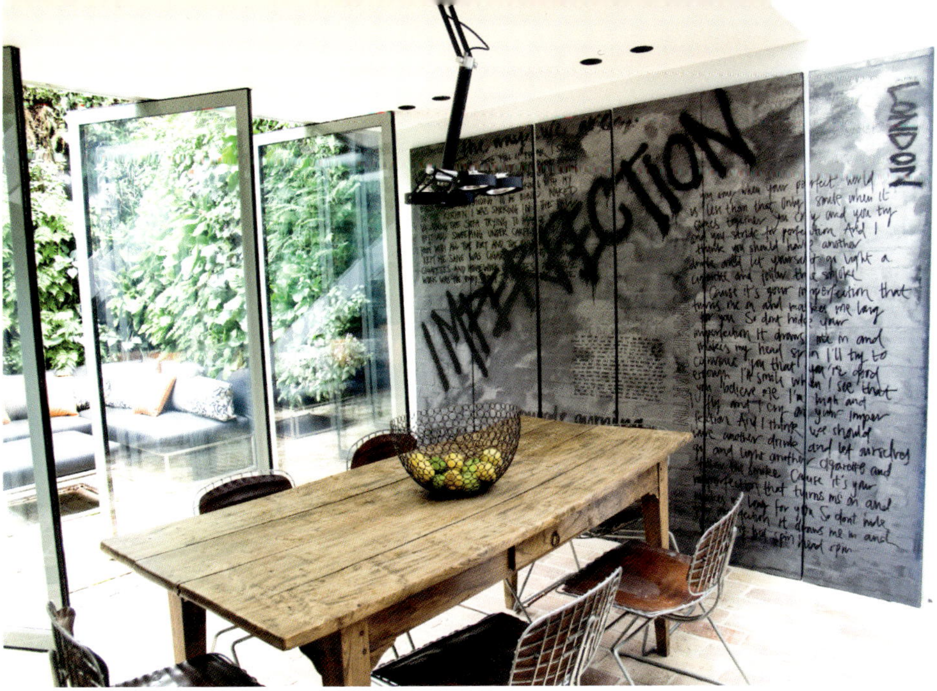

makes me smile. I have one sculpture, which I bought at the Affordable Art Fair, of a blue dog with a human skull and ice cream cone ears, by a French artist called Michael Alacoque. It's a piece that people look at and find 'interesting...' Sometimes I wonder what a psychologist would make of me if they got hold of my art collection...

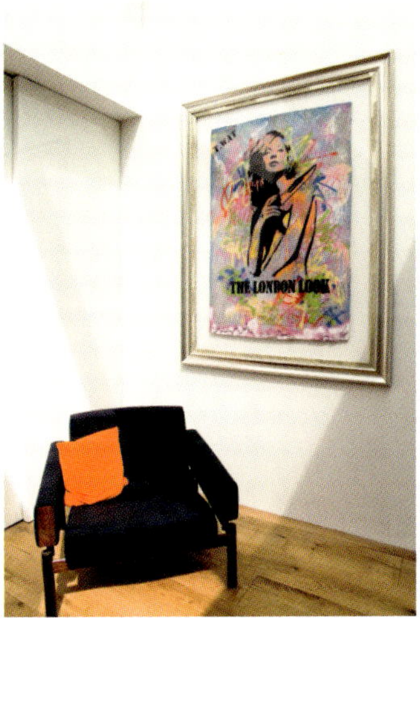

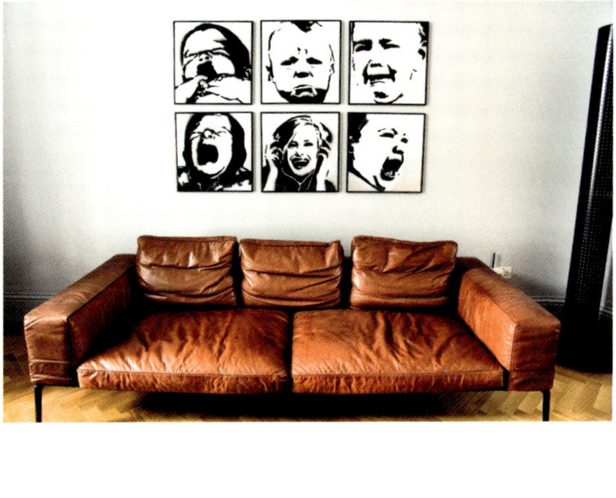

05

Tim Eastop

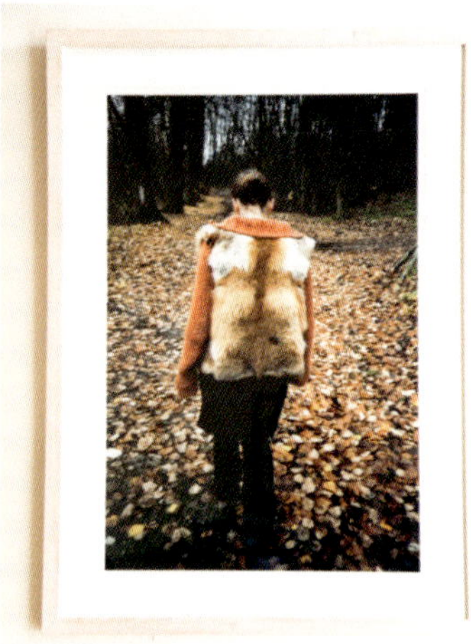

OUR FIRST purchase as a buying collective was a portfolio of 20 prints sold as a limited-edition boxed set of 100, for £1000/€1200/$1600, which we bought at a fundraiser for Cubitt Studios – an important artist studio group. This was 10 years ago, and was the beginning of putting into practice an idea I had first had with my brother-in-law about 5 years earlier about buying art together in small groups; sharing not only the cost, but discussion around the work, and rotating ownership.

After that first purchase we set up a group comprised of seven households who all contributed a monthly amount; at first it was about £25/€30/$40 a month, and over the years it has risen to £40/€47/$65 per household. We're a group of family households so there are a lot of other household pressures and budgets to think about too, so it has to be manageable.

As a group we then agreed on a set of rules and values to follow, and a lawyer formalised them. They were things like: to support artists who are upcoming, to meet artists and have a discussion about their work, to enjoy the work by living with it and sharing it between households.

Initially, we rotated our artwork every 2 or 3 months, but now we do it twice a year when we meet for an 'exchange'. This is a bit of a mad event that takes place on a weekend and is a big social occasion; all the kids come, there's food and discussion and we exchange art works. It's quite an ad hoc process, so if someone particularly wants a piece they make an argument why in front of everyone else and then we vote. At each exchange three new people are selected to be in

Tim's art is shared between seven households.

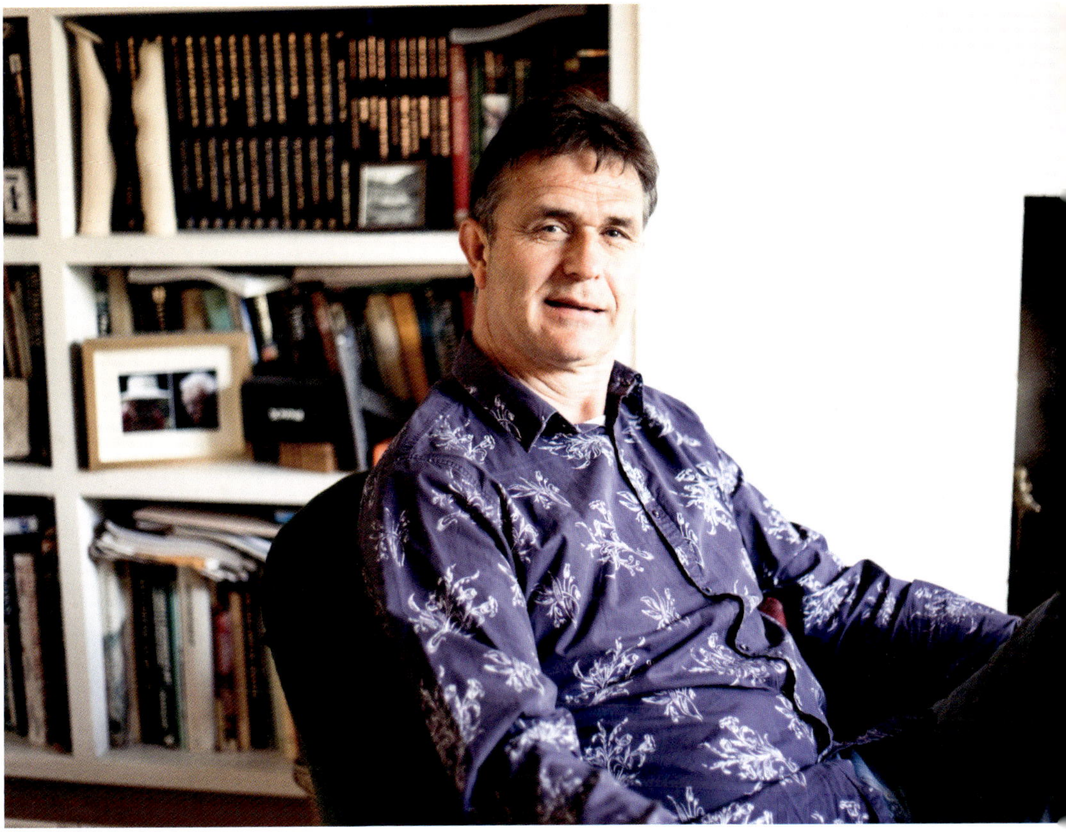

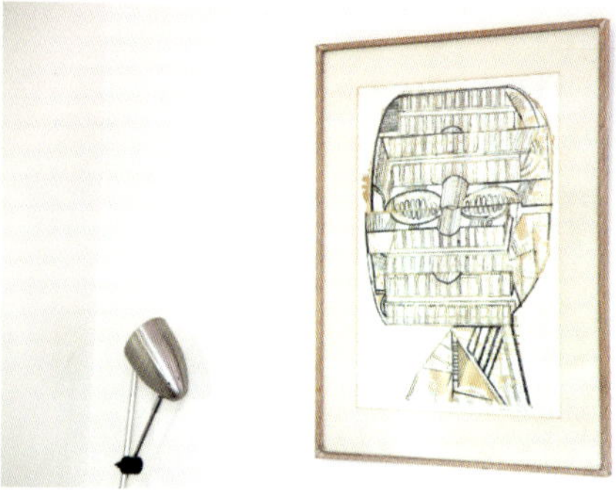

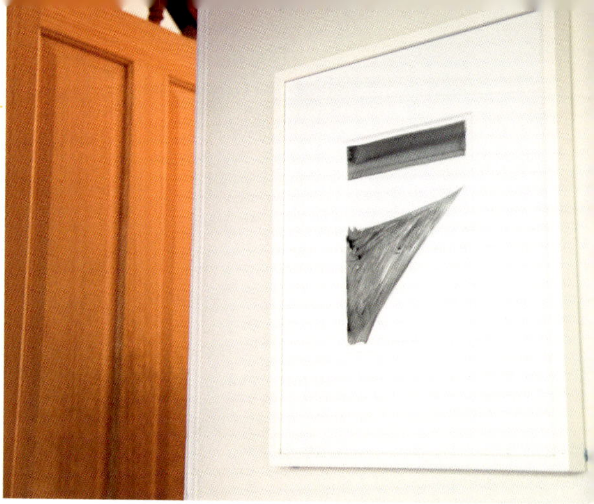

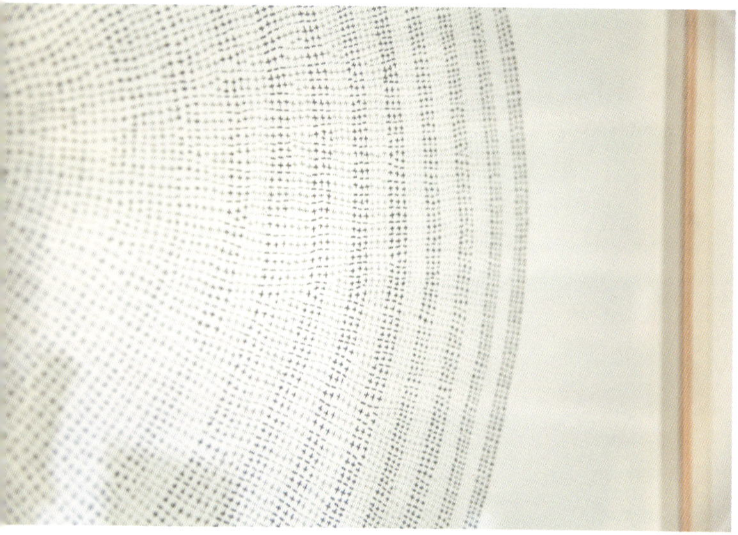

The collective buys work with a political thrust.

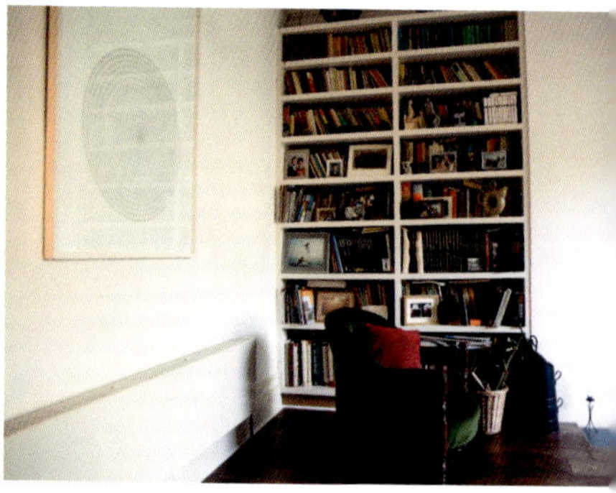

charge of buying the next work. It is their responsibility to spend extra time meeting curators and going to talks and events and artists studios – anyone can join them, but the final decision is theirs.

When we buy art, we don't just jump in with chequebooks, we spend time talking to artists and going to their studios. We have to love what the artist is doing, and understand and engage with the intellectual processes *behind* contemporary conceptual work, and the purchase is a reflection of that. We have to work at it, but we enjoy it.

The members in our group come from quite political backgrounds, and we tend towards artists who address challenging questions in society or politics and whose work is cutting edge, experimental and exciting.

Contemporary artists can give a really critical angle on the issues of the day and it's great that one way to understand our world is through their eyes. One wonderful painting in our collection is by Bobby Dowler – it is made from found bits of chewing gum and torn up Bible; it deliberately deteriorates and is a comment on our throwaway society.

We don't always buy two-dimensional work; we have some video work, sculpture and have commissioned and purchased live art inspired by the way our seven households live, and which was performed in our homes. This was rather an extraordinary process – it triggered tremendous debate and excitement in the group. It was with a young upcoming artist called Katharine Fry (www.katharinewheel.com), you can see two trailers for it on her website.

People always ask, 'how can you hand over the process of collecting to someone else when collecting is so individual and deeply personal?', but we like the fact that we are democratising collecting – not in a missionary way, but in a counter-intuitive way. ”

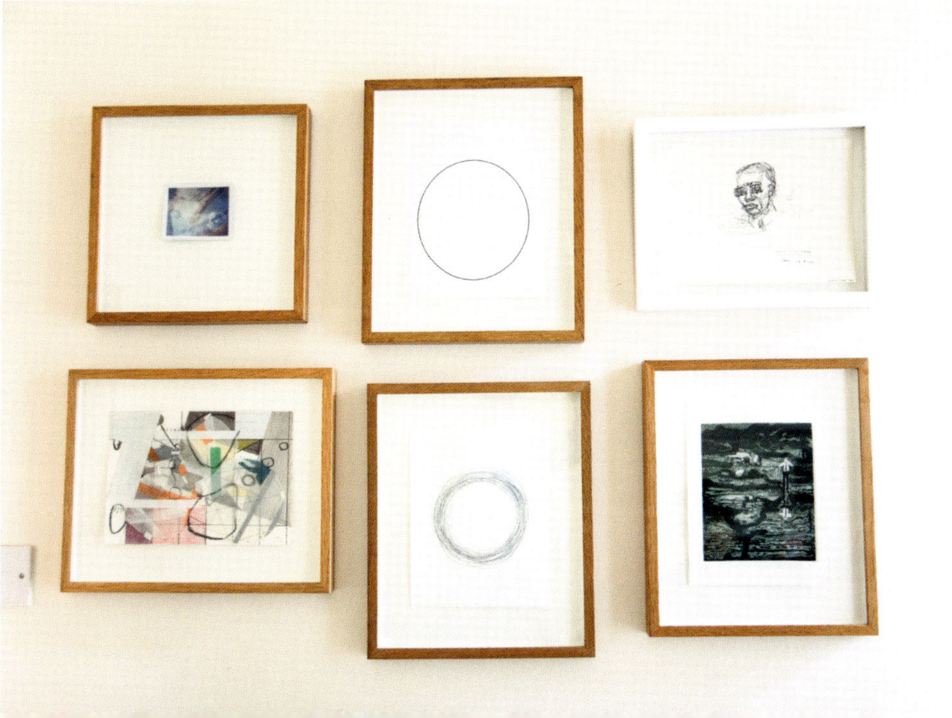

06

Pixie Andrew

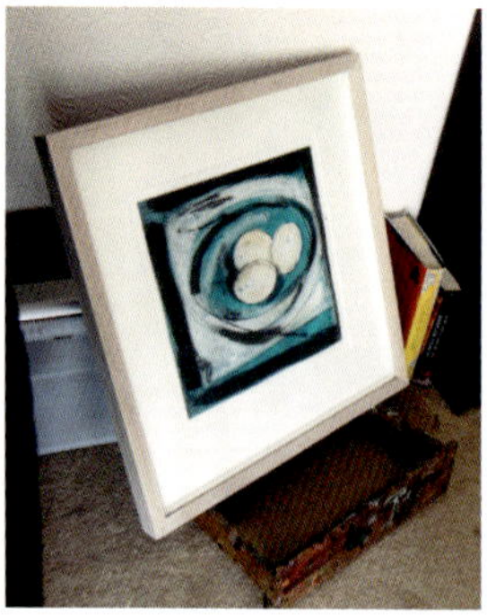

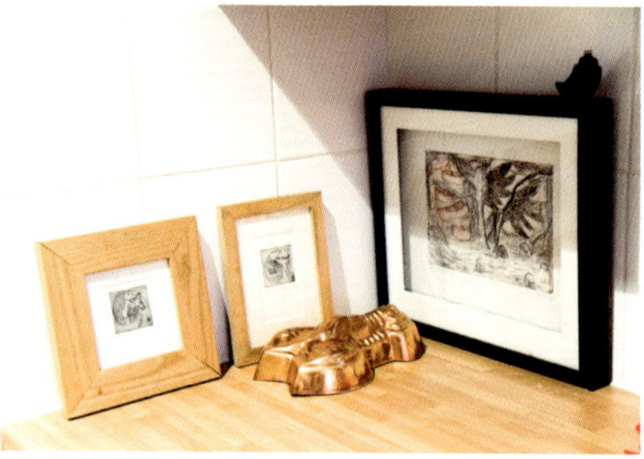

“ILLUSTRATION, and owning original work by contemporary illustrators, is my big passion. Lots of people collect antiquarian illustration, but I tend to collect illustrations from modern children's books, cookbooks, newspaper features, and work by commercial illustrators.

I love the stories behind illustrations, one of the first pieces I owned was an original Peter Weaver drawing from one of the *Alice in Wonderland books*, and one of the most recent is by an Irish illustrator of a little girl sitting under water with an old octopus, and they are reading a story book together. Both are quite typical of the kind of things I like – beautiful but with a dark sentiment; work which often reminds me of being a child.

I have also bought several paintings by recent graduates. Two artists I bought paintings from at degree shows I later found out sold other pieces to Charles Saatchi. I'm ashamed to admit that when I found out that my Christine Aerfeldt painting had gone up in value,

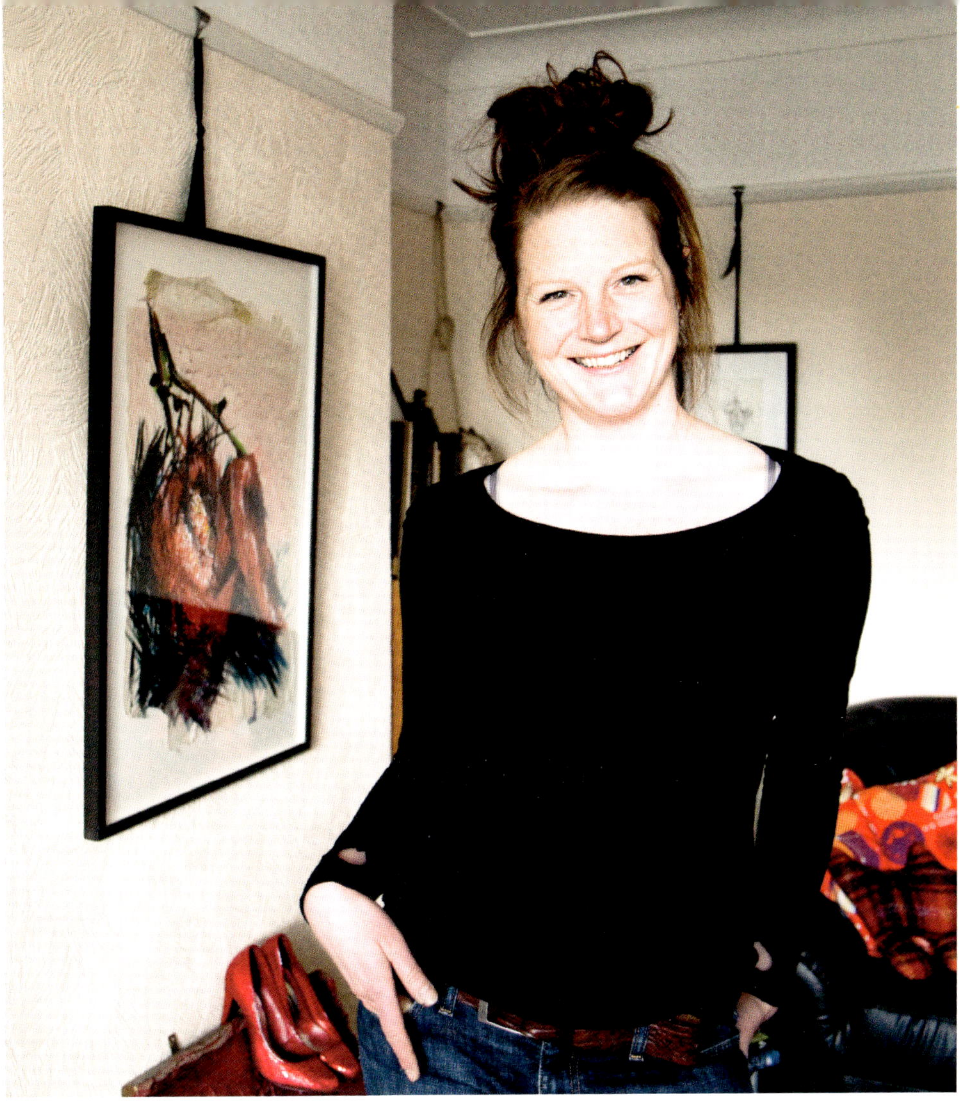

I was excited – but that's *not* why I buy art. I was so cross with myself for having that feeling of glee. I buy pieces because I love them; *I'm* the important one, not Saatchi. But I suppose knowing you've spotted an unknown artist along with someone who is a celebrated art collector is in some ways a validation of your taste and eye. But I am ashamed to admit that. I don't buy for investment; I buy for *me*, what makes my stomach flip, art that I *must* take home and look at every day.

Buying art for Pixie is like falling in love.

I go to art fairs, galleries and shows looking to fall in love with something. That feeling when I have to go and look at something again

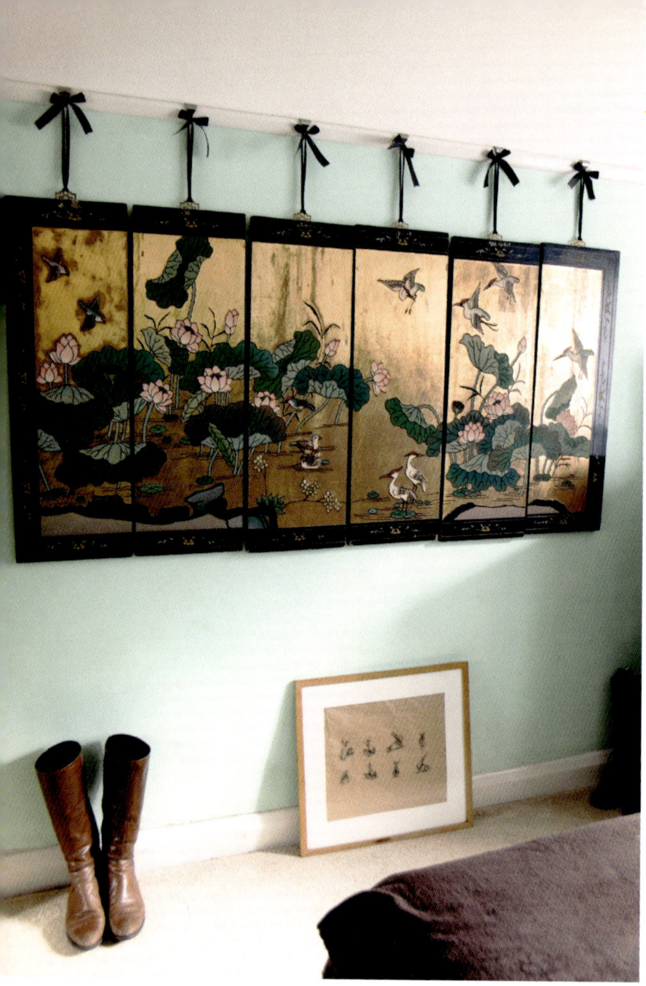

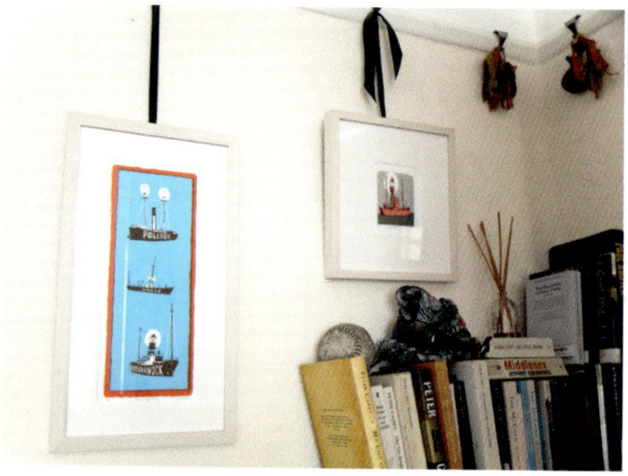

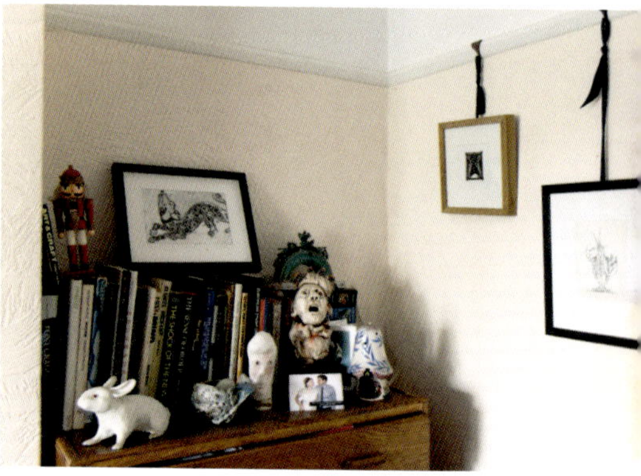

and again. Sometimes I leave empty handed because it's just not there, but when it does happen and I have to have something, taking it home feels brilliant; simply owning it, looking at it – it's wonderful.

I always keep documents relating to each piece in an A4 plastic wallet tucked into the back of the frame. With significant paintings, like the big painting by Christine Aerfeldt, I regularly check what the artist is up to and print off news about any shows they are having, and I keep it at the back in the wallet. It's just for my records, almost a form of mothering, a nurturing, of making myself aware about each piece and the artist. It's not about value, simply interest.

I've probably spent more on art than I've spent feeding, clothing and looking after myself! It may seem ridiculous, but I've got the

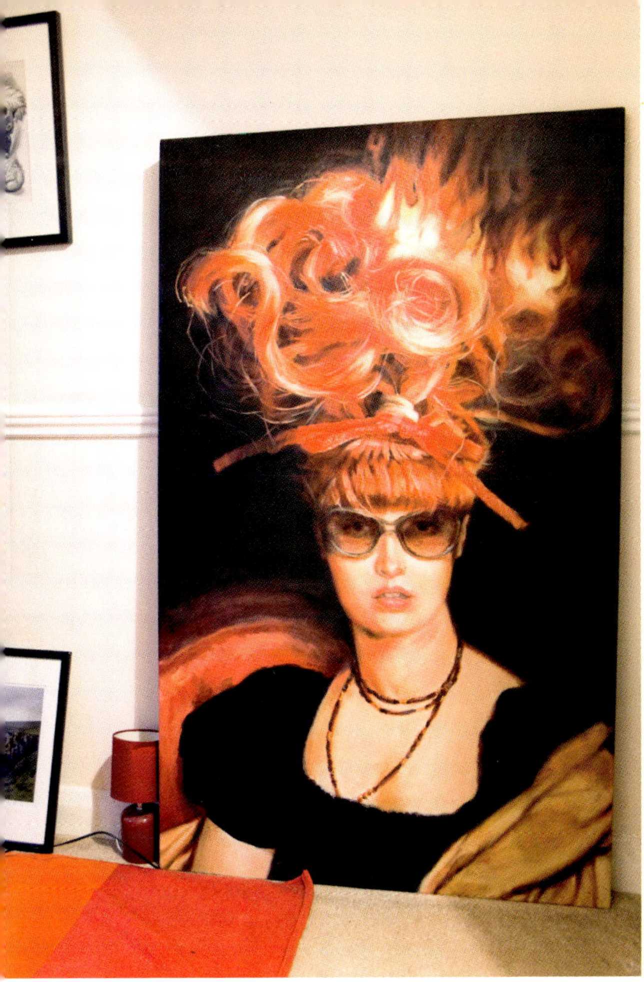

Pixie's beloved work by Christine Aerfeldt, *Madame Tropicana*.

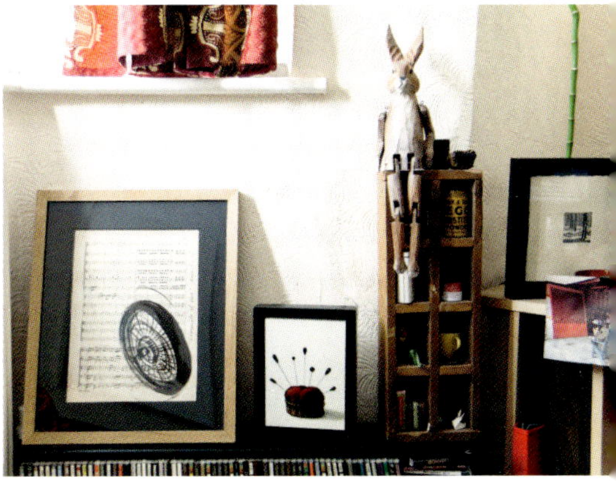

bug. I don't budget for it – every time I see something and fall in love with it, I walk towards the price label and there comes that point where a decision has to be made – is there any way I can actually own this? I do this funny little sum in my head: how much I love it ersus can I afford it. I've often asked the dealer about paying in instalments.

I buy art that will look nice in my life, not my house. I never think about where I'm going to hang it – I just have to have it and it'll have to fit in somewhere. And I don't regret any of my purchases, not one – I love them all the same, the ones that have cost me £50/€60/$80 and ones that have cost me £4000/€4700/$6500. They are my family.

Picture credits

Every effort has been made to credit the appropriate source. Please notify us if there are any errors or omissions and we will put them right in the next printing **Cover:** iStockphoto © ibusca
IFEMA–ARCOmadrid, (2); © Nic Lehoux, (11); © Alamy (14); © David Willems (17); © Ateliers Jean Nouvel (18); © Jennifer Davies (19); © Tim Williams (26); © Art Smart/www.artsmart.com (27); Fin DAC at the Stroke.Art Fair/ © Stroke.Artfair 2010 (34); © Christa Holka for Frieze; David Roche (42); Royal College of Art Show 2010 (work in background Olenna Mokliak, printmaking graduate) (44); Dianne Harris E=MC2, 2011© Alex Robertson (45); Tim Lewis 'Pony', 2008 Image courtesy of Kinetica Museum 2011 (45); ImaOne at Stroke.Art Fair © Stroke.Artfair (46); Jon Buck 'Drawn In' and installation shot © Courtesy of Pangolin London/ Steve Russell (48, 49); Stephen Bishop (Royal College of Art, 2008) © Wright & Wright (49); David Bailey 'Comfortable Skull' © David Bailey, reproduced courtesy of David Bailey/Pangolin London (50); © Image courtesy of The Photographer's Gallery, London (52); © Rafik Aalborg (66); Gagosian Gallery, UK © Alamy (67); White Cube © Alamy (69); Tom Sandford 'Motherless Brooklyn' © Kathy Zeiger (76); Andrea Mastrovito 'The Island of Dr. Mastrovito' © Kathy Zeiger (76); 'Guerra de la Paz Tribute, 2002-ongoing, Found garments' © Julian Navarro for No Longer Empty (77); No Longer Empty's 'About Face' exhibition 2011, © Kathy Zeiger (78); No Longer Empty's 'Reflecting Transformation' Exhibition 2009 © Nicholas Freeman (79); Damien Hirst 'Beautiful Inside my Head Forever' sale of Damien Hirst art at Sotheby's, London 15/09/2008 © John Taylor; Damien Hirst Sotheby's Auction 2010 © John Taylor; Robert Dowling 'Untitled' (painting) (95); © Counter Editions and John Baldessari 'Brain/Cloud (with Seascape and Palm Tree)' www.countereditions.com (99); Cereal Art www.cerealart.com (99); courtesy Other Criteria www.othercriteria.com (99); EMIN International www.emininternational.com (99); Matt's Gallery www.mattsgallery.org (99); Ian Davenport 'Poured Lines' 2006 © Geoff Caddick/epa/Corbis 42-17281970 (127); Michelangelo Pistoleto performs 'Seventeen One Less', 23rd Venice Biennale 03/06/2009 © Andrea Merola/epa/Corbis (129); Venice Biennale plc © Getty . Alberto Pizzoli/ AFP/Getty Images (129); Royal College of Art Show (work by Marcus Foster, sculpture 2010) (139); Art Forum Berlin © Mess Berlin Gmbh (153); © Arte Fiera by Bologna Fiera (154, 155); IFEMA–ARCOmadrid (156, 157); Andro Wekua 'Boy O Boy' © courtesy Andro Wekua; Galerie Peter Kilchmann, Zurich; Piotr Uklański 'Untitled (Fist)', 2007, Galleria Massimo de Carlo, Milan © Berlin Biennale for Contemporary Art, Uwe Walter, 2008 (160-161); © Koelnmesse (162); Opening ART COLOGNE 2011: Gallery Hans Mayer © Koelnmesse (163); Opening ART COLOGNE 2011: Gallery Christian Lethert, Cologne © Koelnmesse (163); Art HK © filination.com (164) ; Venice Biennale © Alamy (165); Peter Friedl 'Brownie' dOCUMENTA 12 art fair © Barbara Sax/AFP/Getty Images (166); © Courtesy Art Basel (167); Atsuko Tanaka 'Work' (1955) at dOCUMENTA 12 © Thomas Lohnes/AFP/Getty Images (168-169); Istanbul Biennale, Platform 2001 © Kenji Morita (171); Daniel Firman 'Butterfly, 2007-2010 and Xavier Veilhan 'The Carriage/La Carrosse, 2010, Galerie Perrotin © Linda Nylind (172 left); Frieze Art Fair 2010 © Linda Nylind for Frieze (172 right); Jeppe Hein, Gallery Johann Konig, Berlin Somergarten at Art Forum © Mess Berlin Gmbh (174); Laden fuer Nichts, Leipzig at Art Forum © Mess Berlin Gmbh (174); Berline Accessible Art Fair, May 2011 © Maria Maslenikova (175); Ambiance 19 Paris Photo 2010 © Delphine Warin–Paris Photo 2010 (178); Artillerie, Supermarket Art Fair 2011 © Jose Figueroa (179);

THE COLLECTORS' artists: Zoe & Mathieu Laroche: Flora McLachlan (184 left); Dodie Wexler (184 top left); Chris Kenny (184 centre, 186 top); Trinidad Ball (185 right); Serena Rowe (186 bottom left); Quentin Blake (186 bottom right); Janine Partington (187 top left); Arabella Harcourt Cooze (187 top right); Kurt J. (187 bottom left); present from Zoe to Mat (187 bottom right). **Bobby Molavi:** Dmitri Shubin (188 top left and centre); Tom Hunter (188 right and centre); Simrin Gill (188 bottom left); Tomoaki Makino (188 bottom centre); Christopher Bucklow (188 bottom right); Georgia Russell (189 left upper and lower); Walid Raad (189 centre top and bottom); Louisa Lambry (190 top left); Idris Khan (190 top centre); Susan Derges (190 top right); Ola Kolehmaimen (190 centre); Dan Holdsworth (190 bottom left); In panel lower right 190: Franz Ackermann (left wall), Izima Kaoru (centre wall, four works), Peter Davies (lower back wall); Staircase left wall from the top 191: Langlands and Bell, Franz Ackermann, Joe Clarke (2 works), Jason Minsky, Carol Fulton (2 works); Wall behind stairs p 191: Izima Kaoru (2 works). **Jo Varney:** Geoffrey Humphries (192 left, 193 right); Jo Varney (192 right on bookshelf, 194 top right, 195 top right); George Hooper (193 left); Jo Bowen (193 top centre, 195 top right and bottom right); Robert Duckworth Greenham (193 bottom centre); Dominic Hills (194 top left); Colin Wiggins (194 centre left, centre, and bottom right); Marcel Marien (194 centre right); Avigdor Arika (194 bottom left, 195 bottom centre); Peter Blake (195 bottom left). **Mark Christophers:** Michael Alacoque (196); Dom Pattinson (197); Teddy Bacon (198); Jimmie Martin (199 top); T. WAT (199 bottom left); Thikent (199 bottom right). **Tim Eastop:** David Bate (200); Eduardo Paolozzi (202 top left); Robert Holyhead (202 top right); Frances Richardson (202 bottom left and right); Paul McCarthy (203 top left); Elizabeth Wright (203 top centre); Suzanne Treister (203 top right); Andrew Bick (203 bottom left); Ceal Floyer (203 bottom centre); Peter Doig (203 bottom right). **Pixie Andrew:** Susan Moxley (204 left); Susan Gabriel (204 centre left and right); Pixie Andrew (204 right, 205, 206 lower right); Simon Tozer (206 top right and centre); Rachel Edgar (206 on top of books); Tatiana Kozmina (206 lower centre right on wall), Peter Weavers (206 lower right); Christine Aerfeldt (207 left); Nana Schioni (207 centre left); Dorion Scott (207 centre); Bella Peroni (207 right).

Index